D0984422

Hari Kunzru

Manchester University Press

Twenty-First-Century Perspectives

Series editors: Kristian Shaw and Sara Upstone

Previously published

Kazuo Ishiguro   Kristian Shaw and Peter Sloane (eds)

Hari Kunzru

Edited by

Kristian Shaw and Sara Upstone

MANCHESTER UNIVERSITY PRESS

Published by Manchester University Press
Oxford Road, Manchester M13 9PL

www.manchesteruniversitypress.co.uk

British Library Cataloguing-in-Publication Data
A catalogue record for this book is available from the British
Library

ISBN 978 1 5261 5520 7 hardback

First published 2023

Typeset by Newgen Publishing UK

For our lockdown companions – Celia, Lúthien and Bombadil

Contents

Contributors

Maëlle Jeanniard du Dot is a tenured teacher of literature, translation and English for Specific Purposes at Université Rennes 2, France. She holds the agrégation in English studies. Her postgraduate research (at Université Grenoble-Alpes) investigates the notion of place in Hari Kunzru's and Mohsin Hamid's novels. She has also authored research on Nadeem Aslam, Salman Rushdie and Monica Ali. Her research more generally focuses on place and space in contemporary British and South Asian novels in English, from the crossed perspectives of globalisation studies, refugee studies and ecocriticism.

Peter Ely is a writer and lecturer based in London. He is a postdoctoral researcher at Kingston University as well as teaching at a number of London universities and institutions. His research works at the intersection of philosophy, critical theory and literature to examine the political potential of 'community' in contemporary British society. He has written a number of journal articles and book chapters and is co-editor of *Community in Contemporary British Fiction* (Bloomsbury, 2022) with Sara Upstone. He is also currently working on a monograph on the same subject.

David Hering is Senior Lecturer in English at the University of Liverpool. His writing has appeared in publications including *The Los Angeles Review of Books*, *The London Magazine*, *Orbit*, *3AM Magazine*, *The Quietus*, and others. He is author of *David Foster Wallace: Fiction and Form* (Bloomsbury, 2016).

Lucienne Loh is Senior Lecturer in English Literature at the University of Liverpool. She is author of *The Postcolonial Country in Contemporary Literature* (Palgrave Macmillan, 2013) and is co-director of the British Chinese Studies Network.

Churnjeet Mahn is Reader in English at the University of Strathclyde and a Fellow of the Young Academy of Scotland (Royal Society of Edinburgh). Her research investigates the history and practice of travel with reference to race, sexuality and nationalisms. She is currently working on a book about queer travel writing which investigates the history of queer travel to, and from, the 'Orient'. She is currently PI on a British Academy grant entitled Cross-Border Queers: The Story of South Asian Migrants to the UK and is an AHRC EDI Leadership Fellow on a project entitled EDI in Scottish Heritage in partnership with Museums and Galleries Scotland.

Bran Nicol is Professor of English Literature and Head of the School of Literature and Languages at the University of Surrey. He publishes widely on modern and contemporary fiction, film, culture and theory. His publications include *Postmodernism and the Contemporary Novel* (Edinburgh University Press, 2002), *Stalking* (Reaktion, 2006), *The Cambridge Introduction to Postmodern Fiction* (Cambridge University Press, 2009) and *The Private Eye* (Reaktion, 2013).

Kristian Shaw is Associate Professor in English Literature at the University of Lincoln. He is the author of *Cosmopolitanism in Twenty-First Century Fiction* (Palgrave, 2017) and *Brexlit: British Literature and the European Project* (Bloomsbury, 2021). He is the co-editor of *Kazuo Ishiguro* (Manchester University Press, 2023).

Sara Upstone is Professor of Contemporary Literature and Faculty Director of Postgraduate Research at Kingston School of Art, Kingston University. Her publications include *Rethinking Race and Identity in Contemporary British Fiction* (Routledge, 2017), *British Asian Fiction: Twenty-First Century Voices* (Manchester University Press, 2011) and *Spatial Politics in the Postcolonial Novel* (Ashgate, 2010). She is the co-editor of *Postmodern Literature and Race*

(Cambridge University Press, 2015), *Researching and Representing Mobilities: Transdisciplinary Encounters* (Palgrave, 2014), *Postcolonial Spaces: The Politics of Place in Contemporary Culture* (Palgrave, 2011) and *Community in Contemporary British Fiction* (Bloomsbury, 2022) with Peter Ely.

Series editors' preface

Kristian Shaw and Sara Upstone

The twenty-first century exists as a site of social, cultural and political precarity. Captured in calls for social, political, and environmental justice, shaped by war and pandemic, it demands a planetary consciousness with the vitality to imagine what might emerge beyond the uncertainties of the current moment.

Twenty-First-Century Perspectives offers a series of edited collections that examine the ways in which contemporary writers have responded to these global challenges, as a clamorous presence that has served to reignite the role of writer as public intellectual and the literary text as an agent of change. The series captures how contemporary literatures are producing striking works of political and ethical power, radically revising metanarratives of nation and identity while searching for original avenues of meaning in order to navigate these uncertain times. It examines the role of texts as daring reappraisals of literary tradition and innovations in form, acting as forces of transformation that – in their interrogations of the past, questioning of the present, and dreams of the future – demand a new critical vocabulary.

Through collections that feature an international range of voices, including some of the most notable literary scholars of the contemporary, the series identifies the key writers at the centre of this cultural moment. Focusing on distinctive individual voices, the series captures the writers in prose, poetry, and dramatic writing whose bodies of work are already establishing them as the defining voices of a century. It also offers first collections on writers who have made their mark in the decades of the current century, alongside new studies of writers whose careers began in the twentieth century, critically appraising earlier texts in the context of contemporary debates to situate them within a specifically twenty-first-century aesthetic. Across the series the dual focus on socio-political contexts and formal invention builds a larger picture regarding emergent developments in contemporary literary culture. What emerges will be a lasting archive – a library of voices speaking in dialogue to the creation of a revolutionary imagination.

Acknowledgements

The editors and publishers are tremendously grateful to Hari Kunzru for his time and support of this project. It is rare to benefit from such generous authorial insights, and the collection is far stronger due to his contribution.

The idea for this collection first derived from 'Transmission: An International Hari Kunzru Conference', which was held at the University of Surrey in June 2014. Thanks to Bran Nicol, Churnjeet Mahn and Bianca Leggett for organising the event and exposing us to the numerous scholars interested in Hari's work.

The editorial team at Manchester University Press have been exemplary – their professionalism, knowledge and guidance is much appreciated. Special thanks must go to Paul Clarke for his advice in developing a new *Twenty-First-Century Perspectives* series and support in bringing this first collection into being.

Thanks also to our contributors for their professionalism and dedication during the unprecedented difficulties of a global pandemic.

Our greatest debts – as ever – are to our families.

Abbreviations

GWM	*Gods Without Men* (London: Penguin, 2011)
TI	*The Impressionist* (London: Penguin, 2002)
MP	*Memory Palace* (London: V&A Publishing, 2013)
MR	*My Revolutions* (London: Hamish Hamilton, 2007)
RP	*Red Pill* (New York: Knopf, 2020)
T	*Transmission* (New York: Plume, 2004)
WT	*White Tears* (New York: Knopf, 2017)

Introduction
'Adding up to an unknown': the elusive fictions of Hari Kunzru

Kristian Shaw and Sara Upstone

In June 2020, the writer Hari Kunzru was asked in an interview to name a writer he had recently taken comfort in and why. One might have expected this 'recovering Pynchonite' (Piccarella, 2019) with a love of the systems novel tradition to cite the elusive author of *Gravity's Rainbow* (1973) or another postmodern classic. His response, however, was that he had been reading the translations of an ancient Chinese poet, Han Shan, who retires to a place called Cold Mountain to contemplate the world. Kunzru prefigures his response to the question with the comment that 'I've fantasized lately about being a hermit' (Bollen, 2020). While this may seem very much to be a contextual response in the midst of the COVID-19 pandemic, it also strikes a chord with the nature of Kunzru's writing. Eclectic, ebullient, often surprising and rarely predictable, Kunzru's impressive body of work is evidence of a truly unique literary imagination.

In *Hari Kunzru*, the first collection to be published on Kunzru's writings, we have aimed to celebrate this distinctiveness and capture the diversity of Kunzru's literary output, with individual chapters on each of his six major novels as well as new interpretations of Kunzru's short stories and his experimental e-book and exhibition fiction. Through these analyses, we not only offer new interpretations of Kunzru's work, we also draw attention to its place within a wider and rapidly evolving world of contemporary literature. Born in Essex in 1969 to an English mother and Indian father (his mother was a nurse, his father a doctor who came to Britain in the 1960s), and now living since 2008 in New York City, Kunzru's global outlook defines a contemporary literature that no longer seeks to be identified via national boundaries. Kunzru, we argue, is a literary shape-shifter whose own expressed interest in performativity has allowed him to reshape his own writing career, creating global fictions that are distinct in their geographical and thematic scope, and their stylistic diversity. The work of Kunzru is therefore essential to understanding the nature of contemporary writing today – a writer who exemplifies the movement beyond the postmodern and the new territories of movements such as metamodernism, digimodernism and post-postmodernism. Kunzru has also proven himself to be a prescient author, warning of the EU immigration crisis and class divides in both the UK and US which resulted in political ruptures such as Brexit and the election of Donald Trump.

Educated first at the public school Bancroft's, before completing his English Literature degree at Oxford University and an MA in Philosophy and Literature at Warwick University, Kunzru's early writing was strongly influenced by his philosophical interests. Yet he found these to be incompatible with his ambitions as a novelist, particularly in Britain. Despite being frequently compared to writers such as Zadie Smith and Monica Ali, his work had little in common with their more overtly realist fictions. In what now reads as a poignant and enthralling discussion between a young novelist and a possible role model, in a 2003 interview with Salman Rushdie the older author gives Kunzru the benefit of his experience by telling him that 'you don't get anywhere in England with French theory' (Kunzru, 2003a). Kunzru and Rushdie share their disdain for the conservative preferences of newspaper literary criticism, while Kunzru reflects longingly on his perception of the 1970s as a moment when there was 'this glorious experimental stuff that was getting written and discussed'.

Yet when Kunzru did emerge into the literary mainstream, his entry was spectacular. Named as one of *Granta*'s Best of Young British Novelists of 2003, Kunzru earned the highest ever advance for a first novel at the time for *The Impressionist* (£1.25 million) on the promise of being a writer who would take 'his place in the constellation of important young British novelists writing about a very new, multi-racial, multi-ethnic Britain' (Mudge, 2002, qtd. in Upstone, 2010: 158). *The Impressionist* went on to win the John Llewellyn Rhys Prize, the Betty Trask Award and the Somerset Maugham Award, and was nominated for the 2002 Whitbread First Novel Prize, signalling the emergence of a major talent on the British literary scene. This reputation was fostered by Kunzru's cultural visibility, which positioned his work in particular ways attractive to a young, liberal reading public. Kunzru's rejection of the John Llewellyn Rhys prize sponsored by the *Mail on Sunday*, because the newspaper was incompatible with 'a novel about the absurdity of a world in which race is the main determinant of a person's identity', identified him early in his career as a vocal opponent of prejudice. He has since then used his literary prominence to bring to light a range of human rights organisations, most notably as the deputy president of English PEN and patron of the Guantanamo Human Rights Commission (Kunzru, 2003b).

In his interview with Rushdie, Kunzru reflects on the lack of representation growing up of Asians on British television. 'I didn't know who to look to or who to be', he declares, 'and that's very different now'. Kunzru found himself part of this shift in the cultural visibility of black Britons. After the publication of *The Impressionist*, he was associated with an explosion in recognition of British Asian talent, what newspapers were calling 'Asian cool'. A phenomenon of the late 1990s and early millennial Britain, 'Asian cool' was defined by an upsurge in interest in British Asian cultures, not only through literature but also on mainstream television and radio through programmes such as *Goodness Gracious Me*, on film in the work of directors and writers such as Hanif Kureishi and Gurinder Chadha, and in the popularity of music acts including Jay Sean, Asian Dub Foundation and Punjabi MC. Mainstream cinema successes such as *Bend It Like Beckham* (2002) and *East Is East* (1999) utilised comedy and narratives of intra-community tensions to foster audience engagement and strategically interrogate racist stereotypes. Kunzru in this respect was identified as part of a larger group of writers including Monica Ali (also one of *Granta*'s Best of Young British Novelists that same year), Nadeem Aslam, Meera Syal, Atima Srivastava and Gautam Malkani who were celebrated for giving voice to a new British Asian generation – born or raised in Britain, and defiant about their rights to cultural belonging. These writers received critical interest through works such as Upstone's monograph *British Asian Fiction: Twenty-First Century Voices* (2010) and Neil Murphy and Wai-chew Sim's edited collection *British Asian Fiction: Framing the Contemporary* (2008), both of which include chapters on Kunzru's work within this context.

Kunzru's work always felt slightly off-centre when taken alongside these other writers. He was aware of the trend, calling 2003 'the year of the trendy Asian in London' (Upstone, 2010: 3). Yet eschewing the tendency for contemporary-set diasporic fictions which dealt with contested notions of Britishness, there was in fact little in common between *The Impressionist* and a semi-autobiographical Bildungsroman such as *Anita and Me* or a heart-breaking depiction of Muslim immigrant life in contemporary Britain such as *Maps for Lost Lovers*. Indeed, Kunzru has never published a novel that is explicitly concerned with life in contemporary Britain. Evoking postcolonial fictions more readily, *The Impressionist* was explicitly directed toward a global audience, garnering significant attention in the Indian press in particular. Kunzru's early comments in an interview that *The Impressionist* was a 'tissue of fiction rather than a narrative' (East, 2002), playfully and self-consciously evoking past imperial tropes, hinted at a career that was going to refuse easy definition. He was acutely aware of the potential to be misread:

> I was in an unbelievably compromised position before I even began, particularly as somebody born in Britain and writing about India and Africa [...] But in the same way that I looked at the literary tradition, I decided that rather than glancing sideways at the problem, I'd try and meet it head-on. I tried to blow up that sensualism to show how it operates and whose interests are best served by it. I don't know whether it works or not. There is always the danger that it's going to be read as just another example of over-blown exoticism. (East, 2002)

The most well-known British Asian novelists, hugely successful with first novels, did not see the success of their early works repeated as they took up new themes and interests, constrained by enduring ideas regarding what constitutes ethnic British fiction. While none of Kunzru's subsequent novels has achieved the same critical acclaim in terms of awards and prizes as his first, his decision to eschew the trend for a novel of contemporary British Asian experience seemed to allow him to break out of such stereotypes. One can compare, for example, Monica Ali's lack of current profile, as she attempted in *In the Kitchen* (2009) and *Untold Story* (2011) to move away from narratives explicitly about ethnic identity, with Kunzru's transatlantic success with *White Tears* (2017). A review in the *New York Times* harshly referred to *In the Kitchen* as 'an otherwise meandering, overstuffed narrative', focusing almost entirely on how the later work is like *Brick Lane* – a narrative of 'multicultural, postcolonial Britain' – in spite of Ali's significant shift in focus (Grimes, 2009). The lack of concern for Ali's trajectory is equally indicated by the *Guardian* review of her fourth novel, *Untold Story*, which the review incorrectly identifies as her third (her second was *Alentejo Blue*, published in 2006) (Tripney, 2012). Despite the novel being a recreation of the life of Princess Diana, it is at its best, the reviewer tells us, when 'exploring the idea of exile' (Tripney, 2012). In contrast, the *New York Times* review of *White Tears* sees no relation to British Asian culture in the novel, other than to note that Kunzru's perspective as a settler in the US may have afforded him a unique vantage point on its culture, with 'an awareness and discernment [that] have particular value in an America of the moment' (Erikson, 2017). This is reflected in Kunzru's position within critical studies; although Kunzru is included in volumes specifically on British Asian writing, he is a notable absence from those which focus more distinctly on questions of inclusion and Britishness such as Dave Gunning's *Race and Antiracism in Black British and British Asian Literature* (2010).

Kunzru's critical success illustrates how, like the protagonist of his debut novel, Pran, he proves himself the master of multiple personas, living in his own literary career his admission that he is 'obsessed with shape-shifting' (Sooke, 2007; qtd. in Upstone, 2010: 145). Shaped by his earlier career as a travel writer (he was the *Observer* Young Travel Writer of the Year in 1999) and as associate editor of technology magazine *Wired* – where he interviewed well-known theorists including Daniel Dennett and Donna Haraway – Kunzru's range of reference points extends over a vast plane. This breadth exists even in his most noticeably postcolonial first novel, and further analysis illustrates why it is important to identify how it only superficially rehearses earlier literary paradigms. Whereas novelists such as Arundhati Roy and Salman Rushdie concern themselves with questions of racial and caste identity, Kunzru broadens his novel's concern with wider issues of religion, gender and selfhood. Pran's difficulties, ultimately, arise not from his lack of acceptance of himself as a hybrid figure, but from a loss of selfhood that means that celebrated poststructuralist notions of performativity are problematised. The issue here is not the postcolonial issue of the self's inherent hybridity, but rather the poststructuralist deconstruction of the self as a social construct in its entirety. As Kunzru admits, it remains 'the most postmodern book I've written' (qtd. in Shaw, Chapter 9 in this volume). For Peter Childs and James Green (2013), Pran's dissolution takes 'the joint postcolonial and postmodernist assault on the imperial/humanist subject to its logical conclusion' (73). Lost in the blank space of the desert, Pran is unable to negotiate his various incarnations, and we witness the brutal deconstruction of Kunzru's protagonist, cast adrift from his cultural origins: 'How easy it is to slough off one life and take up another! Easy when there is nothing to anchor you. He marvels at the existence of people who can know themselves by kneeling down and picking up a handful of soil [...] he is not one of them' (285). Likewise, while gender fluidity is oft-cited as a powerful transgressive potentiality, in *The Impressionist*, Pran's gender is inflicted upon him, so that what was once transgressive becomes a ripping out of what at times appears to be essential. Unafraid of such bold choices, even Kunzru's postcolonial novel is, in reality, not that postcolonial at all. From the very beginning, his own comments reveal a concern not for the specifics of particular identity categories, but for universal questions of homelessness as a human condition (Upstone, 2010: 149–150). In this respect, Kunzru is an important example of what Mark Stein has defined as *post-ethnic* literature, producing work in which questions of ethnicity are displaced on to wider social questions. Indeed, Kunzru has been a vocal critic of the burden of representation which traps ethnic authors in niche markets of identity politics, arguing strongly against the sense that as a British Asian author 'you're only allowed to talk about and relate to certain ethnic and race issues' (Aldama, 2005: 14).

Two chapters in this volume explicitly address this imperative to expand the questions asked of race and identity. The majority of existing criticism on *The Impressionist* focuses on its re-visioning of postcolonial paradigms through a concern for identity that exceeds racial boundaries and which evolves through an intersectional framework that also places priority on questions of gender and class. Extending these concerns, Churnjeet Mahn's '"Walking into Whiteness": *The Impressionist* and the routes of empire' considers the novel within the context of a travel writing genre historically intertwined with questions of racial and colonial othering. Mahn's analysis reveals Kunzru's ironic manipulation of academic discourses surrounding diasporic identity to be played out not only at the level of theme, but also genre, as Kunzru employs a parody of dominant colonial modes of representation in travel writing to expose the apparatus of structural inequalities faced by marginalised minorities in the Western world. Mahn employs the work of Homi K. Bhabha to trace the anxious journey of Pran as he attempts to cross the boundaries of race, gender and sexuality, not in isolation from each other or in favour of straightforward models of hybridity, but rather with a problematised discourse that very much positions Kunzru as an interlocutor in existing post-colonial fictions.

Mahn's detailed reading of Kunzru's first novel emphasises how Pran's successful mimicry of colonial English masculinity provides little route toward a secure or stable sense of self. This concern for the construction of the self, alongside a related concern for questions of consciousness, is a recurring theme in Kunzru's writing. Indeed, he has commented in the past that it was this interest in the hang-over of a Romantic notion of selfhood to the contemporary that motivated his writing, rather than a desire to examine identity specifically through the lens of race (Upstone, 2010: 145). His novels can be seen to offer a fictional counterpart to the ideas of Daniel Dennett, thought experiments that are variously developed through concern for the uniqueness of the human against digital consciousness in *Transmission* (2004), the relationship between self and social construction in *My Revolutions* (2007), the question of subject and object in *White Tears*, and the reflections on Romantic conceptions of selfhood and their resonance with contemporary ideas of the individual in *Red Pill* (2020). For Kunzru, such questions are inherently bound to notions of state intervention, political hegemony and terrorism; repeatedly vocal on the subject of personal privacy, the idea of the individual is not only a philosophical notion but a political imperative.

It is a conjunction that is taken up by Peter Ely in his chapter 'Subjectivity at its limits: fugitive community in Kunzru's short stories'. Though much critical attention has been paid to Kunzru's novels, less emphasis has been devoted to his short stories, which reflect the stylistic strategies evident in his wider body of work.

Ely argues that Kunzru utilises the short story form as a 'vital laboratory to test the limits of narrative voice and subjectivity', expressing
a deep concern over lingering structural inequalities and offering
radical reconfigurations of contemporary society in the process.
Drawing on Jean-Luc Nancy's writings on the exigency of community and the figure of 'fugitivity' in relation to the capitalist state, Ely
looks at short stories from across Kunzru's career, including 'Deus
Ex Machina' (1998), 'Memories of the Decadence' (2005) and 'The
Interns' (2007), to demonstrate how his work aligns with broader
trends evident in the contemporary British novel to represent new
forms of cultural interdependence and belonging. Developing this
line of thought, Ely interrogates Fred Moten and Stefano Harvey's
emergent paradigm of the 'undercommons' to suggest Kunzru's
short fiction resonates with the fugitive framework, imagining new
oppositional solidarities and relational possibilities to abolish dominant structures and their inherent structural racisms. In this way,
Kunzru emerges as a crucial literary voice in the struggle to attend
to forms of capitalist exploitation and racial exclusion which continue to shadow our troubled present.

With his second novel, *Transmission*, Kunzru would push
against definition as both a British Asian and a postcolonial writer
with a novel set in the United States. *Transmission* is the first of
three novels set predominantly in the US, but each of these fictions
situates the nation within a kaleidoscopic global canvas so that,
as Bran Nicol comments in his chapter for this volume, Kunzru's
themes are 'reflective not just of America but of much of Western
global twenty-first-century experience'. This preference for a 'ver-
tiginous range of locations' (Schoene, 2009: 143) has meant that
much of the existing criticism on Kunzru identifies his work with
questions of cosmopolitanism: Berthold Schoene (2009) reading
Transmission as an exploration of the difference between the
capital-driven forces of a homogenising globalisation and the
multicultural promise of a diverse cosmopolitanism (149), Ashley
Shelden (2012) discussing the novel as an example of 'cosmopolitan love', Kristian Shaw (2017) claiming that the novel exposes
the myth of 'digital cosmopolitanism' through its interrogation of
global inequalities, or Caroline Edwards (2019) considering *Gods
Without Men* (2011) as an example of the 'networked novel'.

The political imperatives brought to the fore in Ely's chapter resonate with Lucienne Loh's chapter on *Transmission*, but also Kristian Shaw's chapter on Kunzru's most recent novel, *Red Pill*. Together, these chapters emphasise how Kunzru's early preoccupation with the complexities of globalisation continues to the present, a writer deeply immersed in international affairs, interweaving philosophical concerns for the nature of the subject and reflections of the global place of technology with a concomitant investment in social justice. As Shaw has argued in his monograph *Brexlit: British Literature and the European Project* (2021), Kunzru's satirical depiction of the EU in *Transmission* reimagined as a 'Pan European Border Authority' (PEBA), takes on new resonances in the post-Brexit era. Loh's chapter ' "It was the revenge of the uncontrollable world": *Transmission* and COVID-19' re-evaluates Kunzru's 2005 satirical globalisation novel to indicate how its dissection of digital interconnection gestures towards the insidious confluence of biological and technological forces in the twenty-first century. Forging clear parallels between Arjun Mehta's Leela virus and the recent pandemic, with economic damage becoming the primary concern over issues of national safety, Loh suggests the Western world's attempts to overcome the respective viruses amounts to a 'relentless and committed drive to secure their hegemonic ideological grip on the world'. With this in mind, the efforts of Thatcherite Guy Swift and his branding agency to market Britain as a global leader alludes to recent attempts to draw heavily on national heritage as a belated attempt to retain international influence. In the concluding part of her chapter, Loh argues the novel attains an added prescience, satirising a specific strain of British populism – predicated on imperial dreaming and racist ideologies – which would emerge a decade later and slowly transform into a 'COVID nationalism' that doubles down on the desire to turn towards the bordered world.

The concern for the insidious spread of ideology through technological apparatus is also the focus of Shaw, whose chapter ' "Food for the wolves": the rise of the alt-right in *Red Pill*' reveals how Kunzru's most recent novel marks a close engagement with recent political developments, such as the spread of Western populism, resistance to the Syrian refugee crisis, and the election of Donald Trump. Drawing on a personal interview, Shaw argues *Red Pill* not only reflects Kunzru's own anxieties about the 2016 US presidential election but continues the concern for the haunting legacy of race in the contemporary moment that began with *The Impressionist*. For Shaw, the novel reveals that 'harsh contrast' between those who believe the 'rational progress of humankind will be done by academic progress' and the xenophobic, nihilistic rhetoric of the alt-right, 'where everything is done with a hyper-ironic mockery and nothing actually means anything' (qtd. in Shaw, Chapter 9 in this volume). The unnamed narrator's obsession with the mysterious Anton, a baleful personification of the alt-right, leads him to question the values of a Habermasian public sphere and the morality of what Shaw terms his 'gestural cosmopolitanism'. As he argues, the alt-right's vision of a distorted 'American sublime', predicated on a nativist myth of ethnic unity, aligns with Trump's attempts to tap into a destructive nostalgia untainted by the politics of progress. The second half of the chapter articulates the ways in which the alt-right manipulated memetic discourses to conceal their white supremacist agenda. Kunzru's novel thus connects the spectral echoes of totalitarianism to contemporary cultural debates to expose the historical legacies that continue to scar the body politic.

Shaw's chapter also draws attention to how Kunzru's politics is increasingly invested through decisions of literary style. Immersed in the American literary tradition that has always been, through writers such as Pynchon, an acknowledged influence on his work, Kunzru has increasingly been emboldened to return to the questions of form that preoccupied his early writing experiments, continually pushing at the boundaries of literary taxonomies. The multiple temporalities of *Gods Without Men* and the play with typography in *Transmission* have evolved into more dramatic plays with form and structure. In 2012 and 2013, Kunzru produced two works which defy conventional classification: the e-book *Twice Upon a Time: Listening to New York* (2014), which is designed as a multisensory user experience involving touch, sound and walking, as well as reading, and the *Memory Palace* exhibition (2012) at the Victoria and Albert Museum in London, where Kunzru was commissioned to create a 'walk-in book'. These works connect Kunzru with a burgeoning field of multimodal literature that embraces digital forms, but also with the increasing focus on materiality and the human relation to the non-human world that is foregrounded by new materialist practices and theory.

There is an extension here for Kunzru's concern with posthuman consciousness in *Transmission*, but also a resonance with his fifth novel, *White Tears* (2017). Kunzru has spoken of how this novel was developed alongside *Twice Upon a Time* (Evaristo, 2017), the musical resonances of the earlier work evolving into a larger pre-occupation with cultural soundtracks, an enduring interest that goes back to Kunzru's work during the period of *The Impressionist* as music editor of *Wallpaper* magazine. The novel provides a striking counterpoint to *The Impressionist* with its similar concern for the spectral signifiers of whiteness which continue to haunt the contemporary moment, yet it brings this relationship to a specifically American context through a critique of the power of cultural appropriation in relation to the haunting spirit of the blues. In ' "The ghost is him": the echoes of racism, non-being and haunting in *White Tears*', David Hering demonstrates how Kunzru dramatises musical objectification to provide a satirical swipe at the condition of blackness in contemporary America. Following the actions of two young college graduates, Seth and Carter, as they strive to add old blues texture 344s to musical recordings in order to attain a level of cultural authenticity, *White Tears* emerges as Kunzru's most atmospheric novel, documenting the insidious cultural contamination of the past on the present. As the chapter argues, their Baudrillardian track, 'Graveyard Blues', comes to serve as a liminal object 'which speaks to a broader social concept of blackness as both object and non-existence, one which Kunzru weaponises by transforming this abject, non-existent, ghostly state into a violent narrative of revenge, revoicing and possession'. Hering's analysis – via a sustained conversation with Frantz Fanon – examines how Kunzru's work interrogates the complex interplay of subjecthood and objecthood in relation to the traumatic legacy of racial exploitation, gesturing to the legacies of slavery woven into the fabric of American culture.

In his concern for the fetishisation of the cultural object, Kunzru enacts a formal experimentation that seems to bring such interests into the field of book creation itself. The world of literary criticism has perhaps finally caught up with Kunzru in this regard, and his earlier writing now reads as a prescient forebear of the current literary moment, part of a group of authors including Ali Smith, Jon McGregor, George Saunders and David Mitchell who have found success with experimental prose fictions. That this is a multinational comparison rather than aligning Kunzru with any particular national literature identifies that Kunzru's global consciousness now resonates with a much wider sense of an internationalised literary discourse that challenges notions of 'American' or 'British' literature. *The Impressionist* was translated into twenty-one languages, and despite the important difference in their politics, his narrators have been compared to those of French novelist Michel Houellebecq (Monroe, 2021). Following a period at the American Academy in Berlin in 2016, Kunzru has also become associated with German contemporary literature, with resonances between his work and that of writers such as Daniel Kehlmann. *Red Pill* has been compared to the work of Karl Ove Knausgård and Tao Lin. Alongside this, Kunzru has a high profile in India, and his work is frequently discussed in relation to a body of Indian fiction as well as drawing comparisons with postcolonial writers such as J.M. Coetzee.

Houellebecq aside, the writers identified here combine their formal dynamism with a renewed sense of authorial responsibility and commitment to questions of social and political relevance that has seen them described variously as part of the contemporary post-postmodern, metamodern or new sincerity. Indeed, it is the argument of this book that to turn to Kunzru in this contemporary moment is very much to unravel not only the work of the author, but also a much larger question regarding the future of the novel and the classification of contemporary writing which has gathered pace in the past decade through works such as David Shields's *Reality Hunger* (2010) and famous pronouncements on the death of the novel such as those made by Will Self (2014). Recognising this reaction, Kunzru has asserted his continued commitment to fiction, not as a respite from socio-political realities, but rather as a very necessary strategy of engagement:

> Around the time I was an undergraduate in humanities departments, Derrida was the point around which you had to argue, and this indeterminacy – that language did not relate to the world in any fixed or stable way – again was being mined for liberatory possibilities. More

recently, that lack of anchor has started to feel like a problem rather than the solution to anything. We're in an interesting moment in English-language fiction right now where we've had several years of a kind of nervousness about plot and character from a lot of writers. The autofictional trend that's been around has led a lot of people who I never would have thought had much of a problem with plot and character to suddenly declare that they, too, are sick of the fakery of fiction and want to have some sort of biographically rooted authenticity. I see that as a nervous reaction to the thinness and scary zaniness of our current moment. But I'm quite committed to the forms of fiction, actually. I'm very comfortable with making stuff up, and I think the structures of fiction are quite useful for understanding a very complex, multipolar, multifaceted world. (Piccarella, 2019)

Such questions of form and definition are implicit in all the chapters in the collection, but they are the explicit preoccupation of Bran Nicol and Sara Upstone, whose chapters both argue for Kunzru's central place in emerging critical formulations of post-postmodern writing. For Nicol in his chapter 'The fiction of every-era/no-era: *Gods Without Men* as "translit" ', Kunzru's ironic engagement with the traditions of the 'Great American Novel' resonates with what Douglas Coupland has, in his own discussion of Kunzru, called 'translit': a contemporary literature defined by an atemporality that pulls together multiple timelines and geographies in a simultaneous present. For Nicol, this tendency – encapsulated in the multiple substories within *Gods Without Men* – not only captures the volatility of contemporary culture, it also redefines the novel form. Concerned to distinguish 'translit' from an earlier postmodern fiction, emphasising the loss of the postmodern celebration of heterogeneity in favour of a much more ambivalent, and tense, relationship to questions of chaos and multiplicity, Nicol argues that multiple subjectivities, unreliability and slippage are not for Kunzru the 'party tricks' that Coupland associates with postmodernism, but instead are symptoms of a deeply rooted concern for the impact of hyper-globalisation on contemporary life. Drawing attention to the novel's dominant pessimism, what emerges is an entropic cosmopolitanism and a narrative aesthetic that works against the novel's echoing structure of connectivity, proximity and cross-cultural engagement. For Nicol, this simultaneous indulgence in and concern for the breakdown of traditional meaning produces fiction that modifies rather than rejects the features of postmodern historiographic metafiction: 'an alternative to postmodernism *within* postmodernism'.

In the interest of such concerns with genre, Upstone turns her attention in 'Eyes, ears, head, memory, heart: transglossic rhythms in *Memory Palace* and *Twice Upon a Time*' to Kunzru's experimental e-book *Twice Upon a Time: Listening to New York* and his walk-in story *Memory Palace*, both of which gesture towards the characteristics of the novel while also eschewing its classic forms. Embracing Kunzru's own early love of French theory and reading these works through a detailed engagement with Henri Lefebvre's concept of rhythmanalysis, Upstone reveals the capacity of Kunzru's multimodal literature to engage with a materiality of both the literary and non-literary object. In the second part of the chapter, the implications of this form for Kunzru's ongoing concern for globalised identities and the pursuit of social justice are examined, identifying a discourse of 'resistant rhythms' which question racial, capitalist and ableist norms. For Upstone, the pursuit of these features simultaneously through both form and content defines Kunzru as what can be referred to as a *transglossic* author, a term drawn from work undertaken with Shaw (2021) that aims to evolve a new critical framework for the trends of twenty-first-century fiction. Broader than Coupland's notion of translit, Shaw and Upstone's transglossic takes as its foundation six core literary features – deep simultaneity, planetary consciousness, intersectional transversality, artistic responsibility, productive authenticity and trans-formalism – the conjunction of which typifies a work of contemporary literature. Kunzru's writing provides a model of how such features concretely manifest in contemporary fiction. Despite their differences, each of his works represents a globalised political commitment, simultaneous presence of intersectional identity categories and a renegotiation of concepts of reality. As these are realised through both theme and content – driven by an authorial responsibility evidenced in Kunzru's media activity and political activism – they come to encompass transglossic literature's defining characteristics.

Upstone's work reveals that alongside Kunzru's hauntological concern for the past (and lost futures), he is also a profoundly spatial writer, whose work is shaped by a psychogeographic sensibility.

Maëlle Jeanniard du Dot's 'Turning the tide, or turning around in *My Revolutions*' brings this spatiality into sharp relief. Relatively overlooked in Kunzru criticism to date and his first book without any explicit discussion of India, *My Revolutions* (2007) can be seen as a vital testing ground for many of the ideas of selfhood and consciousness that Kunzru would later bring to fruition, and also the concern for terrorist collectives seen in his most recent novel; its terrorist protagonist, 'Chris', assumes a new identity as a devoted family man called 'Mike', uncovering a relation to the individual that is missing in his terrorist past, which renders its victims inhuman and without substance. Du Dot takes critical readings of the novel in a new direction by considering how these concerns are shaped by a 'poetics of turning and returning in/to time and place'. Reading the novel both as archival and contemporary fiction, psychogeographic motifs of drift forge connections between Kunzru's writing and novelists such as Iain Sinclair and J.G. Ballard, evoking both a literal and figurative use of spatiality. This critical reading does much to reposition *My Revolutions* in Kunzru's literary chronology, offering new connections between *My Revolutions* and other Kunzru works, such as *Twice Upon a Time: Listening to New York*.

The diversity of Kunzru's writing output is unrivalled, moving across continents, thematically diverse and formally varied. At the same time, within this sprawling intellectual landscape Kunzru's work reveals leitmotifs and interconnections, a networked imagination brought to the fore recently with his suggestion that *White Tears* and *Red Pill* are the first two instalments of a loose 'trilogy'. Like viewing a fractal that reveals its patterns only under the microscope, it is in exploring Kunzru's works in dialogue with each other that the nuances of his key prevailing themes of hybridity, cultural appropriation, imperial structures, consciousness and neoliberal systems of control fully emerge. Yet what truly unites his work is its ability to provoke debate, to interrogate dominant discursive positions, and to complicate and entangle. While such characteristics might seem to be common features of postmodern literatures, Kunzru's work is distinct for the ways in which its critique reaches inward to intentionally confound even its own notion of complication. It is the central contention of this book that such quality marks Kunzru's work as defining of the contemporary literary moment – a literature that extends beyond familiar terminology and which offers new interventions not only into many of the most discussed themes in contemporary literary criticism, but also into the very question of how we write about literature in the twenty-first century.

References

Aldama, Fredrick Luis (2005). 'Hari Kunzru in Conversation', *Wasafiri*, 20:45, 11–14.

Bollen, Christopher (2020). 'Ask a Sane Person: Hari Kunzru on the Differences Between Signalling and Seizing Change', *Interview Magazine*, 10 June, www.interviewmagazine.com/culture/ask-a-sane-person-hari-kunzru-on-the-difference-between-signaling-and-seizing-change (accessed 8 August 2022).

Childs, Peter and Green, James (2013). *Aesthetics and Ethics in Twenty-First Century British Novels* (London: Bloomsbury).

East, Louise (2002). 'Making an Impression', *Irish Times*, 12 April, www.irishtimes.com/culture/making-an-impression-1.1084867 (accessed 8 August 2022).

Edwards, Caroline (2019). 'The Networked Novel', in Daniel O'Gorman and Robert Eaglestone (eds), *The Routledge Companion to Twenty-First Century Literary Fiction* (London: Routledge), 13–24.

Erikson, Steve (2017). 'Sonic Youth: Cultural Appropriations of Two Musical Hipsters', *New York Times*, 29 March, www.nytimes.com/2017/03/29/books/review/white-tears-hari-kunzru.html (accessed 8 August 2022).

Evaristo, Bernadine (2017). 'Interview with Hari Kunzru', *Brit Lit Berlin 2017*, https://writersmakeworlds.com/hari-kunzru/ (accessed 8 August 2022).

Grimes, William (2009). 'Londonstan', *New York Times*, 6 August, www.nytimes.com/2009/08/09/books/review/Grimes-t.html (accessed 8 August 2022).

Gunning, Dave (2010). *Race and Antiracism in Black British and British Asian Literature* (Liverpool: Liverpool University Press).

Kunzru, Hari (2003a). 'Salman Rushdie Interview', www.harikunzru.com/salman-rushdie-interview-2003/ (accessed 8 August 2022).

——— (2003b). 'Making Friends with the *Mail*', www.harikunzru.com/making-friends-with-the-mail-2003/ (accessed 8 August 2022).

——— (2014). *Twice Upon a Time: Listening to New York* (New York: Atavist Books).

Monroe, Brendan (2021). 'Enter the Matrix', *Browsing Bookshops*, browsingbookshops.com/2021/05/10/enter-the-matrix/ (accessed 8 August 2022).

Mudge, Alden (2002). 'Identity Crisis: The Many Faces of an Amazing Traveler', *Bookpage*, www.bookpage.com/0204bp/hari_kunzru.htm (accessed 6 August 2010).

Murphy, Neil and Wai-Chew Sim (eds) (2008). *British Asian Fiction: Framing the Contemporary* (Amherst: Cambria).

Piccarella, Stephen. (2019). 'An Interview with Hari Kunzru', *The Believer*, 2 December, https://believermag.com/an-interview-with-hari-kunzru/ (accessed 8 August 2022).

Schoene, Berthold (2009). *The Cosmopolitan Novel* (Edinburgh: Edinburgh University Press).

Self, Will (2014). 'The Novel Is Dead and This Time It's for Real', *Guardian*, 2 May, www.theguardian.com/books/2014/may/02/will-self-novel-dead-literary-fiction (accessed 8 August 2022).

Shaw, Kristian (2017). *Cosmopolitanism in Twenty-First Century Fiction* (Cham: Palgrave Macmillan).

—— (2021). *Brexlit: British Literature and the European Project* (London: Bloomsbury).

Shaw, Kristian and Upstone, Sara (2021). 'The Transglossic: Contemporary Fiction and the Limitations of the Modern', *English Studies*, 102:5, 573–600.

Shelden, Ashley T. (2012). 'Cosmopolitan Love: The One and the World in Hari Kunzru's *Transmission*', *Contemporary Literature*, 53:2, 348–373.

Shields, David (2010). *Reality Hunger* (London: Penguin).

Sooke, Alastair (2007). 'Sign of the Times', *The New Statesman*, 6 September.

Tripney, Natasha (2012). 'Untold Story by Monica Ali', *Guardian*, 15 July, www.theguardian.com/books/2012/jul/15/monica-ali-untold-story-review (accessed 8 August 2022).

Upstone, Sara (2010). *British Asian Fiction: Twenty-First-Century Voices* (Manchester: Manchester University Press).

1

'Walking into Whiteness': *The Impressionist* and the routes of empire

Churnjeet Mahn

The literary self-awareness of *The Impressionist* (2003 [2002]) facilitates a narrative excoriation of the English canon's most persistently racist tropes and techniques through a precisely judged mimicry of form. The novel is replete with literary references which have been the mainstay of English Literature degrees, alongside a recognition of the theoretical arguments and debates which characterised the intersection of postmodern, poststructuralist and postcolonial thought in the 1990s. The critical appraisal of Hari Kunzru's debut novel turns to Homi K. Bhabha's studies of liminality, mimicry and hybridity (Haiven, 2013; Haider, 2004; Aldama, 2005; Graham, 2013; Aydemir, 2006), as well the work of Gilles Deleuze and Félix Guattari, which has produced extremely productive accounts of multiethnic and diasporic experience, securing Kunzru's reputation in the early 2000s as a leading figure in an emerging generation of British Asian writers. While Bhabha's work provides a productive framework for thinking about hybridity and mimicry in *The Impressionist* as literary mechanisms for exploring identities caught between states (in more senses than one), it does not give us a framework for thinking about how the novel takes a critical aim at the histories of travel which have undergirded white supremacy. In some ways, *The Impressionist* is a classic travel text: it follows an itinerant protagonist skimming across different landscapes. The only thing that remains consistent in the text is that Pran will remain on the move. However, by deploying several subplots associated with different kinds of 'travel' (contagious diseases travelling across borders with people, people 'crossing' the boundaries of gender, people 'crossing' the boundaries of race),

Kunzru focuses on the types of drag, inertia and difficulties that minoritised and marginalised identities face.

The Impressionist takes aims at the worst allegations against travel writing. Take, for example, this charge from Debbie Lisle: 'the genre encourages a particularly conservative political outlook that extends to its vision of global politics. This is frustrating because travel writing has the potential to re-imagine the world in ways that do not simply regurgitate the status quo or repeat a nostalgic longing for Empire' (Lisle, 2006: xi). This chapter explores some of the ways in which *The Impressionist* uses travel to 're-imagine the world' by critiquing the freighted history of travel, migration and exile. In *The Impressionist*, the journey to the West is not simply the protagonist's travel from India to Britain, it is his journey to *whiteness*. In this sense, the novel challenges some of the dominant features of travel narratives; as Justin D. Edwards and Run Grauland argue, 'Part of the problem is that "travel" has so often been conflated with "European(ized) travel"' (2012: 3). *The Impressionist* is a European account of travel insofar as it relies on the reader's recognition of stock tropes from colonial-era travel writing; however, its parody of the form reverses the dominant tropes of mapping and representation that pervade travel writing, as *Britishness* (or narrower *Englishness*) becomes a target for ethnographic study through the protagonist's successful mimicry of colonial hegemonic English masculinity.

The basic elements of the plot see the protagonist Pran Nath travel across India, to Europe and then to West Africa, with all of these stages representing different levels of success and failure in his ability to pass as white. The novel does not shift significantly in genre, but it does shift in style, especially as the narrative focalises through some less sympathetic characters for significant episodes of the text while Pran takes on different names. The suspension of belief that is required to follow Pran's *travails* across the colonial world does not necessitate a hesitation over whether some of the key historical events narrated in the text are *real*. Pran may be a hollow character (he is variously described as protean and a husk in the novel), but psychological realism is not one of the novel's ambitions. Instead, we can read *The Impressionist* as a hypotactic montage of colonial scenes arranged in a dense set of textual and historical allusions. This chapter is organised into two sections that work through some of these allusions and textual operations. The first section deals with ideas of 'contagion' and 'contamination' through European contact with Indian society (involving British travel to India). The second section follows Pran's journey to successfully passing as British (concerning the journey to whiteness).

Hygienic identities, contagious fears

In *The Impressionist*, Pran is the fleshy embodiment of a threatening biohybridity that will travel across the colonial world (through his *travails* at the borders of heterosexuality and whiteness). If the Spanish Flu is the real epidemic in the room, then the metaphorical one is the epidemic of miscegenation that appears to threaten high-caste Hindus as much as white British administrators. Another site of border-crossing comes with scenes featuring South Asia's *hijra* community alongside a very white-centred anxiety around homo-sexuality. *Hijras* pose a categorical problem for the colonial Indian state: they are literally and figuratively border-crossing subjects. What remains curious is that while *The Impressionist* is adept at dismantling and reassembling discriminatory structures of racialised difference, gender non-conforming and transgender subjects are collapsed into iterations of a comedic monstrous other. Kunzru uses the Spanish Flu as an epidemic metaphor to trouble the borders of race and caste, alongside gender and sexuality. Contagion becomes a real and figurative device which demonstrates the dangerous and transformative potential of contact.

Kunzru reverses the trajectory of nineteenth- and twentieth-century contagion narratives which used racist assumptions and orientalism as their organising principles. From Mary Shelley's *The Last Man* (1826), which sees a pandemic originating in the East threaten the very existence of humanity, to Bram Stoker's *Dracula* (1897), another threat from the East arriving on Western shores, existential threat to Western civilisation has been continually coded as disease. In her wide-ranging study, *Epidemic Empire: Colonialism, Contagion, and Terror, 1817–2020* (2021), Anjuli Kolb traces the language of contagion and disease as a tool the state can use to naturalise, and medicalise, the equation of a healthy society with whiteness. Kolb argues that 'the imperial disease poetics that casts insurgent violence as epidemic is grounded in narrative and scientific practices central to the management of empire and neoimperial formations' (2021: 4). The slippage between material measures to manage outbreaks of disease which are a threat to life, and metaphors of disease which are a threat to white (heterosexual) lives, creates a framework to operationalise structural racism under the guise of public health. For colonial officials in India in the 1850s, the real fear was not the massive outbreaks of cholera, rather, it was the 'epidemic' of insurgency (Kolb, 2021; Wagner, 2013). The slippery terrain between real and metaphorical virus, disease, and contagion, becomes the fertile ground for *The Impressionist*'s take on contagious mobilities. This section considers two types of contamination metaphors: miscegenation (racial contamination) and orientalised queerness (the contamination of white heteropatriarchy). Both are made literal through the body of the text's protagonist. Pran is an 'Anglo-Indian' of sorts and as Rukhsana is dressed in a sari, seemingly to satisfy the sexual curiosity of Fatehpur's local colonial administrator (his real desires are misread). *The Impressionist*'s lead into this metaphorical emplotting, however, begins with a very different kind of contagion: an actual epidemic, which rather than coming from the East, arrives from the West to pull the trigger on the disorder of Pran's body and life.

Pran's father, Amar Nath, is the embodiment of puritanical high-caste Hindu values, and espouses practical philosophy as an inoculation against the contaminating influence of the non-Indian world: 'He had recently published an article in *The Pioneer* on the question of loss of caste through foreign travel, coming down firmly against the notion of leaving Indian soil' (*TI*: 23). Nath's evangelising is an exercise in futility as the flu epidemic arrives in Agra with soldiers returning from the First World War and the goods flowing across the routes of empire. As he watches people becoming ill around him, one of the most disturbing consequences of contagion is its unexpected effect on bodily distinction, which pervades his nightmares: 'The dream people are horrific and indistinct. At a look or a touch they blur into one another – woman into man, black into white, low into high. It seems the epidemic will obliterate all conceivable distinctions, hybridizing his whole world into one awful undifferentiated mass' (*TI*: 35).

The epidemic engineers the ultimate nightmare: the disintegration of identity through the erasure of embodied markers of difference that have, until now, acted as the guarantors of social distinction and thereby social order. *The Impressionist* finds temporary anchorage in key moments of contact and transmission in the colonial world which reconfigure social relations. As well as being a plot device for dispatching Amar Nath and accelerating Pran's exit into an unsympathetic world, the opening section of the novel allows biological contagion to expand into metaphors of zombie bio-hybridity that become portentous for Pran. *The Impressionist* is preoccupied with the dissolution of literal and figurative borders. In some cases, this is read as celebratory. As Pretty Bobby escapes Bombay, 'He feels the earth moving swift and frictionless beneath his feet' (*TI*: 286). But for most of the novel, the prospect of hybridised, 'half-baked', 'hyphenated' bodies and identities acts as a point of friction that takes the protagonist apart at the seams, only to remake him elsewhere. The revelation of Pran's parentage is the initiation for a contagion narrative that is plotted through the novel in the recurring failure of racial sorting projects that depend on absolute ethnic purity but operate through skin deep readings.

The absolute ethnic purity of Amar Nath is something that can be recited and enumerated through the patronymic listing of Nath's ancestors, which in its recitation evidences a Pandit-caste bloodline of unbroken purity receding into depths of history. Pran's light skin, which was once testament of his Kashmiri Pandit ancestry – along with the attendant associations with Aryan identity popularised in late nineteenth-century anthropological and linguistic accounts of India and Europe – transforms into a biological betrayal that has been hiding in plain sight. Pran's skin, the proof of Amar Nath's untainted bloodline, transitions to the proof of another truth about his parentage which Amar Nath succumbs to (a favoured term in *The Impressionist* as a parody of colonial language for the dissolution of body and character) while bathing in onion skins, a last-ditch attempt to find a desi cure for a foreign contagion.

Pran's mother, Amrita, is described as 'polluted' after her sexual relationship with Forrester, a scene which itself is fuelled by opium and illusory after-effects, taking it outside the safety of 'real' relations (*TI*: 23; 22). Amrita's maid, Anjali, creates an equation which balances the Spanish Flu, on the one side, and miscegenation, on the other:

> She expounds on the theme of miscegenation, and all its terrible consequences. Impurities, blendings, pollutions, smearings and muckings-up of all kinds are bound to flow from such a blend of blood, which offends against every tenet of orthodox religion. Small wonder the city of Agra is suffering a plague. She, for one, would not be surprised to discover that the entire influenza epidemic, all twenty million global deaths of it, was down to Pran. The boy is bad through and through. (*TI*: 39)

The inverted trajectory of this contagion narrative operates by networking associated discriminatory structures, namely race and caste's role in social segregation. 'Pollution' of the Pandit caste's bloodline becomes a metaphor for a destructive and diseased hybridity. What does this critique of mobility mean in a text written at a time when mobile and hybrid characters were so celebrated in British Asian writing? By bringing in the lens of caste, Kunzru creates a space for considering how Hindutva ideologies produce layered fears of miscegenation which co-conspire to ensure the minoritisation of sexually and ethnically diverse communities. Pran travels because there is no community he can call home or that can house his body without requiring censure or alternation.

Pran's itinerant life begins with a journey to Agra's Anglo-Indian community, where he quickly discovers that the practice of living a hyphenated identity is actually the mastery of artifice and disguise. Whiteness reigns supreme in the Anglo-Indian community, with Indian physical characteristics becoming unavoidable biological betrayals which might be hidden by flattering light, but which can safely be eliminated from character and cultural practice, if not environment. Racial mixing introduces the contagion of otherness to whiteness which is consistently figured in terms of hygiene: 'Of course they do not call it that. They have other names. Dirt, grubbiness. She has such grubby skin, dear. No one will ever go near her. And her nose. So flat and broad. Not like yours' (*TI*: 47). This brief episode in the text prefigures the preoccupation with passing in the novel, especially the conditions under which the proper recognition of whiteness operates. In her analysis of *The Impressionist*, Deepika Bahri asks, 'what might the Anglo-Indian experience of passing, hitherto studied poorly in postcolonial theory, teach us about the bioaesthetic dimensions of assimilation?' (Bahri, 2017: chapter 2), While Pran may have the biological assets to pass as white, his accent and accented existence betray something else. *The Impressionist* creatively interrogates the dimensions, and limits, of assimilation and passing through Pran's refashioning in Agra and Fatehpur, as he is named (and becomes) Rukhsana and Clive.

Rejected by Agra's Anglo-Indian community for being insufficiently white, Pran enters a *hijra* community seeking shelter, only to be drugged and kept captive for forced sex. This marks the beginning of Pran's first substantial journey (Agra to Fatehpur) and his first renaming (from Pran to Rukhsana). The basic elements of the plot involve Pran being transported to Fatehpur, accompanied by the Kwaja-sera, and then dressed in a sari and presented to Major Privett-Clampe as part of an elaborate and convoluted blackmail plot that will involve compromising pictures of the Major in flagrante. As a contemporary review observes, 'The tone of the Fatehpur section is uneasily farcical, more influenced by the *Carry On* films than Kipling' (Mars-Jones, 2002). Part of the unease of this farce comes from the utilisation of the *hijra* community as a metaphor that lacks the more complex critique of race that runs through the novel. Rather than seeing gender and sexuality as potentially organising forms of colonial knowledge about the very boundaries of sex and gender, it is reproduced as the literal and figurative butt of a sexual joke.

Critics writing about this point of the text have termed Pran's time as Rukhsana in terms of being a 'transvestite' (Haider, 2004). For example, 'Pran becomes Rukhsana, meaning bright new dawn, a transvestite threatened with a hermaphrodite's identity' (Bahri, 2017: chapter 2). *The Impressionist* does not use the term 'transvestite', which itself is part of a historical, medicalised language used to denigrate forms of non-gender-conforming life. The use of this term by critics is an attempt to identify a disjuncture: in some ways Pran never *becomes* Rukhsana. He is not castrated, and whatever life as a *hijra* might signify for Pran, his adoption of 'feminine characteristics' only ensures he becomes submissive, which is his default throughout much of the novel. Pran is an awkward fit for

Rukhsana, but what does this awkward fit tell us about colonial regimes of racialised and sexualised difference?

Hijras are one of South Asia's historical communities which were, effectively, criminalised during British colonial rule as part of the Criminal Tribes Act of 1871. As Jessica Hinchy deftly shows in *Governing Gender and Sexuality in Colonial India: The Hijra c. 1850–1900* (2019), the *hijra* 'panics' from the mid-1850s amongst some colonial officials in India were attached to the threat of sexual and moral contamination from a community which was poorly understood in terms of gender by colonial officials, as nothing more than deviant criminality. In early European travel writing about India from the sixteenth and seventeenth centuries, the 'eunuchs' described were male-embodied *Khwajasarais*, court servants in *zenanas* (Hinchy, 2019), and not *hijras*. However, various types of non-gender-conforming bodies came under increasing scrutiny as colonial power extended. In *The Impressionist*, a spectrum of 'deviant' sexuality is displayed, but without some of the historical texture (details from colonial archives and history) that gives these plot points any resonance beyond plot functions designed to further the plot.

The combination of the Criminal Tribes Act of 1871, which worked to try and eliminate *hijra* communities, especially in terms of physical reproduction, with Section 377 of the Indian Penal Code (1860), which targeted non-reproductive sex, particularly 'sodomy', meant *hijras* became outlaw subjects. This extended into more generalised observations about *hijra* behaviour which pathologised them as inherent biological threats to colonial order and containment:

> Hijras' periodic travels for alms-collection, though usually of short distance, undermined colonial concepts of centralised political authority by destabilising political borders and were seen as evidence of Hijra criminality. This aspect of the Hijra stereotype was related to long-standing associations between peripatetic peoples and criminality in colonial discourse and law. (Hinchy, 2019: 9)

The Impressionist deploys colonial stereotypes of *hijras* including sexual corruption, kidnapping, dirt and moral depravity: 'To make them go away you must give them money, otherwise they will curse your household. They are outcasts, as ancient as the hills, a human dirty joke which has been told and retold since the hero Arjun was cursed to spend a year as a hermaphrodite conjurer' (*TI*: 72). The 'human dirty joke' remains relatively unchallenged in the text as Pran-Rukhsana agonises over the prospect of castration: 'Pran looks down at himself, at his body modestly swathed in black. He looks across the carriage at the pair of too-tall women, with their raucous voices and strong jaws and exaggerated way of walking. The women smile back. Then he remembers something else, a really bad thing, the other thing everyone knows about hijras. They are eunuchs' (*TI*: 72). The 'too-tall women', the 'strong jaws' and the 'exaggerated' walk end up acting as another kind of failed passing narrative: their gendered excess becomes an aberration. Just as Pran's accent barred him from any hope of being admitted to the Agra's Anglo-Indian community, here the exaggerated walk becomes another kind of utterance that ruins the 'illusion' of properly performed gender.

If part of the colonial project in India attempted to 'clean up' the mess of Indian gender and sexualities, then *The Impressionist* fails to explore how Indian queerness touches and troubles the borders of white heteronormativity; instead, this other gendered reality offers a suite of tropes to suggestively extend the prospect of Pran's borderless existence (which physically continues to remain skin deep). As the Khwaja-sera morphs into a timeless, borderless being, the cut of flesh becomes the promise of a utopian existence:

> 'Such idiocy! All it takes is a cut.' He flourishes the knife. 'This blade is a key, Rukhsana. It opens the door to an infinity of bodies, a wonderful infinity of sexes [...] You may think you are singular. You may think you are incapable of change. But we are all as mutable as the air! Release yourself, release your body and you can be a myriad! An army! There are no names for it, Rukhsana. Names are just the foolishness of language, which is a bigger kind of foolishness than most. Why try to stop a river? Why try to freeze a cloud?' He halts his pirouetting and, ancient again, shuffles towards Pran, holding out the knife. (*TI*: 82)

These kinds of episodes (brief manifestos on the borderless possibilities of identity multiplied by the text, realised through a language that impels them into existence) are a trademark of an increasing number of postcolonial texts using race, gender and mobility to unmake the very idea of discrete or primary categories of identity.

These are texts which mark a clear departure from the boundless possibilities of protean postmodern hybridity in order to feel the possibilities, and limitations, of bodies caught between categories. Aren Aizura's wide-ranging study of how travel, as practice and metaphor, structures transgender narratives in the late twentieth century poses the following question: 'What different accounts might we arrive at by deconstructing the travel metaphor's historical, geographical, and racially specific logics rather than understanding the travel metaphor as impelled by individual autobiographies?' (Aizura, 2018: 34). Aizura's work begins with an examination of colonial tropes in travel writing (through discussing the work of the travel writer Jan Morris) to consider how the backdrop of travel to the 'orient' extracts the exotic *queerness* of non-Western spaces for gender transformations while rendering the 'native' population little more than handmaidens or assistants in the process. In *The Impressionist*, *hijras* and the Khwaja-sera are used as figures to accelerate Pran's transition in circumstance and status with regards to race and 'Englishness', but a critical moment that questions the overwriting of historical and lived sexual difference is lost through uncritical reproductions of homo- and transphobic representations.

Joseph Allen Boone's *The Homoerotics of Orientalism* (2015) is primarily a study of the rich seam of 'ethnopornography' that runs through literary and visual representations of the Middle East. However, some elements of his model can be applied to the workings of *The Impressionist*: 'the ghostly presence of something "like" male homoeroticism [...] haunts many Western men's fantasies and fears' (Boone, 2015: xx). Boone demonstrates how the misreading of figures such as the *Khwajasera* as 'homosexuals' who practice sodomy in literary and visual representations circulating in the West had the ability to reorder the understanding of Europe's queer others. Queerness is always a matter of perspective (what is something queer *from?*). *The Impressionist* riffs off the orientalised fantasies of European travellers and scholars for whom queer forms like homosexuality were cultural *and* environmental markers of degeneration which threatened, however ironically, the borders of European heteronormativity. Nowhere is this overlap of oriental fantasy, pseudo-anthropology and rudimentary sexology more evident than the work of Richard Burton: 'Within the Sotadic Zone the Vice is popular and endemic, held at the worst to be a mere peccadillo, whilst the races to the North and South of the limits here defined practise it only sporadically amid the opprobrium of their fellows who, as a rule, are physically incapable of performing the operation and look upon it with the liveliest disgust' (Burton, 1886: 177). Burton's Sotadic Zone, which incorporates northern India, delineates the crucial distinction: European men may engage in sexual acts (presumably by accident, by force or through active self-loathing or disgust), but there is something *endemic* about queer practices and cultures within the Sotadic Zone. The threat of a moral disease contaminating whiteness through sexual contacts conditions the relations between Pran-Rukhsana and Privett-Clampe. In this setting, *The Impressionist* is able to deploy a deft reminder that whiteness and homophobia were intrinsically linked in the British colonial project.

Pran-Rukhsana provides a complication for Privett-Clampe. Dressed as Rukhsana, he can be presented in the context of an exoticised queerness that seems just about tolerable and comprehensible for his assistant, and for the Prince Firoz and his compatriots. However, behind closed doors, Pran is dressed in an English school boy's outfit and made to recite 'Gunga Din' and 'The Charge of the Light Brigade'. As Pran is renamed Clive, he becomes increasingly adept at mimicking an English accent, performing what Bahri has called a kind of 'sonic drag' (Bahri, 2017): 'Eventually, in the way of things, Privett-Clampe's noble fiction starts to coincide with reality, and even the trouser-fiddling stops. Clive's accent improves and the Major contents himself with mistily watching his protégé. "Oh yes," murmurs the Major. "Ring it out. That's the way"' (*TI*: 111). Privett-Clampe tells Pran-Clive to 'listen to the white' (*TI*: 109) voice inside him, and as his accent and posture change, his successful passing, his temporary permit into whiteness, becomes more possible, something which instantly bars him from being an object of sexual exploitation for Privett-Clampe. Throughout this relationship, the peak of Privett-Clampe's sexual desire is for a Pran (recognised as an Indian adolescent, but with some English blood) in the drag of an English schoolboy. When Pran is Rukhsana, he is *too queer*. But when he is Clive, he is *too white*.

The 'Rukhsana' section may be high camp, but it does utilise different kinds of sexual and gendered 'panic' to interrogate the operation of whiteness. Toward the section's conclusion, Privett-Clampe feels horror and disgust as he is confronted with pornography showing white women's sexual enslavement by non-white men: 'The scene comes to a conclusion, and is rapidly replaced by one in which Sylvia is joined by another female captive. The sight of not one but two white women in peril floods the Major with memories of his darkest days of maharajas and le vice Anglais' (*TI*: 140). The scene drawn on the spectacular popularity of white captive narratives from the mid-nineteenth century. A prime example of this was Hiram Powers's sculpture *The Greek Slave* (1847) which portrayed, in white marble, a naked white woman, in chains, averting her gaze from her supposed Turkish captor. Different versions of this statue toured in North America and Europe with immense and scandalous success. The racial drama of *The Greek Slave* is heightened by her rendering in white marble, her hyper-whiteness caught just before the moment of her sexual contamination.

This is the moment the narrative anticipates one of Pran's most uncharacteristic moves: instead of going with the flow of circumstances, he refuses Privett-Clampe, telling him, 'I'm not your boy', just before Privett-Clampe collapses during a tiger hunt gone wrong (*TI*: 176). If Pran is refusing to be cast in a sexualised white saviour narrative here, then it will not be long before he is cast into another one. The opening chapters of *The Impressionist* riff, recycle and rework a variety of literary and cultural racisms which variously deploy metaphors of contagion. This becomes a strategy for literalising the panic around hybrid identities that underlines that the only successful passing can be absolute passing. The following discussion focuses on that transition to whiteness by *measuring* the experience of cultural difference felt by Europeans in India.

The journey to whiteness

In her 1991 Modern Language Studies keynote, 'Arts of the Contact Zone', Mary Louise Pratt outlines the dangers and possibilities of writing in a space structured by asymmetric power relations, where legacies of colonialism and slavery find articulation in everyday practice:

> Autoethnography, transculturation, critique, collaboration, bilingualism, mediation, parody, denunciation, imaginary dialogue, vernacular expression – these are some of the literate arts of the contact zone. Miscomprehension, incomprehension, dead letters, unread masterpieces, absolute heterogeneity of meaning – these are some of the perils of writing in the contact zone. They all live among us today in the transnationalized metropolis of the United States and are becoming more widely visible, more pressing, and [...] more decipherable to those who once would have ignored them in defense of a stable, centered sense of knowledge and reality. (Pratt, 1991: 37)

Pratt's definition of the contact zone, and her work on the history of travel writing as ethnographic practice in *Imperial Eyes: Travel Writing and Transculturation* (1992), helped to create a travel-specific set of coordinates to understand the odd asynchronicity of contemporary travel writing. Contemporary travel writing's reliance on the all too familiar tropes of unidirectional travel (from global north to global south, from Occident to Orient) and the travel market's obsession with authenticity (exceptional travellers describing 'real' cultures), has left travel writing particularly open to being seen as an antediluvian form unable to adequately remake or satirise its own predilection for the centring of whiteness. Therefore, while Pratt's analysis has focused on travel writing as a kind of literary contact zone, her work has been more successful at seeding discussions of hybridised and diasporic subjectivities outside the field of literal travel. Pratt's description of the contact zone offers a narrative template for *The Impressionist*: the text itself shows the arts of the contact zone in a highly fashioned text which is self-aware of the historical freight of literal journeys, with the view that some creative resequencing of these journeys can recalculate and reorientate some of the vectors of descriptive and discriminatory power.

This second section of the chapter follows Pran's journey to whiteness, which itself involves travelling through the institutions that *produce* whiteness, and the places cast as the most 'other' of European civilisation. This is a journey where Pran will travel to the heart of empire from India, and then end his journey somewhere on the African continent. Literal travel becomes the vehicle for critical explorations of difference. The measurement of various feelings of difference experienced by white Europeans in India is parodied in *The Impressionist* through an obsession with new disciplines emerging in the humanities and social sciences for measuring and quantifying that difference, from ethnography, anthropology and phrenology to geography and cartography.[1] Pran's success in ventriloquising whiteness through the eroticised exercises in elocution delivered by Privett-Clampe leads him to a point in the narrative where he now has to physically measure up to whiteness.

The first step in this journey is made via Amritsar, just as the 1919 massacre of peaceful protesters at Jallianwala Bagh takes place. The Amritsar section of the novel is brief, but curious, because it sits in stark contrast against the comedy, pomp and camp of the preceding section. As the narrative drifts towards a realism that is informed more by colonial historical record than comedic colonial misadventure, there is a question about the purpose this section serves. On the one hand, the narrative cycles through some familiar tropes in the threat of white women being raped during the riots (which brings together white sexual panic with the premonition of the horrors of miscegenation) and the physical disorder of the city (realised in the stench of human excrement drifting through Amritsar). General O'Dwyer is referenced but not met; however, anyone familiar with the story of Jallianwala Bagh knows that the Punjabi revolutionary Udham Singh will travel to London to assassinate O'Dwyer in 1940. To achieve his aim, Udham Singh will cut his hair (kept long and in a turban as a baptised Sikh) and shave his beard in order to pass as an acculturated Indian, travelling to London, the new motherland or home for children of the Empire. Udham Singh was a member of the Ghadar movement, a radical anti-colonial political movement founded in 1913 in the United States and Canada by the Punjabi diaspora who travelled back to Punjab in the wake of the First World War to encourage and initiate more widespread direct action against the British Empire. Udham Singh and the Ghadar movement are part of the extra-textual histories of resistance to empire that act as a counterpoint to Pran's growing desire to be admitted into whiteness.

The penultimate step in this journey is Pran's time as Robert (Pretty Bobby/Chandra) in Bombay with the Scottish missionary Andrew Macfarlane and his wife, Elspeth. Andrew and Elspeth are used to exemplify different stereotypes about the British colonial resident in India: while Macfarlane is preoccupied with hygiene lectures and warning against miscegenation (and it comes as no surprise when the reader later discovers he has a daughter with one of the 'natives'), Elspeth is in danger of 'going native'. With her interest in Theosophy, and gothic romance, she becomes steadily alienated from Scotland, calling Robert 'Chandra'. Her time in the novel is ended by her arrest for contravening the Defence of India Act; Andrew Macfarlane's biological 'crime' can never be as bad as the affective dimension of sympathy and comingling. Macfarlane's preoccupation with racial sciences, however, is the more sustained narrative thread in this section of the novel. Extracts from anthropological textbooks are spliced with accounts of Macfarlane's own exploits in an attempt to show how the potential for manifest hypocrisy to disassemble him is smoothed over by his successful reproduction of whiteness:

> *Compared to the parent of the higher race, the children are a deteriorated product. The mixture, if general and continued through generations, will infallibly entail a lower grade of power in the descent. The net balance of the two accounts will show a loss when compared with the result of unions among the higher race alone.*

> What had he brought into the world? He could not remember what the child looked like. Gradually her face was obliterated by those of his two young sons, born whole and unsullied by their father's previous failure. They were his pride, yet sometimes the price seemed too high. (*TI*: 230, italics in original)

For Macfarlane, Pran-Robert is initially an unwelcome reminder of his daughter, but the gift of Christian disciple and devotion to Pran-Robert's life is one way of exorcising his guilt. Although Macfarlane's sons had been a way to whitewash his history, their deaths left an emptiness which for both Macfarlanes is filled by working on the potential of Pran-Robert (for Elspeth, this will be through Pran-Chandra). Through Pran-Robert, Macfarlane can work to draw out the 'higher' attributes that might be possible in someone 'half-baked'. Here, Pran-Robert becomes the object of phrenological and photographic scrutiny: a body to be captured, measured, described and catalogued, in an attempt to decipher the degree of his biological (racial) degradation:

> Robert is unscrewed and placed on a chair, as the Reverend employs his new measuring devices on the various parameters of his head. Facial angle is fixed at ninety-three degrees, the nose found to be leptorrhine and eyes mesosemic, with a certain upturning at the corners which is announced to be a tell-tale indication of Asiatic origin. The jaw is pleasingly orthognathic, a contrast to the jutting prognathous jaw of the Negro skull illustrated in Nott and Gliddon's *Indigenous Races of the Earth*. This interesting volume is given to Robert to flick through while the Reverend jots down his results. He looks at the pictures of noble Greek statuary and twisted soot-black nigger faces, and feels, as he often does, a peculiar relief at his resemblance to one and not the other. (*TI*: 197)

While describing the process of craniometry, Pran-Robert conducts his own kind of phrenological analysis by flicking through Nott and Gliddon. Why he chooses to see himself in one and not another face is not clear, although the reader has been following him on a narrative trajectory towards whiteness (this is not the first time Pran and white Greek statues are compared). What this scene in the novel demonstrates is how the colonial obsession with measurement and visuality, where faces can become texts that can be read and catalogued, determines the networks and possibilities of affective affinity across the colonial world. Pran-Robert's relief indicates how imbibed racism changes the direction he faces: instead of feeling like an 'other' of Europe, he can begin to see how he might, quite possibly, measure up to other 'real' white men.

As 'Pretty Bobby' outside the mission, Pran-Bobby begins to perfect his mimicry of whiteness by accosting tourists and travellers arriving from Britain and acting as a kind of tour guide for them: 'The point is to tell them a story. Any story will do, so long as it is English. Or rather about being English' (*TI*: 245). After Pran-Robert/Pretty Bobby steals the identity of the murdered Jonathan Bridgeman (naturally this is the 'bridging' character between East and West), he leaves behind his life in India to travel to the 'mystic Occident', where his final transformation into Englishness is guaranteed through his entry to boarding school and university (*TI*: 289). Oxford becomes 'a machine for the formation of character' dependent on conformity and the persecution of outsiders (*TI*: 346). Pran-Jonathan's character is refined to face the ultimate test: through being an able apprentice to Professor Chapel, can he demonstrate his worthiness to marry his daughter? Jonathan (later known as Bridgeman) becomes the most successful transition for Pran because it represents a role that Pran has been in training for throughout the novel: performing Englishness for white men. Rather than being a phrenological curiosity for Andrew Macfarlane to measure, Pran-Jonathan can become part of an anthropological team; he can begin to conduct his own observations and measurements of otherness.

As Pran-Bridgeman plans his travels to West Africa to document the Foste, a highly reclusive, 'primitive' and 'pristine' community, the novel moves into its most directed parody of Joseph Conrad's *Heart of Darkness* (1899) through references to 'blank white space' on maps (*TI*: 315; 363; 370; 431; 448). However, this is a Conrad spliced with Grahame Greene, whose *Journeys Without Maps* embodies more conscious anxiety about travel to unmarked places on British maps of West Africa in search of authentic interactions with Europe's primitive other. Prof Chapel's *Some Months in a Hut with No Plumbing* has a title which tips its hat to accounts of travel from writers such as Greene, whose motivations were felt and described sincerely, but who found themselves at a loss in the field as the elementary forces of plumbing and directions left them to mop their brows, sweating in fear and bewilderment as much as in response to the heat. The journey to see the Foste will also be Pran-Bridgeman's last fixed journey.

Before leaving for West Africa, Pran-Bridgeman visits the 1924 Pageant of Empire where, behind a fence and with an exhibition label reading 'Foste Village/Fosteland/British West Africa', he meets with the 'blank faces' of his first real Fostes (*TI*: 380; 381). The Human Zoos that took people out of their homes to perform as 'savages' for British families on a day out were another visual technology for casting blackness as otherness (Stephen, 2013). As a leisure pursuit, it was the perfect example of how capitalism could mine racist topologies to turn people into exhibits within an experience that underwrote their sense of national belonging to a superior civilisation. The depiction of 'natives' as static, temporally stuck 'behind' Europe in terms of civilisation and progress, is something Arjun Appadurai has aptly called 'metonymic freezing' (Appadurai, 1988: 39). Readers of *The Impressionist* are brought to this moment of the plot by disembarking the metropolitan line at Wembley. The extra-textual irony of this moment, of course, is that if you disembarked the metropolitan line at Wembley in 2002, you would be in the heart of one of Britain's largest South Asian diasporic communities. As with the moment in Amritsar, part of *The Impressionist*'s praxis of recognition involves locations with dense and conflicting accounts of empire and its legacy. The nod to Britain's contemporary South Asian population is important. *The Impressionist* makes an important contribution to British Asian writing by complicating networks of travel that force us to think beyond migration and displacement and consider the longer and more complex ways in which British travel to India has been so formative for what 'Britishness' has meant as an identity (namely through histories of empire).

Even if Pran-Bridgeman acts and thinks as if Pran has been completely erased from his body, his 'uneasy recognition' upon seeing the African continent betrays his residual expressions of inferiority and difference (*TI*: 423). As part of a doomed expedition to meet the Foste, Pran-Bridgeman articulates a realisation that the reader has known for some time: 'He has made himself into an accurate facsimile' of whiteness that is unwanted and out of place (*TI*: 418). As the Foste exorcise him of his hyphenated identities that have insisted on reinforcing the supremacy of whiteness, he turns into a nomad (perhaps a new imitation of a Berber): 'He has no thoughts of arriving anywhere. Tonight he will sleep under the enormous bowl of the sky. Tomorrow he will travel on' (*TI*: 481). Following in the steps of all postmodern travel writers, we are reminded that the journey, not the destination, is the real purpose of travel. Extending from a literal to a spiritual practice of exile, the Impressionist apparently takes control of his peritectic narrative: travel becomes a way to live rather than the narrative engine of displacement. While it may be tempting to read this end as a kind of catharsis or release, it is worth pausing with anthropological writing informed by the tropes of travel writing:

> I hang onto 'travel' as a term of cultural comparison, precisely because of its historical taintedness, its associations with gendered, racial bodies, class privilege, specific means of conveyance, beaten path, agents, frontiers, documents and the like. I prefer it to more apparently neutral and 'theoretical' terms, such as 'displacement', which can make the drawing of equivalences across different historical experiences too easy [...] And I prefer it to terms such as 'nomadism', often generalized without apparent resistance from non-Western experiences. (Nomadology: a form of postmodern primitivism?) (Clifford, 1992: 110)

James Clifford's 'Travelling Cultures' offers a useful warning against taking appropriating terms with specific histories, emptying them of their social and cultural specificity, and repurposing them for figurative models that are can be viewed as emancipatory. The moments where Pran is visually arrested in the field, when he becomes a subject of curiosity, or when he is viewed as a hyphenated aberration, are where the politics and cultural capital of travel make themselves felt in the text.

Conclusion

The Impressionist's intervention in the contemporary politics of travel and migration is sewn into the seams of the text. When Kunzru refused the John Llewellyn Rhys Prize for *The Impressionist*, he wrote, 'By accepting, I would have been giving legitimacy to a publication [the *Mail on Sunday*] that has, over many years, shown itself to be extremely xenophobic – an absurdity for a novelist of mixed race who is supposedly being honoured for a book about the stupidity of racial classifications and the seedy underside of empire' (Kunzru, 2003). Like Jamaica Kincaid's *A Small Place* (1988), Amitav Ghosh's *In an Antique Land* (1992) and Stuart Hall's *Familiar Stranger* (2017), *The Impressionist* uses travel as a forensic tool to understand how empire reordered reality. Ghosh's hybrid academic-ethnographic memoir, detailing his travels across the Muslim world in search of an unnamed Indian slave who travelled to Egypt 700 years ago, brings Ghosh to an archive in Philadelphia:

> At the corner of 4th and Walnut, in the heart of downtown Philadelphia, stands a sleek modern building, an imposing structure that could easily be mistaken for the headquarters of a great multinational corporation. In fact, it is the Annenberg Research Institute, a centre for social and historical research: it owes its creation to the vast fortune generated by the first and most popular of American's television magazines, 'TV Guide' [...] The documents are kept in the Institute's rare book room, a great vault in the bowels of the building, steel-sealed and laser-beamed, equipped with alarms that need no more than seconds to mobilize a fleet of helicopters and police cars.' (Ghosh, 1992: 348)

As Kunzru sat in the British Library researching material for *The Impressionist*, he was performing a similar kind of exercise to Ghosh; his presence in the pristine, air-conditioned building, his handling of residual evidence of lives long lost from view, is the first step in an imaginative reconstruction which itself is always bound up in acts of travel. In both contexts, accounts of lives in India, and Indian lives, become commodities hoarded in the West as part of vast repositories of knowledge, itself a legacy of the imperial urge to collect, collate and document. *The Impressionist* is a novel that treats freighted colonial histories with a light touch. This operates to varying levels of success in this novel but lays the foundations for how travel can be used as a practice and a metaphor for tracing the operation of structural inequalities, something we see revisited in his later texts from *Transmission* (2004) to *White Tears* (2017).

Note

1 For an extensive discussion of the importance of visuality in the period, see Kate Flint, who points out that the Victorians 'were fascinated with the act of seeing, with the question of the reliability – or otherwise – of the human eye, and with the problems of interpreting what they saw' (Flint, 2000: 17).

References

Aizura, Aren Z. (2018). *Mobile Subjects: Transnational Imaginaries of Gender Assignment* (Durham, NC: Duke University Press).

Aldama, Fredrick Luis (2005). 'Hari Kunzru in Conversation', *Wasafiri*, 20:45, 11–14.

Appadurai, Arjun (1988). 'Putting Hierarchy in Its Place', *Cultural Anthropology*, 3:1, 36–49.

Aydemir, M (2006). 'Impressions of Character: Hari Kunzru's *The Impressionist*', in M, Bal, B. Van Eekelen and P. Spyer (eds), *Uncertain Territories: Boundaries in Cultural Analysis* (Amsterdam: Rodopi), 199–217.

Bahri, Deepika (2017). *Postcolonial Biology: Psyche and Flesh after Empire* (Minneapolis: University of Minnesota Press).

Boone, Joseph Allen (2015). *The Homoerotics of Orientalism* (New York: Columbia University Press).

Burton, Richard F. (1886). 'Terminal Essay', in *The Book of the Thousand Nights and a Night: A Plain and Literal Translation of the Arabian Nights Entertainments, Volume 10*, translated by Richard F. Burton (London: Burton Club).

Clifford, James (1992). 'Travelling Cultures', in L. Grossberg, C. Nelson and P.A. Triechler (eds), *Cultural Studies* (London: Routledge), 96–116.

Edwards Justin D. and Rune Grauland (eds) (2012). *Postcolonial Travel Writing* (London: Palgrave).

Flint, Kate (2000). *The Victorians and the Visual Imagination* (Oxford: Oxford University Press).

Ghosh, Amitav (1992). *In an Antique Land* (London: Granta).

Graham, Shane. (2013). 'Memories of Empire: The Empire Exhibition in Andrea Levy's *Small Island* and Hari Kunzru's *The Impressionist*', *The Journal of Commonwealth Literature*, 48:3, 441–452.

Haider, Nishat (2004). 'Hari Kunzru's *The Impressionist*: A Multilayered Bildungsroman Interrogating Diasporic Paradigm', *South Asian Review*, 25:2, 113–123.

Haiven, Max (2013). 'An Interview with Hari Kunzru', *Wasafiri*, 28:3, 18–23.

Hinchy, Jessica (2019). *Governing Gender and Sexuality in Colonial India: The Hijra c. 1850–1900* (Cambridge: Cambridge University Press).

Kolb, Anjuli Fatima Raza (2021). *Epidemic Empire: Colonialism, Contagion and Terror, 1817–2020* (Chicago: University of Chicago Press).

Kunzru, Hari (2003). 'I Am One of Them', *Guardian*, 22 November, www.theguardian.com/books/2003/nov/22/immigration.pressandpublishing (accessed 8 August 2022).

Lisle, Debbie (2006). *The Politics of Contemporary Travel Writing* (Cambridge: Cambridge University Press).

Mars-Jones, Adam (2002). 'East Meets West', *Guardian*, 31 March, www.theguardian.com/books/2002/mar/31/fiction.features1 (accessed 8 August 2022).

Pratt, Mary Louise (1991). 'Arts of the Contact Zone', *Profession*, 33–40.

——(1992). *Imperial Eyes: Travel Writing and Transculturation* (Abingdon: Routledge).

Stephen, Daniel (2013). *The Empire of Progress* (New York: Palgrave Macmillan).

Wagner, Kim A. (2013). ' "Treading Upon Fires": The "Mutiny" – Motif and Colonial Anxieties in British India', *Past & Present*, 218:1, 159–197.

2

'It was the revenge of the uncontrollable world': *Transmission* and COVID-19

Lucienne Loh

It is a salient moment, in the summer of 2021, to revisit Hari Kunzru's *Transmission*, published in 2004, which, in hindsight, offers a particularly prescient narrative centrally concerned not only with a computer virus wreaking havoc throughout the world's technological systems, but also with the construction of a Pan European Border Agency (PEBA). Indeed, the novel appears particularly resonant against the backdrop of the current global COVID-19 pandemic which has changed the world irrevocably since January 2020, as well as the withdrawal of the UK from the European Union on 31 January 2020. *Transmission,* Kunzru's second novel following the international success of his precocious debut novel *The Impressionist* (2002), a sweeping historical text heavily committed to postcolonial ideas, portrays the destructive potential of the digital for an inherently technological, intrinsically interconnected, capitalist world whereby life is wholly mediated, market-driven, constructed and consumer-based. Yet, the novel's epidemiologically inflected title infers the confluence of the biological and technological that defines and shapes life itself in the twenty-first century which has not only led to the spread of COVID-19 globally but has also served as the basis for humanity's efforts to overcome it. The spread of the Leela computer virus across the world in Kunzru's novel through people's electronic devices can serve as an extended metaphor for the transmission of a global pathogen in an interconnected world where viruses, whether electronic or biological, proliferate in uncannily similar ways.

Technological and biological viruses in an interconnected world

Critics frequently laud *Transmission* as a satirical take on 'an eco-nomically and culturally networked world [that] highlights two main driving forces of Westernised modernity: globalised capitalism and instrumental rationality'.[1] Viruses threaten and undermine the pervasive logic of these irrepressible forces while information technology – the cornerstone of twenty-first-century civilisation and globalisation which facilitates the unchecked flow of capital, manufactured goods, services and mass culture – enables global technoscapes and finanscapes to function. These 'scapes' of global-isation, as Arjun Appadurai has conceived them, are the dominant backdrops of Kunzru's novel, but also the metaphorical networks that contour the trajectories of the COVID-19 virus.[2] Yet, these two systems serve as interlinked factors in the spread of zoonotic diseases in the twenty-first century as human society relentlessly encroaches upon natural habitats in the pursuit of 'Western' models of modernity. But they are also the dominant pillars which have circumscribed the political, economic and clinical discourses as well as the technological and scientific approaches adopted to confront the pandemic in the UK and in much of the 'Westernised' world. In other words, overcoming the COVID-19 virus demonstrates the relentless and committed drive to secure their hegemonic ideological grip on the world. As the novel unfolds, the Leela virus exposes the precarity of the fundamental integration of information tech-nology into all facets of modern life and foregrounds the insidious repercussions of this nexus.

Throughout the novel, Kunzru satirises many of the internalised orthodoxies surrounding Westernised modernity which pervade a global collective consciousness. This overriding tone and style is punctuated only occasionally with a sincere narrative voice in a novel which is otherwise saturated with a strident critique of the glibness of postmodern life, enthralled by an age of information technology that only consolidates and further reinforces a capit-alist teleology. 'We've retailed this whole vision of a global future', Kunzru asserts in an interview with the same hallmark sardonic voice layered with self-conscious fatuity that similarly permeates *Transmission*.[3] Yet ironically, as this chapter also argues, the rapid spread of the computer virus throughout the world that was premised on, and precipitated by, the same foundations of 'Western modernity' so recognisable throughout the global North and seemingly so unassailable also paved the way for the inevitable global spread of COVID-19. As with the unremitting transnational dissemination of the Leela computer virus in *Transmission* across all physical and geographical borders, the COVID-19 virus's ceaseless consumption of human bodies *qua* bodies reflects the constructed and superficial nature of national identity even as national borders closed to stop its spread. As I suggest towards the end of this chapter, the novel also satirises a particular brand of reactionary British nationalism and its hubris in an age of globalised capitalism. In more recent times, these affective attachments have manifested in the populist conception of 'COVID nationalism' and in the structures of a global class hierarchy made even more evident in the disparate attempts by nations across the world to control COVID-19, while shedding light on poorer countries which continue to be hardest hit by the effects of the global pandemic.[4]

Kunzru's style and tone throughout the novel create the effects of Roland Barthes's literary 'jouissance', which both reflects and parodies the reduction of human and social life to global capital and its fundamental imbrication in, and with, the global technological networks that contemporary humanity's very survival depends upon. As Ashley T. Shelden has suggested, 'the Internet, or the World Wide Web, [...] serves as the paradigmatic figure of globalization in Kunzru's text' (2012: 365). In the novel, the internet, and its digital permutations, as well as the speed of information transmission, then, all become metaphors for that interdependence, but are suggestive as well of the biological and geographical networks that map the rapid global spread of COVID-19. *Transmission* articulates the mutually constitutive relationship between digital and biological life in a postmodern age: '[f]urther blurring the borderline between life and non-life, the internet had brought computer viruses into their own' (*T*: 109). The rapid transmission therefore of a biological virus like COVID-19 as well as its compulsion to survive and thrive can be likened to the widespread technical dissemination of a computer virus. Richard Brock has argued for the novel's relevance in understanding a more enduring pandemic through examining 'the metaphorical traffic between constructions of AIDS and globalization' (2008: 379). Brock sees *Transmission* as 'a partially displaced allegory of HIV/AIDS, [...] providing a lens through which global responses to the pandemic are invoked and satirized' (2008: 279). The novel could also be allegorically conceived to refract the much more recent context of COVID-19, which is, like HIV/AIDS, a form of retrovirus.

Arjun Mehta, the novel's protagonist and the Indian computer programmer responsible for designing and unleashing the Leela virus on the globe's communications networks, had realised as a teenage amateur programmer that '[a] string of code had hidden itself in an innocuous floppy disk and had used [Arjun's] computer to make copies of itself. Every restart had given birth to another generation. Life' (*T*: 108). These biological analogies acknowledge the way in which computer viruses can be created and multiply, while an uncanny similarity lies in the use of biologically inflected metaphors of human reproduction and regeneration to represent the replication of the computer virus and the spread of the pandemic pathogen, which, like HIV and other retroviruses, replicates itself by integrating parts of its genetic code into people's chromosomes. But the fact that Arjun Mehta, an Indian character and therefore a racialised subject, holds responsibility for the virus speaks to the long history associating metaphors and images of viral contagion with immigrants and the global mobility they represent. Priscilla Wald terms these representative narrative forms 'outbreak narratives' (2008: 2), and Liam Connell has argued that Arjun comes to be aligned with 'technology which is often regarded as the very quintessence of globalization [and] comes to be associated with the threat of otherness as it is transformed into a conduit for an attack on the very institutions of globalisation as neoliberalism' (2010: 281). Similarly, Donald Trump's labelling of COVID-19 as the 'Chinese virus' sparks a lexicon of fear and hate which conflates the Chinese race, contagion and the economic and social instability the pandemic engendered.[5] Yet Trump's racist term speaks more about the threat of the Chinese other alongside economic anxieties around the rise of China as the world's leading economy and its potential to eclipse the US. Writing on *Transmission*, Philip Leonard has suggested that the figure of the hacker, or the cyberterrorist, epitomised by

Arjun Mehta in the novel, 'moves in both the popular imagination and official documents as a predatory, destructive and rapacious force that attacks commercial, personal and national security [...] Hackers are also increasingly viewed as a threat to global, as well as domestic, security' (2014: 268). The rogue nature of COVID-19 similarly collapses national frontiers, deterritorialising the constantly deferred fear underpinning the affective structures inspired by the threat of international terrorism of all kinds, whether in virtual or more material manifestations.

Global

Straddling the boundaries between reality and simulacra, *Transmission* begins with a second-person narrative voice addressing the reader, who is assumedly also an internet user, through text which simulates text on a computer screen:

> It was a simple message.
>
> *Hi. I saw this and thought of you.*
>
> Maybe you got a copy in your inbox, sent from an address you didn't recognize: an innocuous two-line email with an attachment.
>
> Leela.exe. (*T*: 3, italics in original)

The novel thus immediately draws the real-life reader into the novel's fictional realm, simultaneously re-creating an intimately relatable digital world which has been attacked by the virus. *Transmission* also notably begins with an analeptic narrative perspective on the economic and financial impact of the Leela computer virus, reiterating Kunzru's point when speaking about *Transmission* in an interview about 'the logic of market and especially the financialisation of almost everything' (Haiven, 2013: 21). But the global damage wrought by Leela in the novel has an uncanny proleptic effect within the recent history of the COVID-19 pandemic. Each variant of the virus spawned by Leela operates in similar ways as 'an invisible contagion', with its economic damage of primary concern (*T*: 4). The cost of the Leela virus in economic terms was '[i]mpossible to count. Experts have estimated her damage to global business at almost 50 billion US dollars, but financial calculation doesn't capture the chaos of those days'; the result was that '[n]ormality was completely overturned' (T: 4), reflecting the equally surreal retreat from 'normality' that has marked life globally since the pandemic began. The multifarious effects of both the Leela virus and COVID-19 as well as their variants are bewilderingly complex; the source of the computer virus, similar to COVID, is shrouded in mystery and speculation such that 'identifying a point of origin became almost impossible (T: 4). These retrospective efforts to assess the Leela virus are from the point of view of a non-diegetic voice which is established at the start of the novel and which returns occasionally throughout the narrative while possessing a more detached perspective and distanced irony.

During these non-diegetic passages, parallels between the Leela virus of the novel and the COVID-19 virus are discernible. Reflecting retrospectively again on the impact of Leela at a later point in the novel, this narrative voice considers that '[t]o this day much remains invisible to the counters and chroniclers, those whose function it is to announce what happened, to come to some conclusion about how it must have been. There were market movements, jitters and shakes, configurations of money and confidence and power that for the most part were not discussed or even comprehended at the time' (T: 157). The endlessly contingent nature of the current pandemic similarly eludes conclusions for the 'techno-meritocrats (academic and scientific researchers who incorporate technological development into a narrative of human emancipation)' of those who have been tasked to assess, analyse and account for the spread, containment and impact of COVID-19 even as variants continue to emerge in sublimely shifting and enigmatic modes similar to the variants in the Leela computer virus in the novel.[6] In both cases, '[t]he glory of all of these variants, the glamour that caught so many people unawares, lay in their power of metamorphosis' (T: 113). Indeed, COVID-19's transformative, resilient and disruptive power places everyone in a state of sublimity, and the pandemic captures the way in which the Leela virus similarly corrals a global consciousness and psychic trauma in the wake of an event of such seismic proportions in a formulation of Alain Badiou's notion of 'the event', defined by an incommensurability with regard to preexisting contexts or systems.[7] As the extra-diegetic narrative voice asserts: '[a]t the boundaries of any complex event, unity starts to break down. Recollections differ. Fact shades irretrievably into interpretation' (2007: 156), while '[d]ay by day the atmosphere curdles, became vengeful and uncertain' (2007: 158). Though the Leela virus was a relatively short-lived event, the nebulous nature of COVID-19 has resulted in antipathy and hesitancy about the future; the exponential rise in hate crimes, hate speech, racism and hostility against Chinese communities across the world reflects the need for a racialised scapegoat to blame for the multiple personal and economic catastrophes caused in the wake of the pandemic.

In part, the worldwide attack on Chinese communities articulates the fear and trepidation about the toll of COVID's disruption to the normal workings of the global economy and to the gears of GDP. Like the Leela virus created by Arjun, who 'becomes a symbol for more fully articulated rejections of capitalism', COVID-19 threatens to 'cripple the infrastructure of global capitalism' and *Transmission* serves as an unequivocal critique of global capitalism (Connell, 2010: 285). The discourses that surround this critique can, however, also be seen as a critique of the deployment of instrumental rationality within a system of global capitalism that marks the global response to COVID-19. Information and communication technologies are key to this system, and while the Leela virus destabilises the global civilisation in which these technologies are foundational, the world's efforts to marshal a global mass and to systematically manage the efforts of entire populations to overcome COVID-19 rely entirely on information and communication technologies. The novel can thus be realised as a satire of the instrumentalist reasoning in defence of global capitalism that has similarly underpinned the global response to COVID-19. Global brand recognition provides another metaphor for COVID-19's spread, since brands, like the virus, gain traction because – as Guy Swift, the novel's brand guru proclaims – '[h]umans are social' (*T*: 21). The spread and consolidation of global corporate brands dominated by American capital, then, as the quintessence of neoliberal economics, signifies the fundamental interconnectedness of global society and functions as another extended metaphor for the international spread of COVID-19 as well as modes of virus containment which hinge upon curbing human society's innate sociability.

The need to stay ahead of the virus through endless scientific modelling accompanied by technical and clinical verbiage by teams of scientists, consultants and experts also speaks to the instrumental rationality that effectively mirrors the fiscal tools and financial products embodied by Guy Swift, who is CEO of his self-made creative company *Tomorrow**, a company epitomised by Guy Swift himself, who signifies the entrepreneurial Everyman upholding the Thatcherite ideological values of capitalist speed, progress and success so paradigmatic of postmodern life. His luxury flat in the In Vitro housing complex further epitomises the infrangible link between capitalism and biological life. Yet, much like the social surveillance system emplaced following COVID-19, this link also enforces the 'constantly shifting panoptical views' that In Vitro's 'blanket electronic surveillance' (*T*: 118) provides. It is a system reminiscent of Foucault's panopticon, housed in a security post, with its panoply of CCTV monitors and shaped like 'a giant glass oval, reminiscent of an eye' while offering constant and comprehensive security coverage (*T*: 118). Similarly, the UK government's efforts to control COVID-19 by linking personal and collective freedoms exposes the carceral nature of modern social control.

This point is reiterated throughout the novel. All the names of the companies mentioned in *Transmission* are parodied through postmodern irony and display the postmodern convergence of technocapitalism and biological selves. The personified 'Databodies' is the ironically named international human resource company that Arjun first applies to in India to broker his Silicon Valley job in America. Irony is furthered as Arjun stands in for a model of labour practices commonly known as 'body-shopping', where firms obtain US visas for Indian IT workers in order to hire them out to companies based in the United States. Virugenix, the US-based computer security company that finally hires Arjun, is hailed as 'a new-economy success story', since their 'Splat! Product suite was an industry standard' (*T*: 55; 53). The company's name similarly draws on biologically inflected tech-speak. Guy relentlessly believes in the need to 'stay ahead of the curve', an effort frequently distilled into opaque technocratic corporate discourse parodied by Kunzru throughout the novel through phrases such as 'spread spectrum' and 'fiscal responsibility' as well as *Tomorrow**'s USP, a ludicrous method known as 'TBM': 'a proprietary process [that] stands for Total Brand Mutability' (*T*: 20; 95). With TBM, Guy promises to eke out 'the heart-and-mind topography of the consumer'. He asserts that '[n]o one else will be able to do TBM analysis for you, or will provide Brand Mutation Vector Maps, which are the tool we use to help our clients achieve their full Brand Evolution Potential' (*T*: 183). Yet, in a moment of authorial parody, even Guy Swift himself becomes perfunctory over the vacuousness of such terms. While doing the pitch in Dubai, he endeavours to convince himself that he had to 'imagine a truly globalized branding agency, concentrating on the local needs of transnational clients. If *Tomorrow** placed itself at this node, it would potentiate the synergetic emergence of something, thus maximizing feedback in something else and placing everyone at the apex of a place they all wanted to be' (*T*: 180–181). Instrumental rationality, whether constructed around the discourses of finance capital, a computer virus or a pathogen, is frequently steeped in terminology that often obfuscates rather than clarifies. Guy's team, which is entirely committed to 'researching, visualizing, editing, mixing and montaging, arranging, presenting, discussing', reflects a process 'by which he meant convincing people to channel their emotions, relationships and sense of self through the purchase of products and services', effectively encapsulating both the postmodern integration of self and capital and its empty facades (*T*: 122). Yet, these are the same processes which underpin the UK government's approach to tackling the COVID-19 pandemic.

The consolidation of capitalism through COVID-19

The novel's wider satirical critique of global capitalism manifests itself most clearly in the vapidity of those who have profited most from rampant neoliberalism. Guy Swift and Gabriella Caros's privileged and cosseted lives, as well as the mobility and security they enjoy, are parodied throughout *Transmission*. Gabriella's indulged international background is detailed in the novel, but her company, Bridgeman & Hart – a leading international PR agency placed in charge of handling the PR for Leela Zahir, the Indian actress who inspired Arjun's virus and whose image hides the operating system behind the computer virus – further represents the hollowness of contemporary industries such as marketing and publicity which are entirely dedicated to the absolute importance of the image. Kunzru, however, contrasts the self-entitled central characters with references throughout the novel to swathes of unnamed masses leading precarious lives, surviving in the margins of the global economy and exploited within a system of capitalism. Guy Swift serves as the touchstone in the novel for this global rich-poor divide or what Kunzru, speaking about *Transmission* in an interview, has termed the 'a sense of the immense inequity of the global system' (Aldama, 2005: 115). The novel lays bare in a COVID world what Kunzru in another interview has termed 'the condition of people under a globalised world' (Ryan, 2004). As Guy Swift jets about in rapid and pampered comfort in first class, below him lie indistinguishable 'low roofs of patchworked thatch and blue polythene by the roadside' in the Indian state of Uttar Pradesh (*T*: 11–12). While he rides in an air-conditioned car in Dubai, he absorbs the phallic concrete and steel urban iconography of relentless neoliberal dynamism. It is unclear whether he also realises his own class position represented by the upward thrust of 'half-built skyscrapers', on the one hand, and on the other, the incongruity of 'their skeletons criss-crossed by plastic lines hung with the drying dhotis of Indian labourers' (*T*: 178). Kunzru draws our attention to the wilful blindness and disregard to poverty, suffering and exploitation which is the prerogative of first-world privileged subjects. As Peter Kemp observes: '*Transmission* is about mobility – not just the malign mobility of the computer virus but the harassed mobility of the economic migrant and the meaningless mobility of the super-affluent vacuously jetting around the globe' (2004). These two forms of mobility are driven by the same forces underwriting capitalism to create a hierarchy whose strata are interdependent but segregated. Dave Gunning has argued that 'Kunzru's virus suggests that such links between people have to be understood, challenging the fixed divisions of capitalism that Guy brands for PEBA' (2003: 806).

International fault lines cleaving the rich and poor have also become more pronounced in the wake of COVID-19, creating a global COVID cartography of the privileged and dispossessed as evidenced in national vaccination programmes being unevenly rolled out across the world, with the rich world hoarding a disproportionate number of global vaccination supply stocks as well as having power and control over vaccination supply chains. Writing on *Transmission* as a metaphorical account of global responses to the devastating effects of the HIV/AIDS virus and the patent global inequalities evinced through these responses, Brock argues that 'it is an almost self-evident observation that, while the transnational reach of the pharmaceutical giants reflects a certain global homogenisation, access to the drugs they produce – and to other, preventive measures, [...] remains subject to an ever-widening economic gulf between first and third worlds' (2008: 382). Steven Zeitchik, too, thinks of Kunzru as being 'preoccupied with the loss of soul in a techno-fast universe and finds a particular emptiness in pharmacological solutions' (2004: 40).

The disparity between those intrinsically integrated into technology who would be disproportionately affected by the Leela virus and those who stand outside that world looking in is further emphasised by Kunzru, who frequently enlarges the microcosmic world of the novel through a temporal cross-section of the world beyond: on the day the Leela virus was released, '[a]t London's Heathrow Airport two dead Ghanaian boys were found frozen to the undercarriage of a Boeing 747' (T: 127). The fate of these unnamed West African boys speaks to the desperate acts undertaken daily in the pursuit of a better life, even as Guy Swift lunched on bitter sandwiches with Yves, a partner at Transcendenta, 'the venture-capital firm whose investment helped *Tomorrow** get off the ground' (T: 123). Following a drug- and alcohol-infused night with Yves in Brussels during which Guy loses consciousness, he emerges from his nocturnal haze to notice 'a bedroom full of Chinese men, sitting two or three to a bunk, smoking and playing cards beneath lines of drying washing' (T: 279). Despite the farcical mode in which Kunzru portrays this highly unlikely encounter between a member of the elite global class like Guy and the dispossessed global underclass, Kunzru highlights one of the major enduring themes in the novel about a global class hierarchy where 'floating in the margins, are people who are almost invisible' (Cooke, 2004).

In the wake of COVID-19, the organisational apparatus of instrumental rationality possessed by individual states and the global polity has been fully deployed to confront the pandemic. For Kunzru (again in the extra-diegetic voice forming part of what Zeitchik has astutely called Kunzru's 'veiled essayism' that serves as a 'narrative rebuttal to both the global businessman and the entire damn enterprise'), such institutions seek 'to perfect the most modern of European arts: the exercise of control without the display of power' (T: 249).[8] These are institutions that control the levers of capitalism, and in the context of COVID-19, Badiou has argued in a recent blog on the pandemic that 'national states attempt to confront the epidemic situation by respecting as much as possible the mechanisms of Capital, even though the nature of the risk compels them to modify the style and the actions of power'.[9] Indeed, the enactment of control without the outward visibility of power is evident throughout the UK government's efforts to control COVID-19. Central to this control lies the full integration of the body, the body politic and social life as we know it, now congruent vectors branded under the ubiquitous blue banner of the NHS. The all-encompassing nature of this control is akin to the way in which the Pan European Border Agency (PEBA), which Guy Swift is desperate to brand in order to save *Tomorrow**, seeks to control mobility through recourse to biology. One of PEBA's notable and most invidious facets involves a database with biometrics which speaks to the integration of the right to physical and geographical mobility with biological data, to the intermeshing of freedom and the cellular, and to the coalescing of embodied technologies of Foucauldian forms of surveillance and discipline with access to forms of survival. Guy Swift's exclamation that 'the border is everywhere' (T: 252–253) also reflects, for example, in the context of COVID-19, the increasing move to connect access to services and activities to individual vaccination status.

As COVID-19 continues to weaken the global system, borders of all kinds have been erected and, like the regulation of migration movement patterns and migrants, the monitoring of COVID-free or COVID-infected bodies hinges upon information technology being embedded in life itself. These regulatory parameters are also '[t]he question of the border [that] is a question of information', remarks Signor Bocca (T: 230). Bocca, the Chair of the SIS Liaison Committee to whom Guy makes his sales pitch on PEBA, holds a bureaucratic passion for the 'centrality of information technology to a modern customs and immigration regime' (T: 252). While the acronym of Bocca's SIS is never clarified, SIS could perhaps stand for Secret Intelligence Service, or perhaps Strategic Intelligence and Security or some similarly termed organisation shrouded in the secrecy that surrounds essential covert operations around intelligence and security.[10]

The extra-diegetic narrative perspective intimates, with detached irony, the insidiousness of the instrumental rationality that pervades all life in the developed world and which has its roots in the values of eighteenth-century European Enlightenment culture. The EU epitomises the contemporary structural and systemic institutionalisation of these values:

> Regulations, statistics, directives and action plans; in the EU quarter language is order and with order comes violence, coded into the harsh planes of the Verlaymont Building, the uniforms of the bored police on security detail outside parliament. It is a violence that has been coated in language, incrementally surrounded and domesticated by it [...]. Discreet violence, like surveilled privacy and humanitarian war. Typically European paradoxes. (*T*: 249)

The porous borders between bodies and geopolitical boundaries apparent under the COVID-19 pandemic and the responses of the body politic at large to the crisis, which has convinced citizens to cede responsibility of the self to the state, has been fought with the same technologies of rationality codified by the ideals of order and subtended by a language that is, as Kunzru suggested, underpinned by an inherently 'domesticated' and 'discreet' violence. These are not new constellations, and they recall Jacques Lacan's argument that society needs to be inculcated into conforming to the order of regularity and structure governed by the law of the phallic signifier: '[t]his law, then, is revealed clearly enough as identical with an order of language' (1966: 66).

This law and its signifiers determine the power and control of hegemonic institutions such as the EU. In the name of this law, the fight to preserve life against COVID deaths has become increasingly domesticated, reduced to an uncomfortable but tolerable banality, like the 'surveilled privacy' that has become imbricated, for example, in the UK's NHS systems and the disciplinarisation of entire cities and even regions during the UK's 'tiered' system between September 2020 and January 2021. As Jacques Rancière has argued, this is the fullest articulation of what he sees as the politicisation of everyday life for the entire population: 'the boundary between the political and the domestic becomes the boundary between the political and the social' (2010: 28). This pervasiveness

and encroachment on private life has a terrifying inconspicuous-
ness and, like the EU quarter, according to Kunzru, bears 'no fascist grandiosity' (*T*: 249) and is justified within a longer history of
biopower. Nonetheless, the paring down of life to bureaucratic violence in the wake of COVID-19 throughout Europe is a common
and collective European approach, despite Britain's departure from
the EU itself, and appears, as the EU quarter in Brussels does, as
'the outward manifestation of something deeper, which has its
origin in the [European] Union's noble but somehow sinister aim of
a final consensus, a termination of the continent's brutal Dionysiac
history' (*T*: 249). The oblique reference to fascism is not detached
from the comprehensive insinuation of government regulation into
every facet of life in a COVID world. To institutionalise PEBA, Guy
Swift asserts that '[t]he incentive is now there to move towards a
common look and feel to overlay the policy harmonization', so that,
like the way in which a government-backed vaccination programme
impinges on consumer choices around leisure and services, policy
blends seamlessly into consumer lifestyle choices (*T*: 254). Indeed,
an arsenal of communicative technologies – epitomised in the novel
by Gabriella and her PR company, alongside Guy and *Tomorrow** –
has been employed to create a communications campaign which
pits personal liberties against death in the fight against COVID-19,
epitomising Foucault's notion of biopolitics as well as what he calls
'étatisation du biologique' or in other words 'the nationalization of
the biological' (Foucault, 2003: 239). Daniele Lorenzini, writing
on the relevance of Foucault's biopolitics to the COVID-19 pandemic, asserts the fact that 'disciplinary and biopolitical power
mainly functions in an automatic, invisible, and perfectly *ordinary*
way – and that it is most dangerous precisely when we do not
notice it' (2021: 42, emphasis in original). The ordinariness of our
current state of non-exception belies what Carlo Salzani (2021)
has termed the 'medicalization of politics and the politicization of
medicine' as definitive of 'modern politics as such', an aporia that
has also been echoed, for example, by Badiou (2020), who sees in
the COVID-19 situation a 'formidable simplicity, and the absence
of novelty, of the current epidemic situation'. This paradox in itself
encapsulates the undefined trauma caused by COVID-19, which
is not undetached from the collective disquietude caused by the
pandemic's challenge to the purportedly incontrovertible necessity
of a world capitalist system.

Capitalism, COVID-19 control and British neo-imperialism

Martijn Konings in *The Emotional Logic of Capitalism* (2015) has argued for the intrinsic trauma caused by life within a capitalist system. His analysis of such trauma echoes uncannily the prevailing trauma haunting the survivors of the COVID-19 pandemic and their paradoxical relationship to the institutions that seek to maintain their survival in an age of intense anxiety and foreboding:

> We return to the very community that betrayed our trust in it, presenting our problems for treatment but concealing or disavowing the full extent of the trauma that has been inflicted. This means that our attachment to hegemonic institutions is compensatory in nature: they provide ways to manage the effects of an experience we undertake to repress. (2015: 98)

As a human and global society, we have collectively attempted to counter the unruliness of COVID-19 with a pragmatic onslaught of information technology and deference to the hegemonic institutions managing that technology on our behalf, even as we know these institutions sustain our trauma. The media's coverage of the pandemic and its constant insinuation of COVID-19's longevity into the near and distant future fuels this trauma.

Thus, the COVID-19 virus furthers citizens' schizophrenic relationship to institutional power and knowledge. The Leela virus plays a similar role in Kunzru's novel. As Philip Leonard argues, '[w]hat *Transmission* suggests is that [...] viruses [...] interrupt not just the information technology economy but knowledge itself' (2014: 283). Towards the end of the novel, the extra-diegetic narrative voice re-emerges from the perspective of a collective humanity:

> As humans, we want to know what is lurking outside our perimeter, beyond our flickering circle of firelight. We have built lenses and Geiger counters and mass spectrometers and solar probes and listening stations on remote
>
> Antarctic islands. We have drenched the world in information in the hope that the unknown will finally and definitively go away. (*T*: 271)

Just as late capitalism has turned to information as its primary commodity, information, data sets, statistics and computational strategies permeate every personal, socio-economic and political engagement with COVID-19, combined with the deployment of every conceivable scientific and technological discipline to ward off the unknown. The unknowable and elusive nature of COVID-19 similarly lies not only beyond the 'circle of firelight', but also resides in the outer limits of our understanding and knowledge of the world. We are asked by the narrator: 'Do you know of anyone whom Leela did not touch in some way' (T: 272). The rhetorical question posed here finds parallels in the absolute impact of COVID-19 on every individual life on the globe.

The satirical depiction of the Leela virus in the novel thus articulates the insidiousness of human civilisation's dependency on information technology and the control and power it wields over human life, as in the case of PEBA's ambitions in the novel. As depicted in the novel, the Leela virus has the potential to both disrupt and raise consciousness about these levers of control, such as the British government's increasing incursion into private life through mechanisms which seek to ward off COVID-19. Our society's dependency on IT systems and its implications for errors – including in the NHS Test and Trace Service – as well as the possibly grave consequences of a flawed electronic system, is reflected in the novel when Leela infects the system holding the 'Eurodac fingerprint database', which results 'in the system producing a number of false positives, identifying innocent people as known criminals, failed asylum seekers or persons being monitored by European intelligence services' (T: 283). There are similar widespread systems and platforms linked to COVID-19 that are equally vulnerable to the same kind of technical failure which in turn can disavow the identity of individuals and their access to services and places, but which are nonetheless now becoming intrinsic to social life in the UK.

The personal risks posed to such systems by technical failure are encompassed by Guy, who ironically becomes an unsuspecting victim of Operation Atomium, an effort by PEBA to detain as many irregular migrants as possible in a series of flash raids. When he emerges from his dizzying night escapade in Brussels with an Eastern European prostitute named Irina, he finds himself dispossessed of his personal belongings and holed up in an obscure backstreet hostel, a situation exacerbated when he is inadvertently ensnared in an immigration raid by Belgian police while around him Chinese men flee 'clutching trousers and cigarette cartons and pairs of trainers' and '[a] pair of young East African women, one carrying a baby in a sling, ran onto the landing, then turned round and fled back inside' (*T*: 279). In the immigration detention centre, he is treated like these desperate Chinese men and East African women, as a literal 'sans papier', stripped of the identity and denied the rights that information technology and the digital endow him as a citizen of the developed world. At the centre, he encounters 'tall Somalis and tiny Latinos, Nigerians and Byelorussians, Filipinos and Kazakhs' who stand as representatives of the other half of the world (*T*: 280). Guy is introduced to the harsh material realities of the profound global inequalities that have also characterised the global experience of COVID-19 in a class-riven world. Unbeknownst to Guy, the system used by the detention centre had been compromised by 'Variant Eight Leela, the so-called transpositional worm. The "shuffling" action of *Leela08*, which randomly reassociates database attributes, was responsible for the destruction of huge number of EU immigration records before it was finally spotted and the system closed down' (*T*: 283). This system failure results in Guy being labelled as 'Gjergj Ruli, Albanian national, suspected pyramid fraudster and failed asylum seeker in Germany' and treated roughly by the immigration officers before being forcibly deported to Tirana (*T*: 283). While Guy's misadventures are ironically comic, as Ashley T. Shelden has pointed out, the novel critiques 'the hypocrisy of contemporary, Western invocations of cosmopolitan ethics' as a failure of the much-vaunted spirit of contemporary cosmopolitanism conceived as a universal ethos of transnational solidarity and global ethical compulsion (2012: 352). Considering the Leela virus in the novel, Shelden asserts, 'that the virus both destroys and creates unity points to the way in which Kunzru simultaneously embraces and rejects the concept of the universal' (2012: 371). Emily Johansen (2013) similarly sees *Transmission* as a critique of the attributes and assumptions of globalised neoliberal culture and its unequivocal celebratory view of the possibilities opened up by the networks of global mobility and the resultant increased diversity of job opportunities. With this in mind, Johansen instead proposes what she calls a 'viral cosmopolitanism', a vision that acknowledges the global interdependency between privileged cosmopolitans, such as Guy, and those less privileged, such as Arjun, whom the former depend on, and therefore the former's dependency on the latter in order to transcend the global hierarchies structured by neoliberal capitalism.

Instead, viral cosmopolitanism, mirroring the unstable, mutable and contingent nature of the computer virus and other viruses, depends on the constant contact zones between privileged cosmopolitans and 'cosmopolitans from below', to adapt Fuyuki Kurasawa's (2004) term 'cosmopolitanism from below'. Acknowledgement of these quotidian encounters can be abstracted to create novel imaginative models for global connectedness and thus an acknowledgement of the need to recognise the intrinsically global nature of the fight against COVID-19. This formulation of 'responsibility to others throughout the world through adaptive and creative transformations of existing systems in order to produce another world' has the potential to similarly transform our COVID-19-struck world, in which richer countries with high vaccine stocks are being urged to donate vaccines to poorer ones (Johansen, 2013: 429).

Yet, the plot surrounding the Leela virus (as with COVID-19), especially as furthered by Guy, proves the virus to be a social leveller. After presumably escaping from the detention centre, Guy ends up in a small inflatable dinghy alongside a Bangladeshi couple and their two children, all of whom are pitched into the sea by their Albanian traffickers, although Guy eventually washes up on some distant shore and survives. Guy is thus exposed to how the less privileged within a global economy live and struggle to survive. His vocal declarations that he is '*fucking* English' are roundly ignored by the officers. Guy's outbursts inspired by his sense of self as a self-entitled Englishman signify a wider critique in *Transmission* of Britain's post-imperial condition (*T*: 284, emphasis in original). The novel testifies to Britain's waning global power and a definitive post-imperial malaise signified by the commodification of national identity and its sale to Bollywood. In a mouldering hotel in the Highlands where Leela Zahir and her whole production crew stay while her new Bollywood film is being shot, the icons of Scottish identity are reduced to a laughable hodgepodge of cultural detritus: 'a Victorian clutter of stags' heads, [...] golf balls, prints of weeping swains and ruined castles' (*T*: 162–163). Scotland is reduced to lending the Bollywood film an air of foreign exoticness in a postcolonial reversal of fortunes, whereby British 'heritage' is being branded, marketed and commodified for the international market, paradoxically operating both as an index of economic decline and as a belated attempt to assert influence.

Conclusion

The construction of Guy Swift's family identity distils the spirit that underpins both Brexit and the cavalier nationalism that followed in the wake of Britain's successful COVID vaccination programme. Guy pronounces: '*We don't lose.* That was the first principle, the only one that mattered' (*T*: 220, emphasis in original). National British identity for Guy becomes reflected in Thatcherite values of class aspiration, social mobility, faith in financial markets to uplift self and society, and a wilful amnesia about past failure replaced by an endlessly deferred future of success and glory. Despite Guy's 'substitution of the future for the past, long boom for stiff upper lip, he still secretly agreed with that basic handed-down premise: "We are better than other people. We don't lose"' (*T*: 220). The rhetoric that Guy internalises to convince himself of the superiority of the British is reminiscent of imperialist self-confidence and racist ideologies, but also reflects the kind of Tory rhetoric that has couched the fight against COVID as a global competition of hedging bets and survival of the fittest:

> *We* were on top because we were better adapted to the environment of the global city. We took chances and made opportunities for ourselves. We know how to network, how to manipulate the flows of money and information to produce RESULTS. [... Guy] found strength and comfort in this idea. If the world is not doing what *we* want, we have to bend it to our will. (*T*: 221, emphasis in original)

Boris Johnson, for example, has championed the success of Britain's vaccination programme with unabashed neo-imperialist brio backed by capitalist energy: 'None of this [the UK's vaccine success] would have been possible without the innovative genius and commercial might of the private sector' (see Merrick, 2021). Britain's COVID nationalism can be viewed as a response to the Conservative government's efforts to confront and rectify a post-imperial malaise. Suppressing COVID has proven a challenge of tracking and maintaining surveillance over human identity and the international movement of people, one which is not only compounded by the migrant crisis on Europe's southern shores but the pervasiveness of various forms of modern slavery within all of Europe's economies. These are contexts which the novel reflects in its capacious coverage of the UK and of contemporary life in our transnational COVID-19 stricken world in which, despite its apparent temporary arrest, capitalism seems ever more entrenched and enduring.

Notes

1 Alan Robinson writing about the central themes of *Transmission* (2008: 82).
2 See Appadurai (1996).
3 See interview with Zeitchik (2004: 39).
4 On the dangerous rise of COVID-19-linked nationalism as well as the potential for a related rise in ethnic and nationalist conflict, see an engaging discussion by Woods et al. (2020: 807–825).
5 On the link between Trump's 'Chinese Virus' tweet and the rise in anti-Asian racism, see Mishal Reja (2021).
6 For the use of the term 'techno-meritocrats' in the context of *Transmission*, see Leonard (2014: 276).
7 For a useful article on the relationship between psychic trauma and Badiou's theory of 'the event', see Bistoen et al. (2014).
8 See Zeitchik (2004: 40).
9 See Badiou (2020).
10 One such organisation that Kunzru may have had in mind includes the Belgium-based European Strategic Intelligence and Security Center (ESISC), a think tank and lobbying group that collects and analyses intelligence, produces geopolitical, economic and security reports, and monitors threats from terrorism, organised crime and piracy.

References

Aldama, Fredrick Luis (2005). 'Hari Kunzru in Conversation', *Wasafiri*, 20:45, 11–14.

Appadurai, Arjun (1996). *Modernity at Large: Cultural Dimensions of Globalization* (Minneapolis: University of Minnesota Press).

Badiou, Alain (2007). *Being and Event*, translated by Oliver Feltham (London: Continuum).

——— (2020). 'On the Epidemic Situation', translated by Alberto Toscano, www.versobooks.com/blogs/4608-on-the-epidemic-situation (accessed 8 August 2022).

Bistoen, Gregory, Stijn Vanheule and Stef Craps (2014). 'Badiou's Theory of the Event and the Politics of Trauma Recovery', *Theory and Psychology*, 24:6, 830–851.

Brock, Richard (2008). 'An "Onerous Citizenship": Globalization, Cultural Flows and the HIV/AIDS Pandemic in Hari Kunzru's *Transmission*', *Journal of Postcolonial Writing*, 44:4, 379–390.

Connell, Liam (2010). 'E-Terror: Computer Viruses, Class and Transnationalism in *Transmission* and *One Night @ the Call Center*', *Journal of Postcolonial Writing*, 46:3–4, 279–290.

Cooke, Rachel (2004). 'Interview: I'm the Bloke Who Got the Big Advance', *Observer*, 16 May, www.theguardian.com/books/2004/may/16/fiction. features3 (accessed 8 August 2022).

Foucault, Michel (2003). *'Society Must Be Defended': Lectures at the Collège de France, 1975–1976*, translated by David Macey (London: Penguin), 239–263.

Gunning, Dave (2003). 'Ethnicity, Authenticity, and Empathy in the Realist Novel and its Alternatives', *Contemporary Literature*, 53:4, 779–813.

Haiven, Max (2013). 'An Interview with Hari Kunzru', *Wasafiri*, 28:3, 18–23.

Johansen, Emily (2013). 'Becoming the Virus: Responsibility and Cosmopolitan Labor in Hari Kunzru's *Transmission*', *Journal of Postcolonial Writing*, 49:4, 419–431.

Kemp, Peter (2004). 'Review Fiction: *Transmission* by Hari Kunzru', *The Times*, 30 May, thetimes.co.uk/article/review-fiction-transmission-by-hari-kunzru-kcvkmwgbq2b (accessed 8 August 2022).

Konings, Martijn (2015). *The Emotional Logic of Capitalism: What Progressives Have Missed* (Stanford: Stanford University Press).

Kurasawa, Fuyuki (2004). 'A Cosmopolitanism from Below: Alternative Globalization and the Creation of a Solidarity without Bounds', *European Journal of Sociology*, 45:2, 233–255.

Lacan, Jacques (1966). *Écrits: A Selection* (London: Routledge).

Leonard, Philip (2014). ' "A Revolution in Code"? Hari Kunzru's *Transmission* and the Cultural Politics of Hacking', *Textual Practice*, 28:2, 267–287.

Lorenzini, Daniele (2021). 'Biopolitics in the Time of Coronavirus', *Critical Inquiry*, 47:S2, www.journals.uchicago.edu/doi/pdf/10.1086/711432 (accessed 8 August 2022).

Merrick, Rob (2021). 'UK Vaccine Success Down to "Capitalist Energy" Not Government, Says Boris Johnson', *Independent*, 27 March, www.independent.co.uk/news/uk/politics/covid-vaccine-uk-capitalism-boris-johnson-b1823320.html (accessed 8 August 2022).

Rancière, Jacques (2010). *Dissensus: On Politics and Aesthetics* (London: Bloomsbury Publishing).

Reja, Mishal (2021). 'Trump's "Chinese Virus" Tweet Helped Lead to Rise in Racist Anti-Asian Twitter Content: Study', *ABC News Online*, 18 March, https://abcnews.go.com/Health/trumps-chinese-virus-tweet-helped-lead-rise-racist/story?id=76530148 (accessed 8 August 2022).

Robinson, Alan (2008). 'Faking It: Simulation and Self-Fashioning in Hari Kunzru's *Transmission*', in Neil Murphy and Wai-Chew Sim (eds), *British Asian Fiction: Framing the Contemporary* (Amherst, NY: Cambria), 77–96.

Ryan, Nick (2004). 'He's the Millionaire Scribe', *Globe and Mail Online*, 25 May, www.nickryan.net/articles/kunzru.html (accessed 8 August 2022).

Salzani, Carlo (2021). 'COVID-19 and State of Exception: Medicine, Politics and the Epidemic State', https://parisinstitute.org/depictions-article-covid-19-and-state-of-exception-medicine-politics-and-the-epidemic-state/ (accessed 8 August 2022).

Shelden, Ashley T. (2012). 'Cosmopolitan Love: The One and the World in Hari Kunzru's *Transmission*', *Contemporary Literature*, 53:2, 348–373.

Wald, Priscilla (2008). *Contagious: Cultures, Carriers, and the Outbreak Narrative* (Durham, NC: Duke University Press).

Woods, Eric Taylor, Robert Schertzer, Liah Greenfeld, Chris Hughes and Cynthia Miller-Idriss (2020). 'COVID-19, Nationalism, and the Politics of Crisis: A Scholarly Exchange', *Nations and Nationalism*, 26:4, 807–825.

Zeitchik, Steven (2004). 'Speeding Toward a (Cloudy) Future', *Publishers Weekly*, 21 June, www.publishersweekly.com/pw/print/20040621/18630-speeding-toward-a-cloudy-future.html (accessed 8 August 2022).

3

Turning the tide, or turning around in *My Revolutions*

Maëlle Jeanniard du Dot

Mais enfin: qui a jamais cru qu'une révolution tournait bien?[1] (But anyway: who ever said that revolutions turn out fine?)

Commenting on the place of *My Revolutions* in Hari Kunzru's body of work, David Mattin (2011) called it 'a departure' from *The Impressionist* and *Transmission*; 'a radical break' with previous settings and themes, but also 'an intelligent development' of his previous concerns with identity. This dichotomy between rupture and continuity is not only an illustration of Kunzru's aesthetic choices, but also a key dimension of the plot in *My Revolutions*. As we follow first-person narrator Mike Frame on a trip to the South of France with his wife Miranda, this quiet husband and stepfather to teenager Sam starts to reveal an inner conflict, triggered by his impression of having seen a ghost from the past on the square of a small village. From then on, the narrative plunges back into Mike's memories as an activist-turned-terrorist, in the late 1960s and early 1970s. The chronology of this process, from his teenage years to his demise and escape to Southeast Asia, runs parallel to his present conundrum of whether to reveal his real identity – as Chris Carver, the member of an extremist revolutionary group – to his wife Miranda. Indeed, Chris/Mike has been approached by Miles Bridgeman, former photographer and witness to his past activities. Miles's own interests, tangled up in the political machinery of the Blair era, lead him to blackmail the protagonist into turning himself in to the authorities, thus forcing Chris/Mike to an urgent examination not only of his past principles, but also his current life and the people he left behind in the revolutionary struggle.[2]

My Revolutions, published in 2007, has been read as Kunzru's 'most directly political novel' (Mathews, 2020: 4) – a label that could now apply to *Red Pill*, Kunzru's Trump-era exploration of alt-right subcultures. In both novels, politics is first and foremost a personal matter, and exposes Kunzru's lingering preoccupation with identity formation. Both novels also share a concern with history and the narration of pivotal historical events. Whereas *Red Pill* invokes ghosts from the Nazi past through the location of the plot in Wannsee (the site of a conference to determine the so-called Final Solution to the Jewish Question), *My Revolutions* sends the reader back to a London of demonstrations, police charges and squats that might be lesser known to a non-British reader than the swinging Carnaby Street of the 1960s. These events, inspired by peace protests against the Vietnam War, but also by the later violent actions of groups like the Angry Brigade and the German Red Army Faction, are explored at length in a novel that also conveys the writer's journalistic interest in subcultures and their context of emergence. *My Revolutions*, however, is not merely a biographical inquiry. Its dual structure makes sure of that by placing the grounded, eventful 1970s in contrast with the quietly disconnected capitalist lifestyle of the late 1990s. In doing so, the novel branches out to a more universal interest in the conditions of the revolution: what, and who, can cause consciences to stir? Will Blythe (2008) concludes his *New York Times* review of the book by claiming that it is 'less like an elegy for their era and more like a requiem for our own'. Since then, others have observed that the present-day setting of the novel is, in fact, pre-9/11, making the 1990s another past period Kunzru might be looking back on (Hart, 2009: 1063).

This detailed historical setting has led Kunzru himself to nuance one of the labels which have been ascribed to his work, that of 'translit' (discussed in detail by Bran Nicol in Chapter 5), where time and space would have 'collapsed' to allow the novel's swift movement across different subplots (Coupland, 2012). While the term was coined to discuss *Gods Without Men*, Kunzru commented on it by asserting the deeply anchored nature of all his analeptic explorations and denying that his fictions should represent a 'post-historical moment'. He extended this viewpoint to contemporary times, which he described as 'a highly historically specific moment that has its own texture, its own quality and that will in turn be historicised in the future' (Haiven, 2013).

In fact, the minutely informed chronotopes of *My Revolutions*, reaching back to a time and place that Kunzru did not himself experience (he was born in 1969), make it an archival novel as much as a political one. The writer's habit of thoroughly researching the settings of his plots, and injecting them with a plethora of real-life facts, does re-create the 'texture' of an era. It is incidentally remarkable that the narrator himself happens to be working in an antique bookshop, and finds his memories triggered by old pamphlets in boxes of archives (*MR*: 44). As the text – and texture – weaves a thread between past and present, a moment that will '*in turn* be historicised', the novel seems to operate according to a poetics of turning and returning, mirroring the primarily *spatial* definition of the revolution: a recurrence, a cycle, a movement 'round in an orbit or circular course' (OED).

This chapter wishes to analyse *My Revolutions* in light of this poetics of turning and returning in/to time and place, first by looking at the identity quest at work in the novel, then by approaching the spatial and sensorial exploration of past events and, finally, through a philosophical approach via the notions of change, repetition and drifting. Taking into account the influential ideas and ideologies of the 1970s which are reflected in the novel's aesthetics, it seeks to explore how concepts such as drifting (Guy Debord's situationist *dérive*), or 'making noise' in direct political action, guide the reader through the twists and turns of the novel's dynamic.

'Traces of [the] self': circling back to identity

The very title of the novel, with its first-person pronoun, testifies to a preoccupation with identity formation, but also to the close relation of identity and politics. This mock-memoir title as well as the first-person narration and retrospective gaze both betray the identity plot from the beginning. Kunzru denied that *My Revolutions* is biographical, notably in the acknowledgements section at the end of the novel. Even though many events bear a resemblance to the actions of the Angry Brigade, *My Revolutions* seems to be not so much an attempt at a mock autobiography as an inquiry into the perhaps universal yet deeply personal motives that might lead an individual to wish for a revolution and become part of it. In its supposedly selfless aim for a common good, where does the revolution leave one's identity? Forming and transcending one's identity is a fundamental concern in Kunzru's entire body of work, starting with *The Impressionist* – his postcolonial Bildungsroman starring a shape-shifting protagonist – and culminating in *Red Pill*, with a frenzied quest for the poetic and the political self in the context of rising alt-right movements.

In *My Revolutions* as well as *Red Pill*, identity is closely linked with ethics, raising the questions of choice and free will at key moments in one's life journey. Whether or not these choices can be revised is at the heart of *My Revolutions*; what they can ultimately reveal is a collateral concern that proves pivotal in the structure of the novel. The twofold gap between, on the one hand, the narrator's memories and what he is unsure of and, on the other hand, the events he experienced and those he did not also points to Kunzru's frequent concern with authenticity. This constant uncertainty – a homage paid to forms like the psychological thriller or the noir novel – is also explored at length in *White Tears*, which also resorts to an ambivalent first-person narrator. Revolutions, revisions and revelations: all point to the fundamentally repetitive functions of the past and of memory, and to the key role of the narration in retrieving them. In this identity quest, the reader is at times led astray by the protagonist's returns in time and confused chronology. But the plot retains their attention in the main decision-making moments of Chris/Mike's past, as well as the present, urgent choice he has to make: whether or not to reveal the existence of Chris Carver to his new family.

The novel's take on the dynamics of revolution could be illustrated by what Caren Irr identifies as a shift between twentieth-century novels of revolution and those written since the onset of the twenty-first (2014: 149). For Irr, the norms of the former have evolved into more unsettled trends in the latter, involving a movement towards 'viewing revolutionary upheaval in retrospect' or as a 'perpetual present' (2014: 149). *My Revolutions* exemplifies this shift at least as far as the setting and point of view are concerned. Whereas former novels with accounts of revolutions were set during the time of 'civil unrest, public crisis', the contemporary revolution novel is in the 'aftermath, viewing revolutionary upheaval in retrospect or per-petual present'; the narrator, in the former, has a 'restricted know-ledge, limited historical foresight', whereas the latter has a 'cynical, ironic, retrospective' outlook (2014: 149). In *My Revolutions*, it is precisely this narration from the aftermath, from a cynical retro-spective gaze, which fosters the protagonist's confusion and late identity crisis. While it does include forms of irony and cynicism in the novel – especially when Chris/Mike compares his experience to the dullness of the 1990s – the retrospective gaze conveys the puzzle of a fragmented identity that has to be pieced back together by the narrator, and to some extent by the reader.

For Anna, Chris's then-political mentor and idealised lover, the annihilation of individual identity is a necessity to benefit the revolution. She envisions her *self* only to the extent that it is moving and enables her to participate in the revolutionary movement of ideas and people: 'I think she came increasingly to consider herself as unimportant, except as a vehicle for the revolution' (*MR*: 110). Throughout the novel, Anna thus remains a disturbingly flat char-acter, which perhaps makes her ideal to become the symbolic ghost that appears to Chris/Mike in France and leads him back into his memories. Whenever they appear, reminiscences of her indifference to individual identity act as a counterpoint to Chris/Mike's anxious quest for his past.

In fact, it is not so much Anna herself who triggers the character's return into his memories as the written version of Chris and Anna's common experience. Back home after his trip to France, Chris/Mike opens up a box of old belongings and finds drafts of pamphlets he wrote with Anna: 'I found what I'd been looking for: traces of myself' (*MR*: 44). Thus starts the journey of the protagonist-as-writer, attempting to assemble memories and experiences into a coherent story. The other traces of identity that Chris/Mike finds in his return towards the past betray the progressive scattering of the activists' identities caused by their recurrence in media dis-course. While the figure of Anna is discussed repeatedly, and fre-quently fantasised about, Chris is 'almost invisible in those books, a bearded oval in a couple of fuzzy group photos' (*MR*: 96), while Sean, the third member of their group and love triangle, is 'just a footnote in Anna's story' (*MR*: 97). The storytelling surrounding their group and their actions has superseded the memories he tries to return to, and the re-presentation of their group, which once focused on uniqueness and spontaneity, seems like a contradiction in terms. Their dissemination in words and images mirrors the idea of the spectacle, described by Guy Debord in *La Société du spectacle* (1967): for Debord, modern societies have accumulated images and representations, which prevent direct experience from happening: 'everything that was directly lived has moved away into representation' (1967: 3).

The novel is fraught with the practices and views defended by Debord and the *Internationale Situationniste*, notably that of drifting, which will be developed later. Overall, Chris/Mike's attempts to return into the past echo the opposition of experience with representation; the revolutions he experienced in the past, which he desperately tries to make his again, can never quite be retrieved. His group's former claim, expressed on a leaflet, that there is 'no politics but the politics of experience!' (*MR*: 84) reflects back on him retrospectively. While it has been commented that his new identity as Mike Frame is a pun on the present-day narrative that 'frames' his memories (Hart, 2009: 1065), it is also rather telling that the two-dimensional 'framing' of his new identity should be opposed to a previous identity as Chris *Carver*, a three-dimensional revolutionary going through life-forming experiences.

Another reason for Chris/Mike's difficult negotiation with his previous identity is the ultimate derailing of Chris-as-terrorist, which occurs when he leaves his group, reports a violent action he was about to commit, and vanishes into thin air to avoid retribution. Roaming the world in despair, he is finally given a ride by a Dutch couple, and enacts his deviation into a different cycle, a different revolution: '[t]he wheels turned round and I disappeared' (*MR*: 263). As Blythe (2008) comments, this escape from his identity gives way to 'a series of painful turns on the karmic wheel: poverty, heroin addiction, anonymity'. Escape is identified by Peter D. Mathews as a recurring theme and strategy in Kunzru's characters, who follow lines of flight into a variety of directions (2020: 6). He explains how these escapes often fail, with the characters ultimately forced to accept their return to the 'society of control' (2020: 9). In the case of *My Revolutions*, the protagonist's line of flight turns into a spiral, and causes the character to return, if not to his previous self, then at least to the place and time he has fled.

(Re)turning to place, sounding the event

The novel is preceded by an epigraph quoting the Red Army Faction, from their pamphlet *The Urban Guerrilla Concept*: 'The question of what would have happened if ... is ambiguous, pacifistic, moralistic' (2005). The question that is rejected here is, in fact, at the very heart of *My Revolutions*: as Chris revises the events of his youth and the choices he made then, the 'question of what would have happened' keeps repeating itself. At the same time, this analeptic perspective, placed at the onset of the novel, acts as a metafictional warning: the reader is told that the events evoked in the novel are perhaps not the centre of its narrative construction – or at least, they might not be as crucial as what the protagonist eventually makes of them. In trying to answer that counterfactual question of 'what would have happened if', *My Revolutions* displays an obsessive attention to detail and explores, through the senses and the places that made it, the very archaeology of an event. Sounding the event, searching for traces, and listening to its echoes, becomes the main preoccupation of the protagonist.

The resounding return of the event first appears through echoes of the bomb. As a theme and as a motif, the bomb pervades the novel; it is felt by the narrator even in its absence. The novel operates an ironical plot twist as young Chris, at first impressed and scared by the possibility of nuclear disaster, later turns into a bomb maker himself. Through the resounding noise of the bomb, *My Revolutions* approaches the sound, and more particularly, the noise, made by a historical event. Kunzru's interest in noise has permeated most of his works, from the eponymous collection of short stories to the exploration of noise as a disruption of communication in *Transmission*, notwithstanding his auditory experimentation of New York in *Twice Upon a Time: Listening to New York* (2014), as well as the podcast *Into the Zone* released in 2020. In *My Revolutions*, noise is also disruptive, but it exerts an attraction on the characters.

The political formation undergone by young Chris starts with an awareness of the nuclear threat. At first, this threat comes to him as a sound: that of radio waves. Chris is fascinated with it, avidly listening to the news on his transistor radio: '[i]t was like hearing the world think' (*MR*: 53). First mysterious, incarnating a fascinating technical prowess, these sounds of the world become worrying, as the radio brings him the noise of the Cold War nuclear race: '[a]ged fourteen, I tuned in to the missile crisis' (*MR*: 53). The narrative voice then inserts the voice of JFK addressing Khrushchev, and the italics seem addressed to the reader as much as the character. This urgent call and the fear of nuclear annihilation further increase Chris's attention to the radio, as if to hang on to the only thing that would persist – noise: 'This was it. The Bomb was coming [...] Afterwards, noise would be all that was left' (*MR*: 53). Turning to the radio, tuning in to the news, Chris listens to it on a loop before the echoes of activism find their way to him outside an underground station. He joins the Campaign for Nuclear Disarmament – a British organisation which had its heyday in the late 1950s – attracted by Colin and his beautiful girlfriend Maggie. Their house, where the meetings are held, mimics the bomb, with a 'charged, purposeful atmosphere' (*MR*: 56). As Chris listens to the sounds of the world more and more intently, he finds himself unable to perceive the trouble coming from his family, until it becomes atomised in turn: 'That day was the end of something in our family. I couldn't give it a name, but after that it had gone' (*MR*: 58). This disintegration of the aptly named nuclear family is not only an ending; it also announces the beginning of Chris's own dissemination of his identity into various causes and fights.

The second half of the novel thus turns Chris/Mike himself into a bomb terrorist. He is at first reluctant, before he eventually teaches himself the very craft of bomb making. Kunzru's take on the journey of a terrorist in the making is neither anxious nor entirely detached. In a manner similar to Doris Lessing's *The Good Terrorist* (1985), *My Revolutions* provides a cynical outlook on the failures and the apparently confused motives of the armed struggle carried out by young revolutionaries of the 1970s. Commenting on her novel, inspired by the IRA bombing of London's Harrods in 1983, Lessing explained that she wanted to see 'how easy it would be for a kid, not really knowing what he or she was doing, to drift into a terrorist group' (Donoghue, 1985).

Drifting is a translation of the French *dérive* initiated by Debord and the *Internationale Situationniste*. In a now famously vague yet decisive definition, Debord (1958) explained that it is an active and creative practice of urban space, 'the assertion of a playful-constructive behaviour', experienced alone or in groups of two to three, during the course of one day, but that time span was to be extended if necessary. The *dérive* was notably interested in 'aggravating confusion' (Debord, 1958). For Chris/Mike and his friends, this 'aggravation of confusion' first consists in multiplying disruptive political actions, metaphorically bombing society with political messages. This, in turn, leads to literal bombings of symbolic places. Their aim, in short, is to 'make noise': to catch the attention of the dozing masses, trapped in their blind acceptance of what the activists deem to be the capitalist order and authoritarian power of the state.[3] The novel thus focuses just as much on the noise surrounding the bombs as on the effects of a bombing. As Andy Beckett (2007) comments in his *Guardian* review, *My Revolutions* 'dare[s] you to care about a time when bombers still gave warnings'. Whether or not Kunzru chose to set the novel in 1998 to avoid the confusion of post-9/11 discourse, the figure of the terrorist embodied by Chris/Mike is undoubtedly different from those that have since appeared in post-9/11 works of fiction. As a member of his political group, his ideological motives ultimately become too varied and confused to identify. When they start bombing specific sites – 'places, not people' is their motto – their common goal is to be practical before anything else; thus Anna accuses Chris of limiting himself to the theory of the revolution: 'I think when it comes to actual revolution, you'll hate it. You'll hate the noise. You'll hate the people. I think you're a *theorist*' (*MR*: 117, emphasis in original). The noise, and making noise, is what matters: form exceeds content and adds to the confusion.

The novel teems with this accumulation of noise, not only through the characters' actions but also with the constant intertextual play with, on the one hand, the various typescripts of the leaflets and pamphlets scattered by the group on the sites of their actions and, on the other hand, the press reports narrating their actions. The group are indeed intent on finding their actions repeated in writing: they seek visibility in the media as soon as their plans materialise. After leaving a bomb in front of an American bank – a statement against Nixon's foreign politics – they desperately wait for the press reports:

> We posted copies of our communiqué to mainstream newspapers and the underground press. From callboxes we phoned the BBC and ITV,

claiming responsibility. Then we waited. Three days later there had
been no response. No news reports. No commentary. No acknowledgement at all. It was as if the bomb hadn't detonated. But we'd
heard the sound, a muffled crump. We'd seen emergency vehicles
racing towards the scene. The day afterwards the bank was closed.
Wooden boards covered the building's ground-floor façade.

Does something exist if it's unobserved? Does something happen if it
is not reported? (*MR*: 184)

Faced with the limited noise of their bomb (a mere 'muffled crump'),
the terrorists double it up by creating media noise themselves – to
no avail. The last two questions end the chapter, as if to leave time
for them to echo in the reader's mind. It also dawns on us that it
interrogates the position of fiction writing in the face of historical
events – a position that consists not just in reporting events, but in
re-creating them. The narrative itself forms echoes of the event: the
astounding silence of the media lingers over the following chapter,
as if silence itself was echoing. For a year, the terrorists remain
unnoticed, fighting 'a strange, silent war' (*MR*: 186), desperately
trying to 'seed rumours' (*MR*: 188) as the media turn their gaze
overseas towards other armed groups in Europe. Looking for visibility, the group finally aim for the highest of buildings, the Post
Office Tower, in an attempt to 'put an end to the silence' (*MR*: 197).
This action, a straightforward reference to the bombing claimed by
the Angry Brigade in 1971, finally helps the event resonate. Chris
revels as the bombing of the telecommunications building sends
their actions 'propagating through the radio spectrum' (*MR*: 199),
thus symbolising a full revolution back to his youthful fascination
with the noise of radio waves.

   In this growing environment of activism, repetitions of events in
different places and times eventually appear as forms of global connectedness. The novel explores how political consciousness arises
from access to texts, images and voices conveyed from a distance.
It notably dives into the global empathy that emerged together
with the anti-Vietnam War protests of the late 1960s, giving way
to forms of global consciousness that fostered an active anti-state
resentment in 1970s counter-cultures, or, as Chris/Mike terms it,
'the knowledge that elsewhere such horror existed' (*MR*: 31). This
connected consciousness is manifested through the plethora of
historical events mentioned in the novel – be it the Vietnam War

(*MR*: 37) and other Cold War events, or social struggles like those at the Ford factory in Dagenham (*MR*: 156), as well as the May 1968 events in Paris recounted by Anna to the rest of the group (*MR*: 82; 106). This notion of a 'connection' to the outside world (*MR*: 32), and of a limitless commitment to any issue worldwide, is perceived at first as an opening dynamic. But it soon becomes a restricting tie: 'They talked about targets in London, people and places that had no connections with anything I cared about. [...] We weren't autonomous any more' (*MR*: 230). From connection to binding, Chris/Mike reconsiders his journey in light of the relation of individuals to their outside world in the late 1990s: 'Thatcher's gone, the Berlin wall's down, and unless you're in Bosnia, the most pressing issue of the nineties appears to be interior design' (*MR*: 47). Having somewhat lost track of the event's power to raise collective consciousness, aware that the inwardness of materialistic goals has supplanted the outwardness of politics, Chris/Mike is led to revising his past hopes for a revolution. Behind the scathing cynicism of the phrase, one question arises: what change is there left to make?

Change, drift, connect: revolutions and deviations

Through the motifs of repetition and revolution, the novel seems to hint at the disjointed experience of time in the context of postmodernity. The narrative constantly oscillates between the present of the protagonist (the late 1990s), the late 1960s and early 1970s that constitute the time of the narrator's 'revolutionary' acts, and the wider utopian conception of change that Chris/Mike nurtures regularly. These back-and-forth movements seem to illustrate the threefold understanding of time as repetition developed by Deleuze, mostly in *Différence et répétition* (1968) but also later in *Mille Plateaux* (1980) with Félix Guattari, where time is revisited under the guise of the *Ritournelle*. Time as a repetition and a *ritournelle* – a refrain – is indeed very tangible in *My Revolutions*, as the narrative keeps repeating some words, not least the token phrase 'round and round' that indicates the protagonist's return to his memories. But a more strictly epistemological concern arises from the overlapping timelines and invasive memories faced by the character.

Chris/Mike's present in the late 1990s, the starting and ending point of the narrative and the starting point of many flashbacks, is filled with such lexical repetitions and patterns, such as mentally addressing his stepdaughter Sam in a mock-confession style (*MR*: 47; 59; 230). This timeline could be said to reflect Deleuze's first conceptualisation of time as repetition (which he calls 'synthesis of time'): a time which is essentially set in the present and whose repetition is enacted by habit (Deleuze, 1968: 106; 108). For Chris/Mike, habit is embodied by the deeply material and routine lifestyle he has now let himself be drawn to: Miranda's concerns over selling natural candles, Sam's entrance to university, or his day job at a bookshop. As routine as it might seem, the present in that first synthesis of time – the 'passive synthesis' – is always in movement, Deleuze insists: that present is always unfolding, always passing. In this respect it is intrinsically connected to the second synthesis of time as repetition: one where repetition is manifested through our memory of the past. In that process, the past runs parallel to the present, to convoke and make sense of our memories and thus make sense of our present existence. Chris/Mike's memories of his actions as an activist and later a member of a terrorist group call upon this type of repetition, which Deleuze calls 'active synthesis of memory' and which is also turned towards the future, in that it re-activates past desires (1968: 110). As the episodes set in the present are sometimes abruptly interrupted by the protagonist's reminiscing, but also at times by pamphlets or slogans, the active role of memory is made evident on the page and reinforces the repetitive patterns that inform the novel.

In point of fact, these two timelines are challenged by a third understanding of time as repetition, which appears to be more transversal, multidirectional and, for Deleuze, ontological (Lapoujade, 2014: 66). Whether Chris/Mike remembers the past or whether he worries about its return in his present, he remains haunted by the notion of change, and what form or direction he believes it should take. His young idealist self confronts its fifty-year-old avatar whenever he starts reflecting upon the common good, the ideal future or even the sense of an imminent change – a momentum in history – that the revolution would bring forth. Because it is immaterial and strives towards the universal yet remains context-specific, because it is never quite seized and never quite defined, the idea of change that pervades *My Revolutions* strikingly echoes Deleuze's third synthesis of time, concerned with the future and the event. The logic of that understanding of time as repetition is one where the event – or, in this case, the long-awaited *change* – is repeated only because its various incarnations, materialisations, occur at different moments in time. Time, in this sense, is the envelope allowing the change to take form, 'the immutable form of change and movement' (Lapoujade, 2014: 78).

In *My Revolutions*, these incarnations of change materialise in the various shifts in the narrator's perspective. The signifier 'change' is often repeated yet highly mutable in the novel. Whether it is perceived from Chris/Mike in the present or viewed with his young self in mind is always unclear. During an occupation of the London School for Economics with fellow students, young Chris is aware of the Deleuzian issue of actualisation: '[y]ou could make something out, dimly, through the blizzard of opinion that seemed to surround even the simplest question of right and wrong: change, the sense that everything was in play, all verities suspended' (*MR*: 73). In this moment of hanging, change – as a concept, an aim, a wish or an experienced reality – might be found and repeated in several 'verities', all asking to materialise in political action.

The longing for change is then emphasised in the transformation of Chris-turned-Mike, who has converted to Buddhism during his recovery from drugs in a monastery. Change indeed echoes in the doctrine of impermanence, advocating a rejection of things that do not last so as to avoid suffering: 'Nothing is permanent. Everything is subject to change [...] *Annica* is the Buddhist term. The cosmic state of flux' (*MR*: 17). These two sentences frame his memories of running at the Grosvenor Square protest in 1968, as if to turn the movement – physical and political – he was experiencing then into a part of this flux, a continuous flow of experience upon which actions are meaningless. While curing him from his drug addiction, the Buddhist monks attempt to disconnect him from the revolution as well and break the cycle of engagement he is in: 'I gradually began to feel less connected to what I'd thought and done before. The monks taught that to escape suffering one must reject the impulse to act on the world. The desire for change, they insisted, is just another form of craving' (*MR*: 270).

Yet change, Félix Guattari reminds us, is what makes the revolution a unique form of repetition: '[a] revolution is something of the nature of a process, a change that makes it impossible to go back to the same point [...] a repetition that changes something, a repetition that brings about the irreversible' (2008: 258). Chris/Mike's final revelation of his identity to Miranda, despite Miles's promise that he would be able to keep concealing it, acts as the rupture of a cycle of denial, and a final – repeated – commitment to change on part of the revolutionary. Although carefully constructed, *My Revolutions* is not a novel that encapsulates the beginning, middle and end of a fantasised episode of British counter-cultures and would, in so doing, mend the loopholes of history into a self-contained piece of fiction. Rather, the novel disrupts temptations of totalisation and the sense of coming altogether full circle by sending the reader along lines that drift away from the character's seemingly cyclical memory of events.[4]

The term 'drift' appears more than a dozen times on the pages of *My Revolutions*. Repeatedly, the descriptions of the characters' habit of 'drifting' from one place to another, changing directions in space but also in their lives, comes up as a phrasal verb: drifting *around*, showing that drifting is closely linked to a form of circular revolution. This association comes to manifest the activists' way of moving in the same circles, but it is not only cyclical. It notably enables the characters to situate themselves in relation to one another: on one occasion Chris/Mike describes his encounter with Sean by saying that the latter 'had drifted around' (*MR*: 97); retrospectively, he also uses it to recall how he perceived Miles: '[y]ou seemed to be able to do what you wanted. You drifted around, made your films. You always had money' (*MR*: 233). Drifting can thus be a means of moving from one circle to another, or across concentric circles; in the case of Miles's dubious character, who 'drifts' between activist groups and the police when he becomes an informer, it is clear that drifting can also be a kind of derailing.

Drifting or the *dérive* is a practiced example of psychogeography, defined by Debord as the study of the visible effects of the environment on individuals' behaviours (Debord, 1955). On several occasions, the characters seem to indulge in such assessment, notably when Chris/Mike stumbles upon a girl called Alison, who was once part of their group:

> She seemed almost absurdly excited and carefree, as if she were the inhabitant of a parallel world where young people were allowed

to drift around on September afternoons without worrying about raids and explosives and surveillance and the secret state. She was living nearby. And me? 'Round about', I said. 'Staying with friends'. (*MR*: 234)

The spatial semantics used by Chris/Mike enables him to locate Alison on the wider map of his own political geography. Her own use of drifting is misdirected and not conscious enough. However, the protagonist's final answer testifies to a difficulty in locating himself: he lives 'round about', in a closed yet indefinite circle. As Beckett (2007) comments, '[t]he hard, glassy sentences are good reflectors of the geometry of relationships, of shifts in emotional weather'.

The influence of psychogeography on Kunzru's work comes as no surprise given the overall importance of place and space in his writings. Besides, it is mediated by a legacy inherent in British fiction. Analysing the works of Iain Sinclair or science fiction writers like J.G. Ballard, Merlin Coverley (2006) notes the importance of the use of psychogeographical principles and drifting among post-war British novelists. Kunzru's indebtedness towards these figures is acknowledged by the writer himself – he notably wrote the introduction to a 2016 re-edition of Ballard's *The Atrocity Exhibition* (1970). In *My Revolutions*, one of the examples of this legacy can be found in Chris/Mike's endless turns on the Paris *périphérique* after he goes back to France to find Anna – a reminiscence of Sinclair's *London Orbital* (2002), with its descriptions of long explorations of the M25 on foot.

In her discerning article 'Psychogeography, Détournement, Cyberspace', Amy J. Elias draws attention to the current reconsiderations of the concepts of *détournement* and *dérive* in light of the movements of the cyberspace and internet flows (2010: 821). She explains how Debord's definition of psychogeography has often been likened to web surfing, in particular when he claims 'The element of chance is less determinant than one might think: from the *dérive* point of view cities have a psychogeographical relief, with constant currents, fixed points and vortexes which strongly discourage entry into or exit from certain zones' (qtd. in Elias, 2010: 822). Although Elias points to the limitations of the comparison, it is indeed interesting to bear in mind that the *dérive* is directional, that it 'connects' individuals to given places, and in this regard, is different from the detached stance of the *flâneur*.

I would like to draw on Elias's comparison between drifting and the experience of cyberspace and hypothesise that the use of drifting in *My Revolutions* actually functions as a form of intentional re-routing of the plot. This digital metaphor is used by Irr to explain how contemporary fictions of migration tend to redirect the experiences of migration ('an overwhelming multisensory global system') outwards, rather than inwards in the way that previous novels of migration did when they looked at the trauma of migration (2014: 28). I wish to contend that a similar process unfolds from the patterns of the memoir form in *My Revolutions*: rather than looking inwards at his personal conundrums, Chris/Mike finds himself necessarily connecting them to the present and to the wider world. In this context, points of reference are thrust into a centrifugal dynamic, sent into different directions which are for the reader to follow. The thematic and narrative use of drifting informs a hermeneutics of re-routing, where the apparently detached mobility of young activists and the return to blurry memories are in fact highly directive for the reader. This process transpires in Kunzru's own claim that he uses history as 'a way of interrogating the present' (Haiven, 2013). Far from being a disconnected mode of being, drifting is a means of *deviating* the system, the better to make the world your own. For instance, upon realising that Anna is really dead, and that the person he thought he saw is not her, Chris/Mike's final observation is that he is 'completely adrift, without reference or marker' (*MR*: 275). Having lost touch with the practice of drifting, his return to a connected form of living can only occur by reckoning with his past experiences and connecting them with his present life.

Conclusion: cracks in the circle

In trying to return to a revolution, the protagonist of *My Revolutions* is faced with the essential aporia of revolutionary engagement; its actualisation in a tangible result is utterly disengaging. As the protagonist tries to find his way in the meandering streams of memory, the reader is made to see that the revolution can only ever be dreamt, or turn around in infinite circles. The Situationist movement dissected and tested that aporia: they rejected definitions and a canonisation in concepts, advocated the primacy of experience over the 'spectacle' of representation, and thus incarnated a 'revolution that never was' (Marelli, 1998: 7). With *My Revolutions*, Kunzru put his own interest in experience and sensorial descriptions to the test of politics and ideology, and ultimately to the test of time.

The character's problematic return to a long-lost identity shows how the cyclical return to obsessive memories can cause forms of erasure but also reveal cracks in the circle; far from being a continued movement, the past is made of ruptures and disruptions that inform one's identity. The past also appears in the form of echoes and traces which call upon the narration to explore what happened in a given place, at a given time. In this return to the event, one can hear in a returning echo the noise of collective action, which Kunzru plays with as a motif and as a kind of 'bombing' of the reader with information about past movements and political causes. The narrator is fascinated by the event, or at least the idea of it; his longing for change can never quite be found in the past and forces a movement forward: a creative escape which manifests itself in writing through a poetics of drifting.

The main question that seems to haunt *My Revolutions* is whether there is anything left of the Left – or, at least, of the New Left of the 1960s and 1970s. Many paradoxes arise from this quest: what was once new has become old, what was once a rejection of history has become part of it, and the experience and principles of countercultural movements can never quite be experienced anew. But the novel's archival return to this period testifies to the fact that it is not entirely dead and buried – 'left-wing melancholy', as Andrew McCann (2008) terms it, 'has still never quite been given up'. In fact, the re-appropriation of past revolutions makes for a creative incentive that does not only turn around in circles, but is undoubtedly turned outwards, and in particular to the reader's own politics. Here are *my* revolutions, the novel seems to claim – what are yours?

Notes

1 This quotation is borrowed from a discussion between Deleuze and Claire Parnet titled 'Qu'est-ce qu'être de gauche?', published in various venues but notably in *L'Abécédaire de Gilles Deleuze* (1988).

2 For clarity, I will refer to the character as Chris/Mike, except in passages where the 'double' identity is not relevant.
3 See Hart (2009) for a reading of *My Revolutions* through the lens of state power.
4 See Carmen Zamorano Llena's (2016) for a reflection on the refusal of totalisation in Kunzru's works.

References

Beckett, Andy (2007). 'Don't Call Me Comrade', *Guardian*, 25 August, www. theguardian.com/books/2007/aug/25/featuresreviews.guardianreview15 (accessed 8 August 2022).
Blythe, Will (2008). 'Underground Man', *New York Times*, 10 February, www.nytimes.com/2008/02/10/books/review/Blythe-t.html (accessed 8 August 2022).
Coupland, Douglas (2012). 'Convergence', *New York Times*, 8 March, www.nytimes.com/2012/03/11/books/review/gods-without-men-by-hari-kunzru.html (accessed 8 August 2022) .
Coverley, Merlin (2006). *Psychogeography* (Harpenden: Oldcastle Books Ltd).
Debord, Guy (1955). 'Introduction à Une critique de la géographie urbaine', *Les Lèvres nues*, 6.
—— (1958). 'Théorie de la dérive', *Internationale Situationniste*, 2.
—— (1967). *La Société du spectacle* (Paris: Gallimard).
Deleuze, Gilles (1968) . *Différence et répétition* (Paris: Presses Universitaires de France).
Deleuze, Gilles and Félix Guattari (1980). *Mille plateaux* (Paris: Éditions de Minuit).
Donoghue, Denis (1985). 'Alice, The Radical Homemaker', *New York Times*, 22 September, https://archive.nytimes.com/www.nytimes.com/books/99/01/10/specials/lessing-terrorist.html (accessed 8 August 2022).
Elias, Amy J. (2010). 'Psychogeography, Détournement, Cyberspace', *New Literary History*, 41:4, 821–845.
Guattari, Félix, and Suely Rolnik (2008). *Molecular Revolution in Brazil*, translated by Karel Clapshow and Brian Holmes (Cambridge, MA: Semiotext(e)).
Haiven, Max (2013). 'An Interview with Hari Kunzru', *Wasafiri*, 28:3, 18–23.
Hart, Matthew (2009). 'The Politics of the State in Contemporary Literary Studies', *Literature Compass*, 6:5, 1060–1070.
Irr, Caren (2014). *Toward the Geopolitical Novel: US Fiction in the Twenty-First Century* (New York: Columbia University Press).
Kunzru, Hari (2014). *Twice Upon a Time: Listening to New York* (New York: Atavist Books).

Lapoujade, David (2014). *Deleuze, Les Mouvements aberrants* (Paris: Éditions de Minuit).

Llena, Carmen Zamorano (2016). 'A Cosmopolitan Conceptualisation of Place and New Topographies of Identity in Hari Kunzru's *Gods Without Men*', *Transnational Literature*, 8:2, 11.

McCann, Andrew (2008). 'Militancy and Melancholia', *Overland Spring*, 31 August, https://overland.org.au/feature-andrew-mccann/ (accessed 8 August 2022).

Marelli, Gianfranco (1998). *L'Amère Victoire du Situationnisme: pour une histoire critique du Situationnisme, 1957–1972* (Arles: Sulliver).

Mathews, Peter D. (2020). 'Hacking the Society of Control: The Fiction of Hari Kunzru'. *Critique: Studies in Contemporary Fiction*, 62:5, 1–11.

Mattin, David (2011). 'My Revolutions, by Hari Kunzru', *Independent*, 18 November, www.independent.co.uk/arts-entertainment/books/reviews/my-revolutions-hari-kunzru-463612.html (accessed 8 August 2022).

Red Army Faction, Andre Moncourt, and J. Smith (2005). *Red Army Faction: The Urban Guerrilla Concept* (Montreal, QC: Kersplebedeb Publishing).

'Revolution, n.' (1989). *Oxford English Dictionary*, www.oed.com/oed2/00205581;jsessionid=0688A87870A88377A4D42DBDCBC0C1EA (accessed 8 August 2022).

4

Subjectivity at its limits: fugitive community in Kunzru's short stories

Peter Ely

Hari Kunzru's first and only published short story collection *Noise* (2005) comprises five pieces written over a period of seven years. Composed of disparate styles and a wide range of thematic interests in technology, consumerism and fraught social relations, his short stories develop stylistic strategies that have been important for his broader novelistic career. Principal amongst these has been Kunzru's repeated experimentations with narrative voice, where the limits of human subjectivity, relationships and community are explored through unstable, composite or otherwise unconventional narrative perspectives. This chapter argues Kunzru has repeatedly used the short story as a vital laboratory to test the limits of narrative voice and subjectivity, uncovering new forms of unexpected relations and affinities within the changing economic, technological and cultural fabric of contemporary society. Kunzru's short stories are read alongside the philosophical writings of Jean-Luc Nancy, whose recent book on community reaffirms the need to 'dissociate "community" from all projection into a work that is made or to be made' advocating a form of relationality that 'escapes' dominant political frameworks through the elusive 'art of the fugue' (2016: 72). This is viewed alongside the work of Fred Moten and Stefano Harney, who have sought to locate a subversive 'undercommons' from an analogous paradigm of 'fugitivity' where community emerges only in its refusal of restrictive institutions, locating itself only in the 'dislocation' of a 'radical occupied-elsewhere' and the desire to 'build something new' (2013: 152). These thinkers develop a thinking of community that foregrounds its capacity to escape the terms of the present, which, applied to the context of literature, allows for the excavating and preserving of transformational communitarian capacities in the imaginative landscape of fiction. Kunzru engages in a parallel project of capturing fugitive forms of community in his writing, deploying narrative voices and thematic concerns which highlight disruptive modes of life which expand our understanding of human subjectivity and community.

Such a reading broadens the political scope often attributed to Kunzru's work, examining the continued applicability of his identification with 'cosmopolitanism' as critical consensus has established (Schoene, 2009; Shaw, 2017; Jansen, 2018). If Kunzru's short stories may be effectively aligned with broader trends in the British novel to foreground cultural exchange and global interdependence, his short fiction also points to more recalcitrant styles of political thought, encompassing agonistic and destructive elements which call into question the possibility of imagining community in a world where it is increasingly 'put to work' and made 'operative' as part of the function of the capitalist state (Nancy, [1986] 1991). Attending to the narrative strategies of short stories such as 'Deus Ex Machina' (1998), 'Bodywork' (2005) and 'Memories of the Decadence' (2005), which dramatise the various structural barriers to community in contemporary society, as well focusing on underexplored short stories such as 'Magda Mandela' (2007a) and 'The Interns' (2007b) which sit outside of any comfortable designation of the 'cosmopolitan', this chapter will locate the 'fugitive' tendencies detectable in Kunzru's complex evocation of community.[1] By offering close readings which attend to this underdeveloped tendency in his writing and focusing on his development of experimental modes of narrative voice which all engage, in different ways, with questions of human subjectivity and community, the chapter will demonstrate how the figure of 'fugitive community' opens new interpretive possibilities in Kunzru's work.

Narrative voice and community

Kunzru's short stories demonstrate repeated experimentations with literary voice, developing from his early short story 'Sunya' (1999), which depicts an Indian mechanic at the end of his life whose 'corpse will [very soon] be ashes' (Kunzru, 1999: n.p.) through a variety of inventive narrative voices composed of first-person plurals, second-person narratives, instruction manuals and scenes of mythical storytelling. These narrative voices are notable often as they derive from unusual subjective positions, thereby mapping onto another characteristic trope of Kunzru's prose: his penchant for broadly realist scenarios which are disrupted or undermined by subtly magical, satirical, science fiction-inspired or otherwise uncanny and unusual events and characters. If, as Sara Upstone writes, authors such as Kunzru, 'while sophisticated and often lyrical, lack the magical-realist elements of the novels of Salman Rushdie, or the modernist flourishes of Sam Selvon' (2010: 9), it is nonetheless notable, most clearly in his short stories, that Kunzru has a deep investment in formal devices of narration which challenge his reader. For example, the reader is plunged into unfamiliar worlds in stories such as in 'Memories of the Decadence' (2005), 'Love with Impediments' (2014 [2007]), 'Fill Your Life with Win!' (2009a) and *Memory Palace* (2013), or into moments of intense subjective fracture such as in 'Beyond the Pleasure Principle' (2005b), 'Fellow Traveller' (2008a), 'Raj, Bohemian' (2008b), 'The Culture House' (2009b) and 'Kaltes Klares Wasser' (2009c), where memory loss, substance abuse, sickness or paranoia undermine the reliability of the narrator. Likewise, short stories such as 'Godmachine™ v.1.0.4' (2005), 'The Interns' and 'Fill Your Life with Win!' depart radically from recognisable modes of narration, eliding any coherent story-line to replicate genres of writing outside the conventional boundaries of fiction, comprising, respectively: an instruction manual for 'cosmic' software with ambiguous and troubling relations to reality and catastrophe; a political manifesto for unpaid workers who wish to 'smash the system' (2007b); and a magazine-style article with 'top tips for lulzy living' (2009c: n.p.) evoking a dystopian world where failure to adhere to social conventions in fashion, sex and work can lead to violent social ostracisation.

These experiments in narrative voice anticipate a similar trend in Kunzru's novels, which although deploying relatively conventional third-person narration in early works such as *The Impressionist* (2002) and *Transmission* (2004), engage in free indirect discourse and other disruptive narrative techniques which evolve into bolder narrative experiments in his later novels such as *My Revolutions* (2007) and *Gods Without Men* (2011). Most clearly, Kunzru's use of a striking autodiegetic narrative that dramatises its own

subjective fracture in *Red Pill* (2020) may be seen to develop strategies first seen in his short stories such as 'Bodywork' and 'Beyond
the Pleasure Principle'. Unconventional styles of narration consistently characterise Kunzru's ongoing *oeuvre* of short fiction, from his
early short stories and collection *Noise*, as well as his later stories
which have been variously published as part of anthologies, in
newspapers and magazines such as the *Guardian*, *The New Yorker*
and *The New Statesman*, as well as on his website. For example,
the 'Guardian Angel' that narrates his critically acclaimed short
story 'Deus Ex Machina' knows the intimate details of the story's
main character Christina's inner life, but is entirely heterodiegetic
to the story other than a single moment when he allows himself
to 'alter fate' by 'moving nothing larger than electrons' to prevent
her from dying from an overdose (Kunzru, 2005a: 23). Here the
narrative voice works as a kind of magical realist impossibility,
whilst also drawing on elements of science fiction in the detailed
way he interacts with technology, blending it with a secularised and
ironic theological register: 'You will of course find angels at work
in all forms of technology [...] [but in] an era when [...] miracles
and overt manifestations or superhuman power have been banned
under a strict convention, the scope of angelic interventions is
severely limited' (Kunzru, 2005a: 22).

Likewise, the narrative voice of 'Memories of the Decadence' is
told from the perspective of a community which underwent 'the
Decadence', a fictionalised historical period of extremes, where
'we ate and drank to excess until a point came when excess went
out of fashion' (Kunzru, 2005a: 29). Although this generation
of an unconventional composite narrator may be seen to accord
with Kunzru's critical reception, which has identified 'community'
as a foundational aspect of this work, Bettina Jansen's notably
locates this first-person plural narrator as lacking the cosmopolitan meaning she argues most strongly characterises the political
trajectory of Kunzru's short fiction. This is as the story offers a
'depiction of a world-wide community' as an 'integrated totality'
(Jansen, 2018: 261) and therefore lacks the disaggregated and
heterogenous communitarian impulses she finds most laudable in
his prose. Nonetheless, Kunzru's description does not, as Jansen's
analysis suggests, simply imply a homogeneous 'integrated'
experience of 'unitotality' (2018: 261). Although the event is not

differentiated by 'locality', ethnicity or other signifiers of cosmopolitan plurality, it is clearly delineated by a logic of class, an aspect of Kunzru's writing that is arguably underplayed in Jansen's overall analysis. For example, the participants in the 'Decadence' go into 'promenades in the poorer quarters of the city, pausing to examine choice deformities [and to] imitate them' (Kunzru, 2005a: 29). Similarly, the most striking scenes of communal fusion are seen in the 'erotic phase of the Decadence' where '[o]rgasms began to require corporate sponsorship', in which Kunzru foregrounds the class logic that underpins these events, indicating a social body with differentiated fields of experience and status: '[A]n estimated two hundred thousand people participated in a ritual designed solely to produce the little death in a middle-aged software billionaire [...] The energy generated by their activity produced a small quantity of almost-clear seminal fluid on the raw silk sheets of the billionaire's bed, and augmented his bank balance by an estimated twelve and a half million pounds' (Kunzru, 2005a: 31).

The communal nature of the scene is not at first glance entirely incompatible with a cosmopolitan vision. The event runs variously across the world in 'Nuremberg, Shanghai and Hyde Park' (Kunzru, 2005a: 30), combining a global audience in a shared experience irrespective of cultural and ethnic difference. The global matrix of affinity and relation is, however, identified with the logic of capital accumulation and the instrumentalisation of communal desire toward onanistic and monetary gain. This is a theme that suffuses many of Kunzru's short stories, including 'Eclipse Chasing', 'Kaltes Klares Wasser', 'Raj, Bohemian', 'Love with Impediments', *Memory Palace* and 'Fill Your Life with Win!'. These stories demonstrate Kunzru's repeated attention to the way interpersonal relationships and intimate subjectivity can be 'put to work', as Nancy's influential phrasing puts it, through their subordination to the capitalist state which 'actualizes [all] relation' (1993: 112). Kristian Shaw has argued cosmopolitan writing should not be seen as uncritically optimistic about all forms of global community. Rather, writers like Kunzru 'point to the limits of the existing globalised world, in which an emergent planetary ethics has not yet come to fruition' (Shaw, 2017: 186). In this way, any vision of community that emerges in Kunzru's work is made to confront the serious barriers to its being that exist in the current organisation of the global economy and capitalist societies, which make what Nancy terms the 'exigency' of community provisional if not insistent ([1986] 1991: 16).

'Bodywork', the first piece in Kunzru's short story collection, is told from the point of view of a cyborg protagonist who for the duration of the story is gradually replacing his biological body with machinery such that, by the end of the story, he has almost completely erased his organic matter. In this way, the narrative 'I' of the story, who begins the story by informing us of the banal details of his life – 'Sunday mornings I wash my car' (Kunzru, 2005a: 13) – becomes incrementally more alien to the reader in his perceptions and attitudes. At the beginning of the story he disapproves of his wife's failure to 'raise her head before ten-thirty' on a Sunday morning, considering this 'lazy', but by the end his obsession with the finite and organic aspects of her 'rotten toilet smell' and 'pink [...] droplets of sweat' (2005a: 9) belie a perspective that finds all signs of organic life increasingly disgusting and as 'signs of decay' (2005a: 11). As Barry no longer needs to imbibe or excrete organic matter – 'none of that digestive stuff is my concern' (2005a: 11) – his being now resembles precisely the image with which the story started: a 'clean and bright and perfect [...] car' (2005a: 13).

For Jansen, this story contains a kind of cosmopolitan cyborg promise which, drawing on the work of Donna Haraway, 'shows that the cyborg is not a masculinist concept but a boundary figure who holds the potential to deconstruct patriarchy's essentialist notions of men and women' (2018: 64). Attention to the alienating effect of his narration, which is increasingly bereft of empathy, or any emotion other than disgust for his wife, may lead the reader to question whether Barry's final desire to 'know what to do with Cheryl' (Kunzru, 2005a: 13) registers, as Jansen argues, a 'wish[..] to be able to relate to his wife again', or in fact a more ominous outcome. Barry's techno-fetishistic desire to overcome the corporeal and finite nature of his life offers little evidence of an attempt to escape 'his hegemonic notion of masculinity' and still less 'a deliberate choice to construct radically new relations' (Jansen, 2018: 63–64). Rather, the final lines of the story anticipate the arrival of his friend Ted, who must install the final 'unit' to complete the transformation, an act which Barry cannot do himself, implying its installation will work to erase whatever agentic capacity he has outside of his technological matter (Kunzru, 2005a: 12). This suggests a desire not only to erase his being – what Nancy (2000) would term his 'singularity' – with imported mass-produced parts, but by association a desire to renege on his relation to his wife in her alterity and heterogeneity with himself. Nancy's work on community has long noted that technology has no inevitably beneficial relation to our ability to understand ourselves. In response to the question: ' "we," how are we to say "we"?', Nancy suggests this question is made more difficult by 'what [...] we are told about ourselves in the technological proliferation of the social spectacle and the social as spectacular' (2000: 70). Likewise, Kunzru's careful literary disintegration of identity in his narrative 'I' works to question the contours of human subjectivity in its complex negotiation of technology, social relations and self, suspending the possibility of relationality within a technological and political landscape which all but forecloses any positive outcome.

Fugitive community

Thematically it is arguably not community as theme or preoccupation that emerges most clearly in the work of Kunzru, but rather as Upstone has written, 'a detailed and developing vision of selfhood' (2010:144). As his short stories show, however, Kunzru's prose is not invested in the structure of individuality per se, seeking to valorise this ideological structure against the imposition of an encroaching sociality. Rather his rendering of 'self' is always one of crisis and disintegration, where we are each caught in a web of alienating labour, commodification and the increasing power of the state where the possibility of an empowering community can only emerge in resistance to such structures, and indeed *as* resistance to them. For Nancy and Kunzru it is arguably the figure of 'fugitivity', recently proposed by Nancy as a development of his work on community, which best captures the necessity of community to escape being 'put [...] to work' ([1986] 1991: 38), evading the restrictive terms of the present and their inculcation with the capitalist state, that 'negates' community' (1993: 112). In his 2016 text *The Disavowed Community*, Nancy admits his deployment of the political nature of community in his original text *The Inoperative Community* was 'not always coherent or clear', but locates this problem as a fundamental component of political community

itself: 'A crucial paradox lies at the heart of this matter of community (and/or communism): We respond – Bailly, Nancy, Blanchot,
Agamben, everyone – to this question of "communism" that should
be characterised as sur-essential, but whose sense escapes us. Suffice
it to say that it still escapes us' (2016: 13).

Suggesting here a fugitive form of community, Nancy links the
'paradox' of community to the political project of 'communism', a
consistent, if undertheorised touchstone of Nancy's work on community, which is a shared concern for his interlocutors Giorgio
Agamben, Maurice Blanchot and Jean-Christophe Bailly. In each
case the 'sense' of 'community (and/or communism)' is in a crucial way not available, eluding those who nonetheless attempt to
resuscitate its 'exigency', and we can understand this contradiction
precisely in Nancy's enigmatic combining of community and communism as 'parallel and interlocking terms' ([1986] 1991: 8). In
this convergence, Nancy gestures to a material and historical *limit*
which would be the absolute *non-appearance* of 'real communism'
(2016: 2) as an actually existing political entity, deriving from
Nancy's insistence that those regimes that have taken the name of
communism have been faithful neither to its political nor its ontological imperatives. In this sense, the task of thinking community
shares its fate with that of communism, as an ever-present, but by
no means assured potentiality, constantly 'escaping' the terms of
the present, with distant but insistent possibilities.

This figure of community as latent but elusive capacity allies
Nancy's conception with a recent turn to fugitivity in the conceptual
paradigm of the 'undercommons', which is similarly theorised as
something which must 'escape' the terms of the present. For Harney
and Moten, the 'undercommons' is a racialised category linked to
'blackness' where, as the introduction to the book suggests, both
terms denote a shared project of 'reaching out to find connection
[...] making common cause with the brokenness of being, a brokenness' (2013: 5). Taking community as something largely absent from
the instrumentalised relationships of a structurally racist society,
the 'subterranean' figure of the undercommons seeks to preserve
possibilities in community that remain peripheral and fragile. If the
capitalist state works for Nancy to 'negate' community, theories
of 'blackness' have demonstrated the way in which this process
also generates an apparatus of proximity to harm, in relation to

structural racism. Drawing on the work of social theorist and prison abolitionist Ruth Gilmore, Moten follows her definition of this systemic production of racism as 'the state-sanctioned or extralegal production and exploitation of group-differentiated vulnerability to premature death' (Gilmore, 2007: 28). For Moten and Gilmore, the horizon of a politics which harnesses an 'undercommons' seeks to abolish the institutions that perpetrate structural racisms that undermine and harm racialised and exploited communities, whilst also radically reconfiguring society itself. Crucially, this process would necessitate understanding community through the literary figure of the 'uncanny', which 'disturbs the critical going on above it, the professional going on without it, the uncanny that one can sense in prophecy, the strangely known moment, the gathering content, of a cadence, and the uncanny that one can sense in cooperation, the secret once called solidarity' (Harney and Moten, 2013: 42).

Kunzru's short fiction resonates productively with this fugitive framework, where his evocation of community unsettles the terms of reality, emerging from the gaps exposed in the fractured subjectivities of his unstable narrative voices. Whilst his globalised worldview may be allied with the cosmopolitan imagination, his hesitancy in depicting any clear or optimistic instantiation of cosmopolitanism demands precise attention to what is at stake in this more negative valence of his work, where community appears to escape positive representation or clear demarcation at moments of subjective fracture, but also in more fanciful, magical realist or science fiction-inspired moments, where the terms of reality breakdown. For Andrew Bennett and Nicholas Royle such literary devices are aligned with the 'uncanny', whose effect can be to create a process of what Russian formalism termed 'defamiliarisation', where the 'familiar' is rendered 'strange': a process that 'challenges our beliefs and assumptions about the world and about the nature of "reality"' (2016: 35). If the 'uncanny' or *Unheimlich* is for philosopher F.W.J. Schelling 'the name for everything that ought to have remained [...] secret and hidden but has come to light' (qtd. in Freud, 1997: 199), we see in Harney and Moten that the 'undercommons' shares with this an affinity with a 'secret', which 'once [was] called solidarity', unsettling the terms of the present with a form of solidarity or community which might still be retrieved in the uncanny and imaginative world of the fictive.

This uncanny fugitivity, which binds Kunzru's short stories with the thinking of Moten and Nancy, offers a paradigm for thinking through Kunzru's depiction of systems of structural racism, migration and postcolonial environments. For Schoene, the figure of fugitivity can be seen clearly in the final chapter of Kunzru's early novel *Transmission* (2004), which concludes through the miraculous escape of protagonist Arjun, who has been forced to abandon his life as a hyper-exploited computer programmer, having released a computer virus that wreaks havoc in the global economy, and his unlikely companion Leela, who escapes from the set of a Bollywood set in Scotland. Both seem to disappear from the world entirely, forging a mythic alliance in an emerging folklore about their fates, the subject of the final chapter of the novel, which takes place after the narrative arc of the novel, fast-forwarding through time to detail the aftermath of the story and its global impact: 'In its final pages the novel somehow loses sight of Arjun Mehta, the protagonist, who becomes untraceable, quite as if he had made his escape through a thin partitioning into another world whence occasionally, during a momentary lapse of real-world concentration, he rematerialises as a fleeting world-creative promise of subaltern resistance' (Schoene, 2009: 143).

Echoing the language of Nancy and Moten, where community 'escapes' the very terms of the present, forging a life and a relationship which are simply unthinkable and unrepresentable, Schoene captures the uncanny and otherworldly manner through which Kunzru evokes the 'fleeting [...] promise' of community, identifying it with the postcolonial figure of the 'subaltern' that, like 'blackness', must assert itself in a symbolic and material landscape hostile to its very existence. In this way, the 'fugitive' may be located as an important formal device in *Transmission*, emerging in its disjunctive relation to its own narrative structure and narrative voice. It is evident therefore that fugitive narrative strategies, which are found most clearly in his short fiction, precipitate similar effects to his novels, demonstrating the consistent relevance of fugitivity for his general literary project.

The short story and the novel: narrative displacements

The final chapter of *Transmission* is entitled 'Noise', strikingly replicating the title Kunzru gives to his short story collection a year later. In this way we may see Kunzru indicate an affinity between the chapter, which disrupts the narrative unity of the novel, and the narrative techniques employed in his short stories. In fact, through its shift in temporality and its employment of a new narrative style, the chapter embodies an autonomous and self-contained logic which partially replicates the formal conventions of the short story. As Schoene writes, the final chapter creates 'a deliberate disemplotment, which causes the narrative not so much to unravel as fruitfully to disperse. The characters are released into a radical freedom that possesses no clearly identifiable, definitive shape lest it tighten into another formative imposition' (2009: 150). Detailing the fate of Arjun, who is on the run for releasing the 'Leela virus', which caused a world-altering disruption in global capital, destroying stock markets and border regimes, the chapter breaks from the novel's otherwise third-person narrative voice to address the reader in the second person: 'Do you know anyone whom Leela did not touch in some way?' (*T*: 272), thereby implicating them in the fictive world and mythology of Arjun.

Despite events strongly implying Arjun will be detained by the global network of surveillance and state power that seeks to punish him for disseminating the virus, the final chapter refuses to offer an effective denouement to the story. In the previous chapter we see Arjun come very close to capture at the heavily-surveilled 'border between the United States and Mexico [which] is one of the most tightly controlled in the world' (*T*: 266). Nonetheless, it is precisely the temporal break and shift in narrative tone, from the intimate detailing of Arjun's last recorded activity to the historical, social and mythological framing of the story in the 'Noise' chapter that comes after it, which conspicuously denies the narrative expectation Kunzru has otherwise set up as an inevitable outcome. In fact, the chapter serves as precisely the kind of 'noise' with which it begins its description, showing how the desire to 'abolish the unknown' and capture all 'information' about the world is doomed to failure as '[i]n the real world [...] there is always noise' (*T*: 271). Denoting here a form of interference, which like his final chapter, and likewise the narratively disjunctive stories of the short story collection, Kunzru shows how even in the tightly controlled and militarised world of global capitalism, there can be life which escapes this, holding, if only in 'legend', the possibility of disruptive and unlikely relational forms.

This device of disturbing the narrative coherence of his novels with more experimental use of narrative voice drawn from his short-story style is also found in Kunzru's most recent novel *Red Pill* (2020), which integrates an adapted version of his short story 'A Transparent Woman' (2020) as a chapter entitled '*Zersetzing* (Undermining)'. Published in *The New Yorker* in June 2020, a few months before the novel's publication in September of the same year and based on a series of 'interviews' and extensive 'research' into the life of punks in 'East Berlin in the early eighties' (qtd. in Treisman, 2020: n.p.), the story works as a standalone fictionalised account of the effect of the Stasi on 'teen-age punks' who, far from constituting a threat to the GDR at the time, were just 'kids [who] had no real political sensibility' (qtd. in Treisman, 2020: n.p.) until the process of infiltration and state oppression led them to learn the more political implications of social and cultural transgression. Commenting on his decision to include the short story as part of the narrative structure of his novel, Kunzru writes he deliberately wanted to use the story as 'a sort of wedge, to open up the main narrative of the book into something beyond itself', something he comments he 'like[s] to do in [his] fiction' (qtd. in Treisman, 2020: n.p.).[2] Noting that some 'readers' might 'experience this "story within a story" as a distraction, or criticize it as a rupture in the formal unity of the book' as it is only 'indirectly related to the travails of [the] narrator', Kunzru nonetheless affirms that it is 'absolutely central to what [he is] trying to do, and the book would be incomplete without it' (qtd. in Treisman, 2020: n.p.).

'A Transparent Woman' is thematically analogous to many other short stories Kunzru has written, demonstrating the insidious ability of state power to subordinate human relationships and community to its own ends, thereby undermining community as a site of solidarity and mutual care, and subsuming it into a logic of control. The political stakes of Kunzru's critique here are complex, including not only the totalitarian government of the GDR and its violent and abusive secret police, but also inculcating, in stories such as 'Raj, Bohemian', 'Kaltes Klares Wasser', 'Fill Your Life With Win!' and 'Love With Impediments', a reduction of sociality to the totalising profit motive allied with state power. In *Memory Palace* and 'Memories of the Decadence' we see a dystopian regression to a form of neo-feudal, post-apocalyptic social control, and in 'Beyond the Pleasure Principle' we are introduced to historical echoes of Nazism which are also developed in *Red Pill*. In this way, Kunzru's deployment of a fugitive form of community derives from his deep concern with the threat of totalitarianism, which includes not only historical examples of totalitarian states in Nazi Germany and the GDR, but also what he sees as an encroaching totalitarian and authoritarian logic in liberal capitalist democracies in the Neoliberal period, which he claims has seen 'far more pervasive forms of surveillance and control than anything we saw in East Germany' (qtd. in Treisman, 2020: n.p.). The community that would 'escape' therefore abjures not only the explicit totalitarian impulses of the past, but those that develop within the auspices of the present. Like Nancy, Kunzru does not just see the threat of totalitarianism to community only through historical examples, but as part of 'the general horizon of our time, encompassing democracies and their fragile juridical parapets' (Nancy, 1991: 3).

Fugitive promise: revolutionary reticence

Critical attention to the cosmopolitan elements of Kunzru's work has inevitably tended to focus on texts which justify this approach, drawing attention to how the heterogenous characters and narrators of his prose evoke a 'singularly plural cosmopolitan community' through a movement between the local and the global as well as between the individual and the 'worldwide community' (Jansen, 2018: 266). Nonetheless, this pervasive cosmopolitan frame has arguably led to the diminishment of short stories that represent community in ways that are less compatible with this framework. Perhaps most strikingly, two stories that deploy a first-person plural 'we' as part of their narrative structure, and for which this composite speaker is a significant thematic concern of the story, receive very little attention in Kunzru's critical reception. This chapter will conclude with close readings of 'Magda Mandela' and 'The Interns', which produce interpretive possibilities for reading community which indite a set of political concerns and possibilities that move beyond cosmopolitanism. Rather than identifying their political context or meaning with an investment in global dialogue, hospitality and other broadly defined cosmopolitan values as they play

out in the public sphere, their evocation of community is more elusive and recalcitrant, suggesting a fugitive community that escapes
easy capture or representation, but which holds onto incisive and
disruptive relational possibilities.

Published alongside an array of well-known British writers such
as David Mitchell, Nick Hornby, Colm Tóibín and Zadie Smith,
'Magda Mandela' appears in *The Book of Other People,* a charity
anthology for Penguin Books in 2007, a year after the story was
separately published by *The New Yorker* magazine. The concept
behind the collection as explained by editor Zadie Smith was to
create an eponymous character for the story: to '*make somebody
up*' (Smith, 2007: vii–ix), deploying this central creative conceit as
the structuring logic behind the narrative progression of each short
piece. Perhaps surprisingly, as Jansen notes, this protagonist is not
the main narrator of her own story, as is more usual for the largely
autodiegetic narrators of Kunzru's short fiction. Rather, the protagonist of 'Magda Mandela' is described homodiegetically from the
perspective of 'the protagonist's neighbour' (Jansen, 2018: 266).
Recalling the homodiegetic narrators of 'The Maestro's Loss'
(2012) and 'The Culture House', where the main characters are
described from the peripheral perspective of more minor characters
in the story, the narrative voice of 'Magda Mandela' is, however,
distinct in two respects. Firstly, the voice of Magda seeps through
the narrative in the form of frequent free indirect discourse, often
emerging in capital letters implying direct speech that is not denoted
by quotation marks. Secondly, although the narrative is ultimately
told from the perspective of a single neighbour, this voice is largely
rendered in the first-person *plural,* indicating not a just single
narrator but a composite voice of a localised community.

As the story unfolds, we find that Magda occupies a unique
and unsettling position in the fictional 'Westerbury Road' in East
London, disturbing her neighbours at unsociable hours, as well
as upending their expected kinship conventions by cohabiting
with 'Errol', who is 'a widower in his seventies' she met in 'one
of the least salubrious pubs in our little corner of East London'
(Kunzru, 2007a: n.p.). Despite Magda's consistent sonic and symbolic disturbances, her neighbours are strikingly reticent in any
condemnation or even clear opinion of Magda. In fact, the story
evokes a bond between Magda and her neighbours which is deeply

ambiguous, working through metaphorical tropes of 'knowing' and 'love' which disturb any ordinary understanding of these terms: 'All of us neighbors have been known by Magda. Last time she knew me, she pushed me up against the side of my car. I know you, she breathed huskily. And I knew I'd been known' (2007a: n.p.). This 'knowing' takes on a crucial, if under-determined meaning in the story, gesturing to a form of relationality the story cannot seem to state directly. As the story develops the metaphorical weight of 'knowing' is transcribed onto the figure of 'love', which is also part of Magda's exuberant lexicon of community with her neighbours: 'Wake up, my neighbors, she will often command. Wake up and listen. Tonight I love you. I love you, my neighbors. I am filled with love. But you do not love me, so I say to you this: I DON'T GIVE A FUCK ABOUT YOU. That is the truth. Fuck off now. Go. Magda loves us, but she spurns us just as we spurn her. She spurns us out of the vastness of her love' (2007a: n.p.).

This rehearsing of relational intensities, oscillating in the same speech act between intense loving, intimacy and stark rejection, is described as reciprocal: just as Magda is drawn to her neighbours, offering them her 'vast' love only then to spurn them, so too does the collective narration 'spurn her'. The function of the narration is not just to present this unconventional account of love comically, depicting Magda's contradictory passions as simply denoting an unstable or inconsistent character who cannot be taken seriously. The undetermined nature of this 'love' rather works to endow this figure with a strange power over the community, who although ultimately rejecting this love, are unable to do so fully: 'Sometimes I wonder what would happen if we returned Magda's love. If we believed in her, she could do great things for us. But our problem is that we are faithless. Our problem is that we are stupid. Our problem is that we just don't listen' (2007a: n.p.).

For Nancy, '[l]ove conceals a fundamental ambivalence', standing in for many figures Western society feels it has lost: 'religion, community, the immediate emotion of the Other and [...] the divine' ([1986] 1991: 93). Despite its status as a constant preoccupation of contemporary 'Occidental' society, love is nonetheless for Nancy 'rebellious, fugitive, errant, unassignable, and inassimilable' ([1986] 1991: 93). Likewise, the love of Magda, which as Jansen notes is 'exoticised and sexualised by the Western male gaze' (2018: 263), takes on a wider political and philosophical significance of the story, representing the overcoming of a seemingly incommensurable gulf between Magda and her neighbours. In this way, the possibility of this love, as absurd, incoherent and inassimilable as it appears, is nonetheless the final, unavowed promise of the story. Escaping clear intelligibility or representability, poised between its implausibility and a potent promise of reconciliation in the postcolonial environment still characterised by enduring processes of exclusion, exploitation and inequality, Magda's love recalls the 'undercommons' of Moten and Harney. In the figure of the fugitive 'blackness' which 'operates as the modality of life's constant escape', Moten and Harney find a potential to move toward an 'undercommon sensuality, that radical occupied-elsewhere, that utopic commonunderground' (2013: 51) which can unsettle dominant structures with new relational possibilities. If Magda's neighbours cannot ultimately know 'what would happen if we returned Magda's love', this unanswered question nonetheless holds on to a minimal form of potentiality in community. In refusing simple cynicism or dismissal, the unlikely and enigmatic figure of Magda becomes emblematic of forms of being and relation which escape the restrictive norms of the present, creating a literary space where new forms of relation might be imagined.

'Magda Mandela' gestures to a subterranean and radically disruptive reconfiguration of community which, echoing Nancy's own concerns about community, is never fully clear or avowable (2016: 19). We may see this revolutionary reticence in several other Kunzru stories which invoke resistance and transformation at the same time as failing to articulate the terms of what this may look like in reality. Such an impulse may be seen in the ultimately failed resistance of the protagonist of 'Raj, Bohemian' to the subsumption of her sociality into an integrated commodity/advertising nexus; the impulse to 'cut the head off' the digital dystopia of violence and alienation' in 'Love With Impediments' (Kunzru, 2014 [2007]: 65); the inertia and apathy to his work of the protagonist in 'Kaltes Klares Wasser' and the destructive acts of Nicky in 'The Culture House', who burns down the 'Gow House' where he is doing an artistic residency (Kunzru, 2009b: n.p.). Most clearly, this reticent impulse toward political resistance, which is nonetheless not fully avowed by Kunzru, may be seen in his short story 'The Interns', whose narrative voice performs a contemporised proletarian voice of revolution, exploring the potential limits of this articulation. If, for Jansen, this story cannot accord with Nancy's cosmopolitan vision as it explores a 'homogeneous "unitotality" [...] rather than a differential, cosmopolitan community' (2018: 261), and for Schoene, cosmopolitanism would mean precisely the giving up of an 'erroneous [...] Marxian notion of "struggle" [...] [of] two or more partisan factions forever categorically pitted against each other' (2009: 19), Kunzru's explicit drawing on Marxist terminology of 'class enemies' and a logic of class antagonism appears to stand outside the cosmopolitan framing of his work, demanding an expanded perspective on his political vision of community (Kunzru, 2007b: n.p.).

The narrative voice of 'The Interns' is rendered in an adapted manifesto style which, following the rhetorical style of this genre, appears at first to articulate a political argument in the hope of inculcating its reader into a shared vision through rhetorical persuasion. Recalling through oblique allusion Karl Marx and Frederick Engels's *The Communist Manifesto* (1848), the text nonetheless subverts this as its narrative unfolds, establishing itself less as a manifesto and more as a work of short fiction. In deploying language analogous to the famous final lines of Marx and Engels's manifesto, Kunzru's short story shifts its mode of address from the political subjectivity of a proletarian 'we' toward addressing an enemy: the intern's 'masters' who make them perform 'menial' tasks, who they wish to overthrow (Kunzru 2007b: n.p.). Rather than addressing the global proletariat, telling them they have 'nothing to lose but their chains' (Engels and Marx, [1848] 2002: 258), the story instead addresses their enemies, the business managers and CEOs who themselves lack freedom at the same time as exploiting their own interns: 'You know that nothing will make you free, not any more, not ever, that all you've been doing is wrapping your chains more tightly around yourselves' (Kunzru, 2007b: n.p.).

The manifesto form and its implied collective subject of articulation gives way to a dramatisation of an intergenerational conflict where an older economic class are accused of creating an exploitative world which makes no one happy and which makes everyone bored, where interns work unpaid in the hope of entering the world of 'gallerists, publishers, model agencies, production companies, law firms, newspapers, media networks, political lobbyists, non-governmental organisations' (Kunzru, 2007b: n.p.). In this way, Kunzru partially empties the manifesto form of its historic political earnestness, partly undermining its content through digression and a stylistic pettiness. Nonetheless, the story also reacts insightfully to changing dynamics of capitalist society, casting the children of what has been termed the 'Baby Boomer' generation as a new oppressed class. Kunzru's new articulated revolutionary subject, whose political concerns seem at first too 'pampered' and limited to really be convincing, ultimately demonstrate an attention to patterns in labour and power in contemporary society which align the story with Jeffrey Nealon's description of the 'perpetual retraining of flexibly specialised labor in once lucrative and respected sectors of the economy' (2012: 39). The narrative voice of the story ultimately departs from the nineteenth-century call to arms of an emergent proletarian class to radically transform class dynamics in capitalist society, rather responding to increasing intergenerational resentment, inequality, and a lack of a viable political language or collective capacity to overcome this. Nonetheless, the story ends in a striking negation which like 'Magda Mandela' appears to indicate an inchoate, but insistent need for new ways to imagine our political reality: 'Oh, the glory! The pomp of you modern-day pharaohs! We could never ever ever be like you' (2007b: n.p.). Ultimately the configuration of this 'we' is left undetermined, presented not as a positive articulation of a new, transformative community, but simply as a negation of the present. If the naïve oracular insistence of the 'never ever ever' fails to register credibly as a concrete political proposition, creating an unease in the reader that the 'whole cycle of domination' will simply be repeated by this new class of interns, Kunzru's story does not simply leave us with a sense of impossibility or cynicism (2007b: n.p.). 'The Interns' exposes new exploitative dynamics in capitalist society which instructively mirror Kier Milburn's recent claims that generational politics are now important dynamics in contemporary economic and political systems. This emerging politics which Kunzru's story is grasping for may become for Milburn the basis of new 'ideas and practices' for the building of a transformational political community in the context of increasing inequality, climate catastrophe and insurgent nationalism, a project for which the 'stakes could not be higher' (2019: 2–3).

Conclusion

Kunzru's short fiction deploys a variety of experimental narrative techniques to explore the contours, limits and possibilities for community inherent in contemporary capitalist society. His stories serve as laboratories for testing the ability of a narrative voice to build and question human subjectivity and relationships, a capacity which Kunzru has also drawn on in his novels, which deploy devices borrowed from his short stories to explore the ability of prose to create and configure forms of community and relationality. Although often agnostic or reticent in their avowal of communitarian or relational alternatives to the atomism and instrumentalisation of community in society, Kunzru's prose drives toward unstable, complex and disruptive forms of collectivity which suggest an investment in forms of relation that unsettle the operative terms of the present. This facet of his writing replicates a paradigm seen in the works of Nancy alongside Harney and Moten of 'fugitivity', where community may only be glimpsed in its ability to 'escape' the terms of the present, residing in a subterranean capacity that literature can imaginatively capture and sustain.

If the international and multiethnic make-up of Kunzru's prose may indicate an investment in a cosmopolitan project, as broad critical consensus has established (Schoene, 2009; Shaw, 2017; Jansen, 2018), it is clear that Kunzru's short fiction also disassociates itself from any clearly identifiable political project as well as any simple celebration of globalisation or contemporary multiculture. In their indeterminate, but often insistent evocation of communitarian possibility, Kunzru's short stories involve a wider and more antagonistic set of political concerns, attending to material conditions of exploitation, proletarianisation, and technopolitical subsumption which implicate the capitalist state in practices that instrumentalise community in often inegalitarian ways. In stories such as 'Magda Mandela' and 'The Interns', close reading can find incalcitrant gestures to insurgent, undetermined and transformative communities that may yet emerge in the present. Fugitive community is ultimately a way of holding onto the possibility of provisional futures, even if they must inhabit the uncertain time of the 'one day', which falters between fantasy, naïveté and exigent political conviction. Writing recently in *Harper's Magazine*, Kunzru expresses deep concern over shifts in digital technology and an increasingly regressive, nationalistic political landscape in the COVID-19 era, leaving his reader with a powerful, if characteristically oblique sense of an emerging political community founded in justice: 'One day we shall be paid for the work we have done. One day we shall go viral' (Kunzru, 2021: n.p.).

Notes

1 As Bruce Robbins and Paulo Lemos Horta's recent collection on cosmopolitan thought argues, cosmopolitanism is definitionally 'irreducibly plural' and therefore difficult to capture as a single 'idea' (2017: 8; 16). Nonetheless I refer here to major currents in the literature: intercultural dialogue, hybridity, hospitality, and a broadly optimistic worldview as broadly defining features. For Ulrich Beck (2006), such ideas have become at least partly integrated into the 'banal' facticity of contemporary global capitalism, presenting problems for preserving cosmopolitanism's more radical trajectories.

2 Similarly, Douglas Coupland (2012) in his well-known essay 'Convergences' describes Kunzru's *Gods Without Men* (2011) as a series of 'substories' that 'combine to make a novel'.

References

Beck, Ulrich (2006). *Cosmopolitan Vision* (Cambridge: Polity Press).

Bennett, Andrew and Nicholas Royle (2016). *An Introduction to Literature, Criticism and Theory* (London: Routledge).

Coupland, Douglas (2012) . 'Convergences', *New York Times,* 8 March, www.nytimes.com/2012/03/11/books/review/gods-without-men-by-hari-kunzru.html (accessed 8 August 2022).

Engels, Friedrich and Karl Marx ([1848] 2002) . *The Communist Manifesto* (London: Penguin Books).

Freud, Sigmund (1997). *Writings on Art and Literature* (Stanford: Stanford University Press).

Gilmore, Ruth Wilson (2007). *Golden Gulag: Prisons, Surplus, Crisis, and Opposition in Globalizing California* (Berkeley: University of California Press).

Jansen, Bettina (2018). *Narratives of Community in the Black British Short Story* (Basingstoke: Palgrave Macmillan).

Kunzru, Hari (1999). 'Sunya', www.harikunzru.com/sunya/ (accessed 8 August 2022).

——— (2005a). *Noise* (London: Penguin).

—— (2005b). 'Beyond the Pleasure Principle', *Guardian*, 25 June, www. theguardian.com/books/2005/jun/25/originalwriting.fiction3 (accessed 8 August 2022).

—— (2007a). 'Magda Mandela', *The New Yorker*, 13 August, www. newyorker.com/magazine/2007/08/13/magda-mandela (accessed 8 August 2022).

—— (2007b). 'The Interns', www.harikunzru.com/tag/interns/ (accessed 8 August 2022).

—— (2008a). 'Fellow Traveller', *Guardian*, 25 August, www.theguardian. com/books/2008/aug/25/chineseliterature.originalwriting (accessed 8 August 2022).

—— (2008b). 'Raj, Bohemian', *The New Yorker*, 10 March, www. newyorker.com/magazine/2008/03/10/raj-bohemian (accessed 8 August 2022).

—— (2009a). 'Fill Your Life with Win!' , *Mute*, 8 December, www. metamute.org/editorial/articles/fill-your-life-win (accessed 8 August 2022).

—— (2009b). 'The Culture House', *The New Statesman*, 30 December.

—— (2009c). 'Kaltes Klares Wasser', in Mark Ellingham and Peter Florence (eds), *Ox-Tales: Water* (London: GreenProfile).

—— (2012). 'The Maestro's Loss', *Guardian*, 1 January, www. theguardian.com/books/2012/jan/01/the-maestros-loss-hari-kunzru (accessed 8 August 2022).

—— (2014 [2007]). 'Love with Impediments', in *The Mechanic's Institute Review: New Stories from Birkbeck*, 11:1.

—— (2020). 'A Transparent Woman', *The New Yorker*, 29 June, www. newyorker.com/magazine/2020/07/06/a-transparent-woman (accessed 8 August 2022).

—— (2021). 'Attention', *Harper's Magazine*, July, https://harpers.org/ archive/2021/07/attention-hari-kunzru/ (accessed 8 August 2022).

Milburn, Kier (2019). *Generation Left* (Cambridge: Polity).

Moten, Fred and Harney, Stefano (2013). *The Undercommons: Fugitive Planning and Black Study* (New York: Minor Compositions).

Nancy, Jean-Luc ([1986] 1991) . *The Inoperative Community*, edited by Peter Connor, translated by Peter Connor, Lisa Garbus, Michael Holland and Simona Sawhney (Minneapolis: University of Minnesota Press).

—— (1993). *The Birth to Presence* (Stanford: Stanford University Press).

—— (2000). *Being Singular Plural*, translated by Robert D. Richardson and Anne E. O'Byrne (Stanford: Stanford University Press).

—— (2016). *The Disavowed Community* (New York: Fordham University Press).

Nealon, Jeffrey T. (2012). *Post-Postmodernism, or, The Cultural Logic of Just-in-time Capitalism* (Stanford: Stanford University Press).

Robbins, Bruce and Paulo Lemos Horta (eds) (2017). *Cosmopolitanisms* (New York: New York University Press).

Schoene, Berthold (2009). *The Cosmopolitan Novel* (Edinburgh: Edinburgh University Press).

Shaw, Kristian (2017). *Cosmopolitanism in Twenty-First Century Fiction* (Cham: Palgrave Macmillan).

Smith, Zadie (ed.) (2007). *The Book of Other People* (London: Hamish Hamilton).

Treisman, Deborah (2020). 'Hari Kunzru on Privacy, Surveillance, and Paranoia', *The New Yorker*, 29 June, www.newyorker.com/books/this-week-in-fiction/hari-kunzru-07-06-20 (accessed 8 August 2022).

Upstone, Sara (2010). *British Asian Fiction: Twenty-First-Century Voices* (Manchester: Manchester University Press).

5

The fiction of every-era/no-era: *Gods Without Men* as 'translit'

Bran Nicol

When it was published in 2011, *Gods Without Men* was described by one reviewer, Lisa Appignanesi, as 'Kunzru's great American novel' (2011). There is a note of irony in this description, partly because the very idea of the Great American Novel, or 'GAN' as Henry James called it, the encapsulation of the 'essence' of a nation as vast, multifaceted, and multicultural as America in novel form (see Buell, 2014), is ironic in itself. But it is also because Hari Kunzru is neither American nor indeed easy to pigeonhole in any one national or racial category, for anyone minded to do so: 'Depending on who I'm talking to, and how I feel, I might describe myself simply as a Londoner, British (that one's only crept in since I came to live in New York – to anyone in the UK, it's weirdly meaningless), English, the son of an Indian father and an English mother, Kashmiri Pandit, rootless cosmopolitan' (qtd. in Kumar, 2012). Yet it is in fact appropriate in some ways to compare *Gods Without Men* to the Great American Novel. Insofar as its subject can be condensed into a single set of themes, those themes outwardly revolve around what America is and the kind of people and behaviour it produces.

Gods Without Men came about directly after Kunzru had travelled to the United States in 2008 to take up a fellowship at the Cullman Center in the New York Public Library initially intending to write a novel set in sixteenth-century India. Once in New York, however, he 'just couldn't concentrate on anything that wasn't set in America' (Barron, 2017). The need to write about America had been with him for some years but was formed especially on 11 September 2001, the day of the terrorist attacks on the World Trade Center, when Kunzru had realised that he would be unable to fly home to the UK the next day as planned. Acutely aware of how he might be profiled racially in such a volatile international climate, and unable to return his hire car, he drove into West Hollywood and found it 'full of freaked out hipsters telling each other someone was about to fly planes into the Hollywood sign. People were losing their minds'. Kunzru decided to get out of LA 'and drove to Death Valley, which seemed quiet and appropriate. I had a very intense few days' (Kumar, 2012).

'Rootless cosmopolitan': Kunzru and the global novel

Prompted by this origin story, by Kunzru's professed enthusiasm for elements of American popular culture (such as the blues, explored in his 2017 novel *White Tears*) and admiration for post-modern American writers (Piccarella, 2019), and by *Gods Without Men*'s preoccupation with some of the core features of American culture – race, violence, faith, paranoia and conspiracy-thinking, system versus chaos, the yearning for the mythic West – it is logical to regard *Gods Without Men* as 'a distinctly American novel worthy of comparison with Pynchon and DeLillo' (LeClair, 2012). But the journey into America which *Gods Without Men* represents in fact makes it reflective not just of America but of much of Western, global twenty-first-century experience. Appropriately enough, given the role of cars in American culture and Kunzru's own five months researching the novel by driving around the United States (Kumar, 2012), we might suggest that America is a vehicle for the novel's exploration of more contemporary global social and literary themes.

Gods Without Men is in fact an example of one of the distinguishing features of literary fiction over the first few decades of the twenty-first century: its global or 'world' status. For Adam Kirsch, what he calls the 'global novel' is not a genre, but 'a per-spective that governs the interpretation of experience'. It is a form which does not abolish place (and it would be hard to imagine a novel which is more about a specific place than *Gods Without Men*) but uses 'the global' 'as a theme by which place is mediated' (Kirsch, 2017: 12). The global novel, Kirsch suggests, in different ways 'addresses the question of what it means to write across borders' (24).

These preoccupations are most immediately visible in the central plot which runs through *Gods Without Men*, which narrates the lives of characters who represent the 'hyphenated identities' whom Peter Boxall argues appear throughout his own category of 'world fiction' (2013: 68), a form dedicated to 'imagining national and postnational identities under contemporary global conditions' (2013: 168). Kunzru's novel depicts a critical period between 2008 and 2009 in the life of an affluent young Brooklyn family, a second-generation Punjabi-American, Jaz Matharu, his wife Lisa, a non-observant Jewish American, and their four-year-old son Raj. Jaz is a mathematician who has designed a 'big data' model for a finance company, which they call 'Walter', and which is designed to predict markets. His and Lisa's marriage has settled into a mundane and unfulfilling routine, its trials exacerbated by their mixed marriage and the difficulties of raising an autistic son. During a day trip to the Mojave Desert, Raj wanders off and disappears. A few weeks later he is miraculously found just as suddenly, appearing in a desert military base ten miles from the nearest road. The mystery is never explained. Despite their initial relief, Raj's reappearance serves to intensify Jaz and Lisa's estrangement. There is something different about their son. He now seems supremely gifted, and able to engage articulately and intelligently with others. Where Lisa appears able to accept this, Jaz cannot, and questions whether this Raj even is his son.

This plot is gripping and eerie and meditates themes about racial mixing (Jaz is estranged from his Sikh family in Baltimore), the power of late capitalism, and the destructive, aggressive, shaming power of social media – none of which are subjects confined purely to American experience. Indeed, if this story was the only one *Gods Without Men* told, the novel would be a worthwhile contribution to the kind of world or global fiction critics such as Kirsch and Boxall have defined. But it is its distinctive form which ensures that the novel adds something else to the understanding of how a novel can reflect 'contemporary global conditions'. The most distinctive feature of *Gods Without Men* is the fact that this main story is accompanied by a number of other stories which occasionally overlap with it (which I shall discuss in more detail below) but which, more intriguingly, are discrete, feature – for the most part – different characters, and take place at alternate points in history. Nevertheless, the stories are all linked spatially, for they are set in the same geographical place, the place where Raj disappears. This is a rock formation in the Mojave Desert which resembles three fingers pointing upwards, known as the Pinnacles (which seems to be based on the real Trona Pinnacles in San Bernardino County, California).

Two central intrigues thus provide the narrative impetus of *Gods Without Men*. The first is: what happens to Raj? Can there be a rational explanation for his disappearance, reappearance and apparent change in personality? The second is: what do all the narratives and occasional convergences within and between them mean? Overall, this complex novel invites readers to ponder how the second intrigue relates to the first. The implication is either that Raj has been inhabited by another person from the past, or that he somehow has been transformed by the sublime mystical energy of the Pinnacles region. Either way this requires readers to compare what they know from the novel's validation of reality – that Raj *did* disappear and transform from a troubled, autistic child to a benign, gifted one – with the potential explanation for this. This explanation is never forthcoming, and the mystery is never solved.

At its most general the mystery about convergence – even more than 'America' – is what *Gods Without Men* is 'about'. While the novel is clearly 'about America', as Kunzru has himself directly acknowledged (Gilbert, 2012), it is more profoundly about 'how people handle the unknown' (Piccarella, 2019). This is what the characters throughout the story, as different as they are, and as literally unconnected as they are, are trying to do. The tension between an unfathomable metaphysical set of truths or values and an attempt to capture these or to measure them through a particular system is repeatedly foregrounded, through, for example, the efforts of an eighteenth-century monk to make sense in terms of his faith of the vision of an angel's face he sees in the desert; a desert hippie community's attempt to co-opt the manifestation of entities from outer space in the form of UFOs into their manifesto; or the 'ultimately quixotic' (Kumar, 2012) project Jaz and his company are involved in, the project to use big data to gain knowledge that can enhance trade.

This sense of vast unknowability explains the function of the desert setting in the novel. As Kunzru himself has explained, referring to the first of the novel's three epigraphs, 'Dans le desert, voyez-vous, il y a tout, et il'y a rien […] c'est Dieu sans les hommes', the title's primary meaning comes from this Balzac story, 'Passion in the Desert', where an old soldier in the Napoleonic War in Egypt is asked, 'What is the desert?' and he says, 'It's God without man'. That was very much my feeling when I was in the Mojave. It's got this metaphysical quality, a vast emptiness, and a feeling [...] it's almost like, behind a very bright light there's something that you can't quite grasp. (Gilbert, 2012)

There is a danger that such remarks encourage a somewhat banal interpretation of *Gods Without Men* which fails to do justice to its complexity and narrative exuberance: namely, that the novel affirms there are mysteries beyond our comprehension, that life is full of potential meaningful connections and patterns if only we could figure out what these are. This is why I think Douglas Coupland's analysis of the novel in an influential review-essay, 'Convergences', which first appeared in *New York Times* in 2012 and was later republished in the essay collection *Shopping in Jail* (2013), provides a more fruitful way of understanding *Gods Without Men*. Its starting-points are that the novel is precisely of its moment, and that it is unmistakeably global. Yet Coupland conceives of its global nature in a way which is different from (though compatible with) the definitions of Boxall and Kirsch. Most significantly, Coupland shows that the key to *Gods Without Men* is to recognise – to quote Fredric Jameson in a reading of contemporary fiction which I shall also consider in due course – 'that the most valuable works are those that make their points by way of form rather than content' (1991: 311). Its form makes *Gods Without Men*, as I argue in what remains of this chapter, a self-reflexive enquiry into the nature of fiction itself as much as a philosophical or political treatise delivered through fiction. Kirsch contends that the global novel is 'a basic affirmation of the power of literature to represent the world' (2017: 13). This, I think, is the real value of regarding *Gods Without Men* as a global or world novel rather than a Great American Novel, yet it is one which suggests that this affirmation is anything but basic.

Coupland, Kunzru and 'translit'

For Coupland the defining experience of the first decades of the twenty-first century is the sense that we are now living in 'an aura-free universe in which all eras coexist at once – a state of possibly permanent atemporality' (2013: 24). Ours is a world, he contends, with no dominant 'era' because of the advent of the internet, the smartphone, Wikipedia, Google, YouTube, Twitter, all of which have collapsed both temporal and geographical distance. Coupland would go on, with co-authors Shumon Basar and Hans Ulrich Obrist, to categorise this condition more precisely as 'the extreme present' (Basar, 2015). But what is most interesting about his 'Convergences' essay is that it suggests how the experience is reflected in and has shaped contemporary fiction.

Coupland describes *Gods Without Men* as a paradigmatic example of what he terms 'translit', the product of this distinctive 'aura-free' temporality – or rather atemporality – which typifies twenty-first-century Western culture:

> Translit novels cross history without being historical; they span geography without changing psychic place. Translit collapses time and space as it seeks to generate narrative traction in the reader's mind. It inserts the contemporary reader into other locations and times, while leaving no doubt that its viewpoint is relentlessly modern and speaks entirely of our extreme present. Imagine traveling back to Victorian England – only with vaccinations, a wad of cash and a clean set of ruling-class garb. With Translit we get our very delicious cake, and we get to eat it, too, as we visit multiple pasts safe in the knowledge we'll get off the ride intact, in our bold new perpetual every-era/no-era. (Coupland, 2013)

Using *Gods Without Men* as his paradigmatic text, Coupland goes on to sketch out three further distinctive features of translit which result from the way this kind of novel transports itself across time and space. What is most distinctive about Kunzru's novel, he argues, is the way it alternates between a 'core' story and 'multiple substories'. Coupland lists eight of these 'substories', but actually I do not think they are fully representative of the novel, even though it is hard to improve upon Coupland's witty, pithy summary of them. So here I will retain much of Coupland's description, but regroup his list of substories into what I consider is a more accurate way of isolating the principal six interlocking narrative/temporal worlds which make up *Gods Without Men*:

1. 'In 1775 [and 1778], Kunzru sends an Aragonese friar, Padre Fray Francisco Garcés, on a mission into the desert, where he

sees [...] the face of an angel? It's not quite clear, but something primal and possibly dreadful';

2. 'In 1871, a Mormon silver miner with a checkered past lies dying of mercury poisoning';

3. 'In 1920, a badly scarred linguist and his wife, caught in a passionless relationship, study what remains of a local American Indian dialect. In a moment of jealousy, the husband unleashes vengeance on his wife's Indian lover, setting off a tragic chain of events.' Then, 'In 1942, the military investigates the linguist, by then a husk of a man living in a cave beneath the Pinnacles, and a cruel trick of the gods is revealed';

4. 'In 1947, a former aircraft engineer named Schmidt sets up a station at the Pinnacles to await the arrival of aliens';

5. 'In 1958, a UFO cult uses the rock formation as its energy center to make alien contact. A young girl goes missing. [...] Ten years later, a scuzzy, Keseyesque hippie commune has taken over the Pinnacles. People come and go, damage is done, people return and some vanish.' This narrative world actually continues into 1969, 1970 and 1971 featuring some of the same characters grown older, especially two women, Dawn and Joanie, who move from impressionable kids on the fringe of hippiedom to mature adults, unable to forget their cultist past;

6. The sixth world is the most expansive and frequently returned to. This is because 2008–2009 is the period of the main story involving Jaz, Lisa and Raj. But it also contains two other related stories. As Coupland describes them: 'In 2008, a peyote'd British rock star (to be played by Noel Gallagher in the movie) crashes and burns in a desert motel', and 'In 2008–9, a teenage Iraqi refugee has assimilated into American culture as a goth, but she works as a simulated Iraqi villager in a simulated Iraqi village used to train soldiers in assault' (Coupland, 2013).

These stories which make up the sixth narrative world are separate but, because they overlap, are clearly part of the same narrative world (or occupy the same diegetic level, to put it in more narratological terms). This is not the case with the majority of the other stories. After a drug- and alcohol-fuelled dispute about 'musical differences' with his band, Nicky has driven out into the desert and, when too exhausted to go any further, has checked in to the motel. This is the same motel at which Jaz, Lisa and Raj are staying while on vacation. It is also where Laila, the teenage Iraqi refugee, who is a fan of Nicky Capaldi, meets him by chance. Laila is the person who will find Raj in a military base in the desert. The motel, the *Drop*

Inn, is the location which points to a way in which one of the other narrative worlds, number five, bleeds into this main world, as it is owned by the adult Dawn who bought it with a stash of money she came across in a drug-fuelled escapade (an episode narrated in one of the chapters). Worlds five and six converge when one of the later 2008 chapters (*GWM*: 351–357) is focalised through Dawn, and when Laila listens to the trippy LP recorded by the Ashtar Galactic Command, the hippie commune of which Dawn was a member.

Kunzru's novel uses the comparison between historical moments and the present to encapsulate the volatility of our age, a volatility caused by the fact that technology has ensured we have more knowledge, or at least information, and are more connected than ever before as a result of digital technology (but are also less and less convinced of a stable pattern or belief system). Contemporary technology, in the form of Jaz's big data modelling, is the most outwardly sophisticated method of trying to make sense of the incomprehensible, but it is no more capable of bending the complexity of the world into a clearly understood system than religion or Ufology.

The 2008–2009 main story ends with Jaz, Lisa and Raj reunited by going back to the Pinnacles but unable to get there because police are turning people away after what they say is a 'serious incident [...] an explosion. Some kind of chemical release' (*GWM*: 279). When turning back, Jaz impulsively veers off the road to get there another way, but when they arrive at the rocks, 'They could see no evidence of anything wrong. There was no cloud, no column of fire, no toxic mist. The air was blue. Ahead of them lay only a vast emptiness, an absence. There was nothing out there at all' (*GWM*: 381).

What is striking about the substories is that the echoes and potential connections between them are numerous and tantalising, yet never clear. We cannot be sure whether Laila's listening to the Ashtar recording, whose music is tuned to 'the harmonic vibrations of the Universal Field' (*GWM*: 277) and imparts a message about being 'Children of Light', has somehow conjured up the reappearance of Raj, '[a] little glowing boy', 'as if he'd dropped from space' (*GWM*: 309). Nor does the order of the stories reveal an enlightening pattern. Instead, the 'present and multiple substories' coexist in a manner Coupland (2013) describes as 'elegantly pinballing' together, all linked by the 'thematic, geographic and chronological tether' of the Pinnacles rock formation.

'Convergences' is designed to counter another, highly influential review-essay from some years earlier by the literary critic James Wood, 'Human, All Too Inhuman' (2000). Wood uses a review of Zadie Smith's novel *White Teeth* (2000) to define a series of 'big, ambitious' novels published by high-profile British and American novelists – Salman Rushdie's *The Ground Beneath Her Feet* (1999), Thomas Pynchon's *Mason & Dixon* (1997), Don DeLillo's *Underworld* (1997) and David Foster Wallace's *Infinite Jest* (1996) – as 'hysterical realism' (Wood, 2000). Such novels, he contends, are founded upon an excess of elaborate and fantastic storytelling as a way of hoodwinking readers into thinking they are reading something powerful and meaningful when in fact it is a gratuitous display of the writer's imagination. They are packed full of different stories, all of which 'intertwine, and double and triple on themselves', the events in each interconnecting in implausible ways as if born of a fear of random, contingent events. Wood's interpretation is that in doing so the conventions of realism (the coincidences, parallels) are being 'overworked' in such fiction. The reader is expected to believe that the characters are all linked by a deep symbolic texture when in fact they 'are not really alive, not fully human' (Wood, 2000). The connectedness of the characters and events is *insisted upon* rather than developing naturally or plausibly, because ultimately the novelist is concerned with using the coincidences and details to advance a message – in the case of *White Teeth* it is 'the need to escape roots' (Wood, 2000) – rather than reflect the reality of human being.

Wood does not refer to Kunzru, of course, as his first novel, *The Impressionist*, was published two years after Wood's essay, but one suspects that the criticisms he levels at other writers might apply to *Gods Without Men*, too. It could be accused of 'overworking' parallels and creating characters who are vehicles to demonstrate a connectedness, in order to advance an overall message: 'how people handle not just the unknown, but the unknowable' (Romig, 2012).

What is at stake in Wood's and Coupland's debate-by-review-essay is the very definition of the novel. Wood, conforming to a tradition of champions of realism before him (such as John Bayley in his 1960 study, *The Characters of Love*), assumes that because a novel does not trade in realistic character and plausible plotting (plots that reveal a meaningful, symbolic texture but which nevertheless respect the random, unplanned nature of real life) it is not a novel. For Coupland, what makes a translit novel a novel is precisely the interconnectedness of the multiple stories – and he is at pains to note that the 'long-form solidity' Kunzru achieves affirms *Gods Without Men* as a novel and not 'a collection of short stories that seems like a novel' (like Alice Munro's work) (Coupland, 2013). Nowhere does Coupland refer to character. Indeed, he thinks Wood's argument feels 'dated', and explains that to criticise such fiction for being 'hysterical' misses the point that 'what once seemed like hysteria in our culture has now become a staple of daily life. The translit reader knows there is a spirituality lacking in the modern world that can only be squeezed out of other, more authentic eras' (Coupland, 2013).

This is an insightful comment about *Gods Without Men*, for it suggests that as much as it is about the desert signifying a world of 'Gods without men' (the mysterious plan behind everything) it is also about 'men without God'. A recurring context for contemporary fiction – in which we can place Coupland's own fiction – is the search for meaning in a post-religious world.

Historical novels of the future: Kunzru's post-postmodernism

According to Coupland, then, *Gods Without Men*, as translit, reflects the reality of a mediated, interconnected world governed by internet technology. It would be an over-simplification to argue that translit is the literary counterpart of the smartphone, but strictly in terms of its approach to crossing time and space 'without changing psychic place' (Coupland, 2013) it is a form of writing which is unmistakeably a product of the digital age. Its ability to create the effect of accelerated transportation is paralleled by what Coupland regards as its preference for 'genre-bending'. 'I do wonder', he states, 'if being a writer in 2012 means needing to be able to write in multiple genres, as do Kunzru, David Mitchell et al., but not as some sort of post-modern party trick. It's more a statement of fact about the early-21st-century condition' (Coupland, 2013).

Coupland's remark raises the question of translit's position in literary history and in particular what distinguishes its approach to genre and history from postmodern writing. The narrative made up of many interlocking stories is a typical feature of many celebrated postmodern narratives, such as Georges Perec's *Life: A User's Manual* (1978), Calvino's *If on a Winter's Night a Traveller* (1981) or Salman Rushdie's *Midnight's Children* (1981). The contiguous placing of narratives from previous historical periods beside present ones is a device associated with one of the definitive postmodern modes, which Linda Hutcheon (1988) famously termed 'historiographic metafiction', examples of which include Peter Ackroyd's *Hawksmoor* (1985) and *Chatterton* (1987), A.S. Byatt's *Possession* (1990) and Michael Cunningham's *The Hours* (1998).

This is not the place to rehearse what is by now an extensive debate involving theorists and literary critics about cultural dominants and whether we are still in a kind of late postmodernism or have moved into a fully 'post-postmodern' moment. More relevant for the task at hand is to note that Kunzru and his work exhibits the kind of ambivalent attitude towards the legacy of postmodernism which is – paradoxically, because it cannot be definitive – representative of literary novelists of his generation. Coupland's eagerness to equate postmodern technique with mere 'party tricks' is revealing. Kunzru has also been keen to distance himself from postmodernism. As a young writer he was attracted to the fluidity and hybridity of postmodernism because he felt it had the potential 'to allow us to put together a new way of understanding identity that wasn't on this spectrum between those perceived as having a "fully present" authenticity and the rest of us, who were a bit lacking or broken in some way' (Piccarella, 2019). In literature he admired the way that Thomas Pynchon, in particular, demonstrated in his anti-realist fiction the fact that 'informational excess, and our inability to process everything and the kind of absence of stability in tone and reality, is a liberating force' (Piccarella, 2019). But in time he felt that this anti-realist irreverence had become 'domesticated as a set of forms'. Worse, in social terms, 'in this political moment', postmodern fluidity has become 'a very threatening force' (Piccarella, 2019).

In this respect Kunzru and his work is definitively post-postmodern, or as he puts it more wittily, he can never be any more

than a 'recovering Pynchonite' (Piccarella, 2019). His remarks on
how contemporary political reality has effected a *détournement* of
postmodernism to explain why Pynchon's approach cannot work
now might figure as a shorthand description of *Gods Without
Men*. The novel presents its characters as threatened rather than
freed by the tension between the excess of information and their
inability to process it. Perhaps the most pertinent contemporary
example it contains is its glimpse into the unpleasant modus operandi of those internet users who become hystericised by Raj's mysterious disappearance and miraculous return and marshal the tools
of the internet to make his parents the objects of a process – all
too familiar to us now, a couple of decades into the twenty-first
century – of investigation, speculation, public shaming and accus-
ation. Lisa is alarmed by these anonymous people's

> outrage when something unknowable reared up before them, not just
> unknown for now, because they or their designated expert had yet
> to enquire into the matter, had yet to Google the search term [...]
> Their fear made them dangerous – murderous even – for in their
> blind panic they'd turn on whoever they could find as a scapegoat,
> would tear them into pieces to preserve this cherished fiction, the
> fiction of the essential comprehensibility of the world. (*GWM*: 358)

Yet, at the same time, for all Kunzru's rejection of postmodernism,
and despite the fact that his novel simply does not *feel* the same as a
novel by Calvino, Pynchon or Byatt, *Gods Without Men* might actually be understood as modifying some of the staple literary techniques
associated with postmodernism rather than rejecting them. The
novel's liberal coursing through historical periods might be seen as a
variation on historiographic metafiction rather than an alternative.
To start with the most obvious fact: the way its chapters are titled
and organised serves as an invitation to readers to receive it as a historical novel. Its six narrative worlds, summarised above, are divided
up in a way which draws attention to their historical specificity.
The novel begins with a Prologue entitled 'In the time when animals
were men' (which is undated though seems to involve characters we
later meet from narrative world five, 1958–1971), and then features
twenty-three chapters, each of which is titled simply with a specific
year and no additional text.[1] Reading the book is partly a process of
bearing in mind the year of the events described in each chapter and

attempting to establish a kind of order to the chapters. It is thus an active, self-conscious process of orienting oneself in history and comparing different historical moments. Unlike historiographic metafiction, though, in Kunzru's novel these are indeed little other than extended moments, almost like film clips rather than in-depth self-conscious reconstructions of a particular historical period. In most the reader is plunged into a dramatic narrative in a style which recalls an adventure story, and has quickly to become acquainted with its world: 'His hands quivered and the skin under his eyes burned and above him a whirlwind came out of the north' (1871); 'The raid, when it came, was sudden and brutal' (1971) (*GWM*: 190; 260).

This effect is comparable to the kind of 'experiential' or 'immersion' tourism which characterises the age of translit. The carouselling through specific moments in time is also different from the immersion in a carefully constructed historical period which is the speciality of both the classic modern historical novel – such as Pat Barker's *Regeneration* (1991) or Hilary Mantel's *Wolf Hall* (2009) – and postmodern historiographic metafiction. *Gods Without Men* is not 'set' in the past in an attempt to understand the spirit of a particular age. It only 'visits' previous moments at the Pinnacles like a tourist, and then leaves. Nor does it involve a systematic contrast between a time in the past and a time in the present in the manner of historiographic metafiction. In considering its historical snapshots we have to take into account the imbalance between the sixth narrative world, set in the near-present, and to which a total of ten chapters are headed 2008 and two 2009, and the others (the only other recurring period, twice, is 1920). This suggests that the purpose of visiting the past is not for the reader to become immersed in it but to look for connections – flashbacks, premonitions, coincidences – with the present. The adventure style suggests that the novel is not just about the fleeting, hallucinatory way we 'experience' history, but how literature acts as a medium for this experience, by packaging history into drama.

This method of reconstruction – especially Kunzru's 1775 and 1778 chapters (narrative world number one) which are, respectively, representations of eighteenth-century diary-writing and letter-writing – conform to Jameson's famous identification of pastiche as one of the signature modes of postmodernism: 'blank' parody, a means by which historical periods are experienced superficially, as 'styles' (1991: 17). Jameson's more recent work confirms that he is not one who has subscribed to the conviction that we are beyond postmodernism, not least because the practice of pastiche remains dominant in cultural production. To return to his recent reading of contemporary fiction I referred to above, which he develops in his 2013 book *The Antinomies of Realism*, Jameson notes that we are still subject to the 'enfeeblement of historical consciousness and a sense of the past' (2013: 259). He does, however, suggest that a 'Science-Fictional' approach to writing the historical novel provides an antidote to this impoverished understanding of history because of how it invites the reader not to inhabit a particular historical world but to understand history itself by self-reflexively showing us how our cultural memories of its periods operates through pastiche. It is an argument which complements Coupland's view of translit by suggesting how a novel like *Gods Without Men* invites its readers to understand both history and how literature represents history.

Jameson's example of just such a 'historical novel of the future' (2013: 276) is David Mitchell's *Cloud Atlas* (2004), a novel which Coupland also refers to in 'Convergences' as an exemplary work of translit to set alongside *Gods Without Men*. Both novels indeed share a number of features. *Cloud Atlas* contains six separate interlocking narratives which sweep from the nineteenth century through the present day into a post-apocalyptic future, most of which are set in one geographical place, the Pacific Rim. As with the narratives in *Gods Without Men*, these sections are different from each other stylistically, and feature different characters and events which nonetheless echo across each historical period. They are stacked together without overall authorial guiding explanation, and this leads Jameson to conclude that, like the interpretive drive associated with modernism and with Freud's notion of 'overdetermination' in the 'dream work', the onus is placed on the reader to draw connections between them, 'to invent as many connections and cross-references as we can think of in an ongoing process' (2013: 303).

The effect is to make it possible that either we are being presented with a random sample or 'a coherent picture of the stereotypes which govern our current view of history, past, present and future, or even project some ideal caricature of that Pacific Rim culture'

(2013: 303). More precisely, what Jameson believes underpins *Cloud Atlas*'s method is a way of reading 'the present as history' (2013: 298–299). Readers are able to experience the present day as a kind of 'named period, and to endow it with a period style, on which we look back' (2013: 299), just as we do in postmodern nostalgia films about, say, the 1920s or 1950s. This means using the practice of pastiche, but self-consciously so, to draw attention to the very function of pastiche in enabling readers to access history.

Jameson's reading of *Cloud Atlas* opens up a productive way of understanding *Gods Without Men*'s commingling of the present and the past. Kunzru's novel also presents history as 'shapes of time' rather than seeks to construct any linear model. Like Mitchell's novel it presents readers with its snapshots of other worlds and other lives without overall authorial guiding explanation. Similarly, the reader is invited to draw connections and make cross-references between the stories. The device of remaining in one specific place while traversing through historical periods – in this case, of course, the Pinnacles – means that history is essentially laid out *spatially* in Kunzru's novel rather than temporally or sequentially. Like *Cloud Atlas* the effect is to create what Jameson terms 'an absolute present' (or what Coupland might call an 'extreme present') by which previous moments in time and history can be inhabited *now*. The present day is depicted as a historical period, which the reader has been 'taught', by the process of visiting the moments in history represented by the various substories in the novel, to view in the same way, as if looking down on a total picture of history.

There are notable differences between the two novels. *Gods Without Men* does not include the directly 'Science-Fictional' element of having narrative sections which are set in the future (and which, for Jameson, adds to *Cloud Atlas*'s effect of scrutinising history as a totality because it invites the reader to consider 'what comes next' (2013: 305)). Nevertheless *Gods Without Men*'s narrative worlds do figure as a version of what Jameson sees as the Science-Fictional trope used in Mitchell's novel (and much less successfully in a contemporary generic Sci-Fi movie such as the 2010 Christopher Nolan film *Inception*) where time is presented as 'an immense elevator that moves us up and down in time, its sickening lifts and dips corresponding to the euphoric or dystopian mood in which we wait for the doors to open' (301).

The other key difference between *Cloud Atlas* and *Gods Without Men* is that the structure of Mitchell's novel does ultimately provide an overall piece of authorial guidance which makes sense of the interlocking narratives by showing how they relate to each other. Its chapters are sequenced into a kind of nesting pattern in which the narratives are presented in chronological order with each one broken off for the next to begin before 'peaking' and being picked up again in reverse chronological order, so that the effect is, to Jameson, like scaling and descending a mountain. This kind of modernist patterning is something Kunzru was keen to resist. Indeed, one of the defining characteristics of Kunzru as a novelist – which marks a clear distinction between his form of 'translit' and Mitchell's – is his desire to resist system and to allow fictional creation to flourish. He has said of the process of writing *Gods Without Men*,

> I made the decision to hold the novel "open" formally for as long as possible as I was writing. I made a rule that anything that felt important would go in, even if I couldn't rationally understand why it was connected. I wanted to write a book that was structured, not so much by conventional plot or causality but by a kind of rhyming or echo. (Kumar, 2012)

While *Gods Without Men*'s contiguous historical narratives go some way towards enabling readers to understand the present 'as history' in the way that Jameson's exemplary 'historical novel of the future', *Cloud Atlas*, does, there is no pattern to the stories in *Gods Without Men* which can enable us to make sense of how they fit together. Another way of putting this is that Kunzru's novel is, in the end, not actually as interested in history as Mitchell's. The non-schematic echoes point to more of an interest in the potential of literature to cause readers to reflect on time and human relations. In the absence of authorial guidance or pattern, readers are left alone in their efforts to draw connections and to point to convergences in the novel. Confluences abound but remain mysterious. Could the child who appears in the third narrative world (1920) – 'Boy about five years old. Walking along hand in hand with an Indian man' (*GWM*: 223) – somehow be Raj, suggesting that either his 2008 incarnation is a repetition or that the present can somehow impact on the past? Is the mysterious trickster figure, Coyote, a single, history-traversing character or a series of echoes or apparitions? The characters in the novel who experience such echoes and seek to draw connections are surrogates for the readers – in ways that recall the function of Tzvetan Todorov's '*hommes-récits*' whose role in the text subtly directs readers to read it in particular ways (1977: 70–75). One such is the linguist Deighton, required professionally to make connections, but preoccupied by more mysterious echoes:

> As Deighton lay by the fire, his head propped uncomfortably on his saddle, many things seemed to collapse into one: the runner disappearing and reappearing instantaneously at his destination, the wandering Spanish friar, Coyote clinging to the reed and weaving his way into the Land of the Dead. Was this where Garcés had journeyed in his lost days? Was this where the running Indian had led them? (*GWM*: 236)

Another is Dawn. We wonder with her whether the transition between her life as a hippie in the late 1960s and 1970s and her later life as a motel owner (which crosses narrative worlds five and six) is actually between two separate incarnations, a transition from one state to the next in the manner of the Buddhist *bardo*: 'Every moment is a bardo, suspended between past and future. We are always in transition, slipping from one state to the next. She'd had doubts over the years, wondering if this was where she really was, if this person Dawn even existed, or was just a momentary confluence of forces, a ripple on the pond' (*GWM*: 351).

'Something larger than itself': the liberation of writing fiction

Kunzru's approach to writing the novel is to ensure he himself remains open to surprise as he writes. He has linked – perhaps surprisingly – this open, non-schematic impulse to postmodernism:

> In this novel there are things which absolutely defy explanation and which I don't explain. Which in a way is a breach of contract between the writer and the reader. And perhaps this is where postmodernism

comes in, what it means to tell stories and to explain and to provide satisfying endings. I'm trying to deal with situations in this
book where there isn't a resolution which will keep everything nicely
ordered. There's something disturbing about these absences and
silences. And that's where Coyote comes into the book, I suppose.
Coyote is the one who messes everything up. (Gilbert, 2012)

Kunzru seems to be suggesting here that in refusing to provide a
resolution which ensures order presides over the novel he is subtly
inviting readers to consider not just what reading literature is, but
what writing it involves too. The writer can himself be 'disturbed'
about what his imagination has generated. Kunzru himself does not
know who Coyote is and appears just as intrigued by the persona
as Deighton or Dawn.

In this respect *Gods Without Men* might be seen a progression
in metafiction in the same way that *Cloud Atlas* is considered by
Jameson as a progression of the modern historical novel: an alternative to postmodernism *within* postmodernism. It is metafictional
in this sense, but not in the systematic, fully self-conscious, sense
we were once familiar with from historiographic metafiction, which
deliberately sets out to compare writing fiction to historiography
though carefully constructed pastiches of previous 'named periods'.
Gods Without Men's metafiction is more subtle and resists the kind
of didacticism which is a core element of the approach adopted by
authors of 'high' or 'classic' postmodern narrative (see Hutcheon,
2014). The impression is that Kunzru is not in possession of all the
facts. Nor is he trying to educate the reader about something or
other; the convergences and echoes are mysterious to him too. This
is more in keeping with the new kind of 'post-ironic' metafiction
critics have described emerging in a generally 'post-postmodern'
era, characterised more by the effort to 'think one's way into a
shared space between one being and another' (Boxall, 2013: 116)
or to create a 'pact, rather than a dialogue' between writer and
reader, which reduces the danger of authorial insincerity to enable
ethical communion between author and reader' (Clements, 2015).

An invitation for author and reader to share a meditation on the
function of literature lies behind the subtle analogies with fiction
which are made in *Gods Without Men* and which magnify and
extend the novel. There is, for example, the discussion amongst
the hippie community Dawn belongs to in the late 1960 about
'multiplexing' or 'muxing', a method used in telecommunications or

computing: 'It's a way of combining multiple messages into a single signal, then sending it over a shared medium' (*GWM*: 76). This calls to mind the ways stories coincide in *Gods Without Men*, both on a spatial level (as we engage with different parts of the same 2008 world) and on a temporal one (as we enter different periods in the same place), which might well be understood as 'combined signals'. What happens if we think of stories as signals, or narrative as signal processing? Even more obviously, the Walter system developed by Jaz invites comparison with the novel when described by his enigmatic manager Bachmann as a form of art rather than data-gathering:

> As with most art, this is an attempt to stand outside time. That's per-haps its most luxurious quality – one could even say a sign of deca-dence. What a moment to deny history! […] There's a tradition that says the world has shattered, that what once was whole and beautiful is now just scattered fragments. Much is irreparable, but a few of these fragments contain faint traces of the former state of things, and if you find them and uncover the sparks hidden inside, perhaps at last you'll piece together the fallen world. This is just a glass case of wreckage. But it has presence. It's redemptive. It is part of something larger than itself. (*GWM*: 138)

In *Gods Without Men* Kunzru produces a work of art which con-vincingly gives the sense that it is 'part of something larger than itself', even though what this something is remains obscure both to writer and reader. It opens the way to thinking about the present as history, as well as pointing subtly to itself through self-reflexive analogies like muxing or programming in a way which recalls but differs from earlier postmodernism. This is not to conclude that *Gods Without Men* is definitively post-postmodern or postmodern. But it is certainly self-reflexive. Josh Toth has recently evidenced his scepticism that postmodernism is actually over by noting that, des-pite proclamations of its demise, the production of metafiction, 'the postmodern modus operandi par excellence' (2021: 4), has never let up across a range of art-forms.

Conclusion

Kunzru, despite his awareness of contemporary theory and tech-nology, at times advocates a surprisingly traditional view of the novel. In a 2019 interview with *The Believer* he dissociated himself from the 'autofictional trend that's been around', a trend born of an impatience with 'the fakery of fiction' and determined to counter it with 'some sort of biographically rooted authenticity'. By contrast, he articulated a commitment to faith in plot and character that is essentially realist: 'Novels are just never going to be reducible to a kind of modernist rigor. You can look at things like the *nouveau roman* as various interesting experiments that test out the novel as a formal apparatus, but essentially the novel is baggy and messy, and bits get stuck to it, and it gets mixed up with the writer's life and the writer's world in a very unsatisfactory way' (Piccarella, 2019). The delight in mess, and the allusion to Henry James's famous description of novels as 'loose, baggy monsters', at once positions him in the same category not just as Pynchon but as an altogether different kind of novelist, such as Iris Murdoch.

But rather than helping us categorise his work, these remarks remind us that there is in fact something more personal, more biographical, at stake for Kunzru when it comes to the liberations of writing fiction – something we might risk suggesting is not as much of an issue for David Mitchell. Kunzru's strong preference for openness and echoes over pattern, relates implicitly to the liberation writing fiction provides for a rootless cosmopolitan son of an Indian father and an English mother. It enables him to counter what he has argued powerfully is 'the central claim of artistic whiteness', namely the capability white writers exhibit

> of transcending whatever their individual position might be in order to speak universally [...] whereas the rest of us have to inevitably think about our identities, these bloody millstones around our necks that we've always got to go, Oh, I've got to write about my identity. I've got to think about my identity. What we all want is for us all to be able to freely imagine, but without that culpable forgetting that you are an individual with a particular window on the world. (Piccarella, 2019)

That these remarks were made in a discussion about *Gods Without Men* underlines the fact that this novel, more than anything else perhaps – more than a desire to analyse History, or even to make sense of America – is the product of free imagination, exercised without denying its author is an individual with a particular window on each of the worlds conjured up by the process of writing the novel.

Note

1 In chronological order, the chapters are: 1775, 1778, 1871, 1920, 1942, 1947, 1958, 1969, 1970, 1971, 2008, 2009. In chapter sequence, they are: 1947, 2008, 1778, 2008, 1958, 2008, 1969, 2008, 1920, 2008, 1970, 2008, 1871, 2008, 1920, 2008, 1971, 2008, 1942, 2009, 2008, 2009, 1775.

References

Appignanesi, Lisa (2011). '*Gods Without Men*, by Hari Kunzru', *Independent*, 23 October, www.independent.co.uk/arts-entertainment/books/reviews/gods-without-men-by-hari-kunzru-2335939.html (accessed 8 August 2022).

Barron, Michael (2017). 'Interview with Hari Kunzru', *The White Review*, May, www.thewhitereview.org/feature/interview-hari-kunzru/ (accessed 8 August 2022).

Basar, Shumon C. (2015). *The Age of Earthquakes: A Guide to the Extreme Present* (London & New York: Penguin).

Boxall, Peter (2013). *Twenty-First Century Fiction: A Critical Introduction* (Cambridge: Cambridge University Press).

Buell, Lawrence (2014). *The Dream of the Great American Novel* (London & Cambridge, MA: Harvard University Press).

Clements, James (2015). 'Trust Your Makers of Things!: The Metafictional Pact in Dave Eggers's *You Shall Know Our Velocity*', *Critique*, 56, 121–137.

Coupland, Douglas (2012). 'Convergences', *New York Times,* 8 March, www.nytimes.com/2012/03/11/books/review/gods-without-men-by-hari-kunzru.html (accessed 8 August 2022) .

———(2013). 'Convergences: Gods Without Men by Hari Kunzru', in Douglas Coupland (ed.) , *Shopping Jail: Ideas, Essays, and Stories for the Increasingly Real Twenty-First Century* (Berlin: Sternberg Press), 24–28.

Gilbert, Erin (2012). 'That's Where Coyote Comes In: PW Talks with Hari Kunzru', *Publishers Weekly*, 13 January, www.publishersweekly.com/pw/by-topic/authors/interviews/article/50172-that-s-where-coyote-comes-in-pw-talks-with-hari-kunzru.html (accessed 8 August 2022).

Hutcheon, Linda (1988). *A Poetics of Postmodernism* (London & New York: Routledge).

——— (2014). *Narcissistic Narrative: The Metafictional Paradox* (Waterloo, ON: Wilfrid Laurier University Press).

Jameson, Fredric (1991). *Postmodernism, or the Cultural Logic of Late Capitalism* (Durham, NC: Duke University Press).

——— (2013). *The Antinomies of Realism* (London & New York: Verso).

Kirsch, Adam (2017). *The Global Novel: Writing the World in the 21st Century* (New York: Columbia University Press).

Kumar, Amitava (2012). 'Hari Kunzru on *Gods Without Men*', *The Paris Review*, 6 March, www.theparisreview.org/blog/2012/03/06/hari-kunzru-on-'gods-without-men'/ (accessed 8 August 2022).

LeClair, Tom (2012). '*Gods Without Men* by Hari Kunzru', *Barnes and Noble Review*, 6 March, www.barnesandnoble.com/review/gods-without-men (accessed 8 August 2022).

Piccarella, Stephen (2019). 'An Interview with Hari Kunzru', *The Believer*, 2 December, https://believermag.com/an-interview-with-hari-kunzru/ (accessed 8 August 2022).

Romig, Rollo (2012). 'Staring into the Void with Hari Kunzru', *The New Yorker*, 13 March, www.newyorker.com/books/page-turner/staring-into-the-void-with-hari-kunzru (accessed 8 August 2022).

Todorov, Tzvetan (1977). *The Poetics of Prose*, translated by R. Howard (Ithaca, NY: Cornell University Press).

Toth, Josh (2021). *Truth and Metafiction: Plasticity and Renewal in American Narrative* (London & New York: Bloomsbury).

Wood, James (2000). 'Human, All Too Inhuman', *The New Republic*, 24 July, https://newrepublic.com/article/61361/human-inhuman (accessed 8 August 2022).

6

Eyes, ears, head, memory, heart: transglossic rhythms in *Memory Palace* and *Twice Upon a Time*

Sara Upstone

In a 2012 interview to publicise the publication of his novel *Gods Without Men* (2011) on online literary magazine *The Millions*, Hari Kunzru responds to a question regarding his interest in literary form by saying

> You know, you can still make books where stuff happens. I don't think you necessarily have to be some kind of high postmodernist and refuse any kind of stability of meaning. One way I've found is through the use of silence and the use of incompleteness, because that demands a kind of active reading. (Yoder, 2012)

With his next novel published in 2017, Kunzru would spend the two years after this interview engaged in his most experimental writing projects. Published in 2013, *Memory Palace* was created as part of a collaborative project with the Victoria and Albert Museum in London – a physical gallery exhibition was combined with a printed text in which the artists' concept drawings for their exhibition pieces were reproduced, interspersed by a fantasy text written by Kunzru, in which an unnamed narrator exists in a dystopian future London. While this chapter focuses predominantly on the printed object produced to accompany the physical space, one can equally discuss the exhibition itself given that, as the accompanying essay to the book explains, it was designed to 'explore the idea of an exhibition as a walk-in book' (*MP*: 84). Rather than a catalogue, the physical book strategically omits or re-orders the exhibition; so as the curators' desire was for a walk-in book experience, so the book itself functions conversely as an exploration of the idea of a read-in exhibition. Published a year later, *Twice Upon a Time: Listening to New York* is an experimental e-book published by Atavist Books; a collage of autobiographical text by Kunzru, photographs, and typographic word art, it has been described both as an essay (Tipper, 2014) and as a 'kind of three-dimensional tone poem' (Ulin, 2014) and takes the reader on a walk around New York to a soundtrack of city noises, words appearing on the pages through swipe functions to generate an immersive experience. These projects, whilst distinctly different in both form and subject matter, are united by their commitment to the realisation of Kunzru's enduring belief in the potential of books to produce meaning through an active reading process in which the reader is explicitly positioned as a participant in the narrative experience.

In this chapter, I want to examine how Kunzru's use of these contemporary multimodal literatures facilitates a dynamic movement through virtual and imagined spaces which align with real-world physicalities in the service of the creation of meaning. Constructing a virtual and physical mobility, *Twice Upon a Time* and *Memory Palace* offer an engagement with movement through space and in space that is inherently multisensory, and which resonates with contemporary concerns for the potential of psychogeographic experience to reveal and construct a relationship to not only place, but also identity and self. Kunzru's experimental works thus echo with his more well-known novel output, whilst at the same time advancing new facets to his engagement with these concerns that are only made possible through the use of multiple registers. As such, these texts not only nuance Kunzru's critical perspective and the potential of literary engagements with space, they also contribute to a growing understanding of the potential of less conventional literary form.

While it is profitable to advance such understanding via contemporary critical theory, in particular affect theory, mobility theory and new materialism, I root my discussion of such concerns in the dialogue between these contemporary methodologies and the work of French theorist Henri Lefebvre. Operating at the conjunction of Marxist and poststructuralist thought, recent geographic criticism has attempted to examine how Lefebvre's work can be opened up to contemporary debates around questions such as race, gender and disability (Reid-Musson, 2018). In this context, Lefebvre's concept of rhythmanalysis foregrounds the sensory properties of the body in space and its interdependence with a vibrant materiality without the loss of social and political relevance that is often implicated in critiques of new materialist methodologies. Resonant with Lefebvre's theory, Kunzru's work offers a distinct use of rhythmic movement through space to advance a cultural imaginary that intervenes in discrete notions of cultural identity in favour of a productive hybridity where genre evokes intercultural empathy. Such literary presence situates Kunzru's work at the centre of contemporary literary innovation, a conjunction of form and meaning that can be described as 'transglossic', a new term developed by myself and Kristian Shaw (Shaw and Upstone, 2021) to describe the movement across formal positions which defines contemporary cultural production.

Literature that moves

Both *Twice Upon a Time* and *Memory Palace* are concerned with the creation of an experience of movement for the reader. In *Twice Upon a Time* the reader is invited to walk with Kunzru through the streets of New York. The digital format of the text creates a portable guide with which readers might wander either through New York itself or through another physical space, with the text's soundtrack playing through headphones. Likewise, *Memory Palace* as an exhibition was constructed as a physical movement around a book, while the printed output is constructed with the aim of giving readers a textual experience commensurate with yet distinct from the physical experience of the exhibition; the curators' choice of Kunzru was motivated by his elusive fictional landscapes that they felt might echo the non-linearity of the physical exhibition space (*MP*: 85). The text begins with a discussion of the memory palace, a technique used to recall memories via their association with a mentally reproduced physical space, the suggestion that memory is rooted in physical movement around a place that is then returned to so that 'you can tour it in your mind when you are not there' (*MP*: 9).

   Kunzru's focus on mobility in this regard can be seen as a central part of his concern for the ability of texts to construct meaning, pushing the boundaries of the literary form to examine its ability to touch the material, extra-literary world. In this respect, his works can be identified in terms of what Kristian Shaw and I have defined

(2021) as contemporary literature's transglossic characteristics – an alternative framing of post-postmodern literature which emphasises contemporary literature's conjunction of genre and thematic concern in the interest of a renewed commitment to artistic responsibility and productive authenticity. Transglossic literature as we define it is inherently *transformal*: it eschews traditional definitions of form and identifies works such as Kunzru's – which refuse to fit neatly into existing categorisations – as defining works of literary newness. As *Twice Upon a Time* and *Memory Palace* are both concerned with movement conterminously both literal and figurative, likewise the concept of the transglossic defines through its use of the suffix *trans* (meaning 'to move across') literature's concern for both a figurative movement across subject positions and an investment in mobility as a defining feature of globalised twenty-first-century culture. The concept of the transglossic explicitly acknowledges the spatiality of contemporary culture, and more specifically its association with tropes of movement. This focus places the transglossic in contradiction to the dominant trend in literary theory to append a 'modernist' suffix to new conceptual framings. The continued recourse to the modernist suffix in theorisations such as post-postmodernism and metamodernism, we suggest, encloses literary theory within a discourse of periodisation that naturally privileges the verticality of historical thinking over the horizontal thought encouraged by an emphasis on spatiality, and as such limits the potential of such discourse to create cross-cultural and cross-historical empathy that might produce narratives which contribute radically to social, political and cultural change.

Kunzru's transglossic attention to space thus resonates with a wider attention to movement as an essential feature of the contemporary return to meaning making in the post-postmodern period. The new mobilities paradigm (Sheller and Urry, 2006; Cresswell and Merriman, 2011) has been associated with a concern for the conjunction of movement and meaning within the context of everyday life. In the field of literary studies and related humanities, this motif of mobility is increasingly evident in dominant critical paradigms, in particular through concepts allied to affect theory. Ann Werner, for example, has written about 'the intersection of motion and emotion in mundane cultural practices [...] mundane forms of mobility and emotionality that are easily overlooked, taken for granted' (2015a: 169), while Sara Ahmed has written of happiness as affect both informed by a politics of globalised movement through experiences such as migration, and of mobility as a rationale for xenophobia where unhappiness is associated with increased migration and post-imperial nostalgia (Ahmed, 2008; Ahmed et al., 2003). Affect theory in this regard draws attention to both the feelings and emotions felt within the individual body and within the broader cultural body when movement takes place, and argues that it is through emotion and feeling that such meanings take place, not just for the individual, but with broader relevance to social and political power structures. Likewise, new materialist thinking, particularly the work of Jane Bennett (2009), has been concerned for movement as part of a wider concern for the significance of material space and its relationship to questions of subjectivity.

Such theoretical approaches undoubtedly have relevance for both *Twice Upon a Time* and *Memory Palace*. Both texts focus on a mundane, quotidian act of movement – walking around a city or an exhibition space – and utilise the literary text as a form of evocation that might stimulate affective response. Yet the focus in Kunzru's texts on a movement that exists not in pure physicality, but rather on the liminal border between real and imagined space, is one that resonates even more powerfully with the work of an earlier theorist, Henri Lefebvre. Well known for his work on the city, Lefebvre is highly influential for a range of contemporary theorists relevant to the study of space – particularly geographers such as Edward Soja, Doreen Massey and Nigel Thrift. His evocation of a conception of space in his 1974 work *The Production of Space* (1991 [1974]) posits its existence as simultaneously real and imagined, a fusion of mental influence and physical engagement that parallels Kunzru's multimodal concern for the reader's mental engagement with the book as an imaginative journey alongside a corporeal connection to physical space. In *Memory Palace*, the narrator's mention of a previous London, at once recognisable and yet not, with familiar place names altered, invites the reader into a relation with a physical space simultaneously real and imagined, both shared with the narrative voice and set apart from it. The physical exhibition space likewise opened with a quotation – not in the printed book – 'my fellow Londoners, can't you see how we're diminished', with the effect of offering visitors an alternative vision of the space in which the gallery itself is located. In *Twice Upon a Time* the reader walks as the narrator does, and yet even if that space is New York, it is not the New York of the narrative.

In a later and less known work, *Rhythmanalysis*, first published posthumously in 1992, Lefebvre extends his concern for simultaneously real and imagined space to a concern for movement – movement both through that space and of that space. For Lefebvre, rhythms are what define our spatial situatedness. When we move, his work suggests, we move both with rhythm and through rhythms. There is a powerful connection with the transglossic nature of Kunzru's fiction in Lefebvre's theory of rhythm. In particular, the work emphasises both the complex relation between material and imagined space during movement, and the import of this movement for political meaning. Rhythm, Lefebvre tells us, is both the mathematical and the visceral, the body and the calculation, and as such it has the answer to 'strange questions' (2004 [1992]: 14), bringing together the elements of the material world in an 'ensemble full of meaning' (2004 [1992]: 23). Turning to Lefebvre in this critical context is to seek his relation to contemporary theorists who seek to find meaning in everyday encounter; his work powerfully foreshadows, and in some cases perhaps offers a corrective to, the emphases of theories such as new materialism and affect theory.

In her introduction to *Cruel Optimism* (2011) the affect theorist Lauren Berlant writes:

> But everyday life theory no longer describes how most people live. The short version of this argument is that the vast majority of the world's population now lives in cities and has access to mass culture via multiple technologies, and is therefore not under the same pressure to unlearn and adapt that their forebears might well have been. At the same time, as Nigel Thrift has argued, the reflexive scanning that provided relief for the *flâneuse* and the *flâneur* no longer does, but rather exemplifies the mass sensorium engendered by problems of survival that are public and that induce a variety of collective affective responses to the shapelessness of the present that constant threat wreaks. (2011: 8)

In response to this shift, Berlant states that 'Instead of the vision of the everyday *organized* by capitalism that we find in Lefebvre and de Certeau, among others, I am interested in the overwhelming ordinary that is *disorganized* by it, and by many other forces besides' (8, emphasis added). Berlant refers to this as a glitch, and indeed calls their own practice of reading it a rhythmanalysis, yet not of the modes that enable one to live in the city, but rather of a disturbance in the situation of the present and the adaptations improvised around it (198).

Berlant's reading of Lefebvre in this context overlooks Lefebvre's rhythmanalysis as a process which is precisely concerned with both the order and disordered elements of everyday life – with what he refers to as polyrhythmias, eurhythmias and arrhythmias (17). Berlant's argument is that 'This ordinary is an intersecting space where many forces and histories circulate and become "ready to hand" [...] inventing new rhythms for living, rhythms that could, at any time, congeal into norms, forms, and institutions' (9). Yet rather than seeing this as distinct from Lefebvre's project, I instead see these two approaches as deeply aligned.

By paying attention to rhythms as much as to the underpinning of affects, we work within a wider canvas for meaning making that is particularly useful within the framework of the transglossic. We are able to identify the dialogue that exists between the ordered and disordered imposition upon the everyday, but also foreground how meaning exists in the dialogue between matter and human or non-human animal agency, where that matter has an intrinsic rhythm which exists of itself, and not only in the mediation of that rhythm through subjectivity. It is in relation to these social realities that, perhaps most crucially, *rhythmanalysis* is of importance, demanding that we make sure that concrete materiality and its political consequences are at the centre of any concern for how meaning is made in and through space.

Lefebvre's own most striking account of rhythmanalysis in his text is the experience of the city, in his case Paris, and the movement through it:

> He who walks down the street, over there, is immersed in the multi-plicity of noises, murmurs, rhythms (including those of the body, but does he pay attention, except at the moment of crossing the street, when he has to calculate roughly the number of his steps?). By con-trast, from the window, the noises distinguish themselves, the flows separate out, rhythms respond to one another. Towards the right, below, a traffic light. On red, cars at a standstill, the pedestrians cross,

feeble murmurings, footsteps, confused voices. One does not chatter while crossing a dangerous junction under the threat of wild cats and elephants ready to charge forward, taxis, buses, lorries, various cars. Hence the relative silence in this crowd. A kind of soft murmuring, sometimes a cry, a call. (2004 [1992]: 28)

Twice Upon a Time illuminates the power of the multimodal to bring this experience to life, to communicate the rhythms of the city to another who is not physically present. Kunzru's original text combines these written sensory fragments with recordings of the city that he has described not as music, but as sounds that are 'tonal or rhythmic' (Tipper, 2014). This is combined with movable text that coalesces on the page as the user swipes. In between the prose, blocks of conventional text, large print and stylised typography visually construct the sound rhythms of the narrator's movement through the city – one page, in bold, stylised and underlined print, reads simply 'broken bottle smashes/argument by benches/dog barking/honk rattle'. An image of street writing is overlaid by large-print text which reads 'Be a hobo and go with me'. Later in the book the bold text again marks auditory rhythms, but this time the words are laid over one another to give the impression of syn-chronous sounds. In *Memory Palace*, there is no physical sound, but rhythm is constructed in the reading experience through the disjunction of text and image. The commissioned images do not illustrate the text in conventional fashion, rather they serve as interlocutors that adjust the text's rhythm. Haunting this is the physical exhibition, which did not represent all of Kunzru's words but instead used them selectively, visitors not given a prescribed route so the narrative experience would be different for each viewer.

The central feature of Lefebvre's rhythmanalysis is a complexity of movement that can only be registered by a fully corporeal engagement which extends beyond any single sensory experience. 'No camera, no image or series of images can show these rhythms,' writes Lefebvre; 'it requires equally attentive eyes and ears, a head and a memory and a heart'. As Elden discusses, for Lefebvre the distinction between an analysis of rhythms and rhythmanalysis lies in a practice in which the body serves as metronome, a tool as well as its first point of analysis (Elden, 2004: xii). *Twice Upon a Time* replicates this multisensory experience of movement with the use of a soundtrack to accompany the text and the need to physically swipe the pages. The creation of the text was itself a corporeal process. As Kunzru describes it in interview with Bernadine Evaristo (2017), he arrived in New York and found himself living in a ground-floor apartment on the East Side, disturbed by noises that led him to begin recording the sounds of the city. Kunzru used a binaural recording method which is designed to create the effect for the listener of being in and moving through the space where the recording takes place; he describes it as 'like you're inside somebody else as they're taking a walk' (Evaristo, 2017). Alongside this, the narrative of the book emphasises the narrator's own multisensory relation: the text begins with the narrator lying in bed, their own thoughts a fusion of sights, sounds and smells – the orange light filtered through blinds, an unfamiliar smell, and the fused sounds of street noise, R'n'B playing in a car outside, and an unattributed laughter, while the sound of a mechanical timer echoes amidst their thoughts. Later, Kunzru emphasises this human body as a source of rhythm in a scene which recounts the experience of composer John Cage, who on entering a silent anechoic chamber at Harvard University was certain he heard two sounds, one high, one low. On asking the engineer about his experience Cage is told, 'The high one was your nervous system in operation. The low one was your blood in circulation.' In the chamber, the body as sound is exposed.

Likewise, for those visiting the *Memory Palace* exhibition the notion of the gallery as a book also literally creates a multisensory experience where the gallery stands as synecdoche for the book and walking is metonymically situated as the act of reading. In the experience of the printed text the reader's awareness of a parallel physical experience foregrounds the sense of reading the text as one would walk a gallery – alongside the primacy of sight, the haptic experience of page turning draws readers into a physical realm where they are connected to a sensory experience that evokes the conditions of walking. The reader walks without walking – the rhythms are those of the physical book, which has been converted to a polyrhythmic space through the interweaving of Kunzru's text with the visuals of multiple artists. The book mimics the gallery in which rhythms shift with the encounter with each artwork – the slow rhythm of mock-Renaissance painting bustles against the clipped rhythms of schematic drawings, the languorous rhythms of sketches and the fast paces of graphic art. Interspersed with this

diverse variety of reproduced artworks, Kunzru's text is an elusive, fantasy narrative. As Alison Gibbons notes, the printed text
has largely been overlooked in studies of multimodal literature
(2008: 107), yet the 'imagetext' novel in which image is an equal
partner in the construction of meaning rather than an illustration of
textual meaning is a rich source of multimodal experience. Through
the employment of cognitive poetics Gibbons' work stresses the
form as one with a particular impact on the reader, the destabilisation of authorial presence with multiple subjectivities providing
new avenues into the reader's engagement (115). As such, it fulfils
Kunzru's transglossic desire for a text in which the 'silences' open
up the space for the reader's construction of meaning.

Material rhythms

'Silence' is in this respect a kind of rhythm and, indeed, the representation of a rhythm without sound is crucial to Lefebvre's concept
in which rhythm constitutes a vibration of space rather than aud-
ible noise. It is a tendency in criticism to consider Lefebvre's notion
of rhythm as one which is about the subject that moves, or the
movement of that subject through a physically moving space. Yet his
focus on the body as tool reveals how it is nevertheless also the case
that Lefebvre emphasises the vibration of space as a material property of that which does not obviously move. Indeed, Lefebvre gives
an explicit dictate that we easily confuse *rhythm* with *movement*
(2004 [1992]: 5). Kunzru's movement is also, inherently, one
which contains a rhythm that escapes kinetic action. In part, this is
constructed via the materiality of the book itself as an object, the
unique sensory quality of which Kunzru has spoken of in effusive
terms (Evaristo, 2017). The cover of *Memory Palace* is an ornate,
gold-leaf-inspired hardback, published on premium paper, which
engages with what can be seen as the movement towards a premium, anti-digital text as part of what is defined as 'bookishness';
as Liedeke Plate has argued, this bookishness is interwoven with a
material culture that establishes the book as an object which has a
body (2015: 96). Within this context, the varying qualities of the
book construct its rhythms without physical action or sound. The
fast rhythm of dialogue sits on the page opposite the slow rhythm

of a hand-drawn portrait. And while *Twice Upon a Time* may have a more direct association with literal movement, the text also translates this kinetic energy into the digital movement of multimedia. Atavist, the e-book's publisher, folded in 2014, and the app which ran the text was closed down in 2015. As a result, the sound version of *Twice Upon a Time* has become obsolete, no longer supported by operating system updates. Even Kunzru himself no longer has the complete work, and all that remains are two different versions of the physical text. Ironically, the loss of the book's soundtrack and swipe function makes the power of polyrhythms evident; without its sound, without the text's movement, the pages without narrative seem cast adrift, stripped of their dynamism.

Kunzru thus creates material objects which hold a rhythm within themselves. As the association with the reader's engagement has indicated, such rhythm may forge a dynamic interaction between material object and the human audience. In this respect, the works resonate with Karen Barad's conception of new materialism as a movement founded upon the underlying principle of the dialogic intra-action of human and non-human. In Barad's thinking the notion of space as a passive container is called into question (2007: 224), but the interrelation between these two elements is always paramount. The object only has meaning in a discursive interaction. Reality for affect theory, likewise, is principally and foremost a matter of 'mediated affects' rather than of objects (Berlant, 2011: 4).

Without disavowing such potential, it is nevertheless interesting to consider whether Kunzru's texts also, simultaneously, hold a rhythm that is intrinsically imbued with intra-active operation. Like Barad, Lefebvre sees meaning in both material objects and corporeal forms. Rhythm, in particular, Lefebvre argues, is a matter of both affects and bodily experiences, and the rhythms of objects as well as those experienced by human and non-human animals. Yet unlike Barad, for Lefebvre the object has a rhythm that exists in and of itself. In a later essay on the theme co-authored with Catherine Régulier, 'The Rhythmanalytical Project' (2003), Lefebvre writes, 'the surroundings of the body, the social just as much as the cosmic body, are equally bundles of rhythms [...] this meadow, this garden, these trees and these houses [...] You at once notice that every plant, every tree has its rhythm' (80). This draws us towards alternative new materialist models, most notably prefiguring Jane

Bennett's new materialist theory on the vibrant matter of things, 'the active powers issuing from nonsubjects [...] the nonhuman powers circulating around and within human bodies' (2010: ix). Bennett's objects, too, have movement. Yet she appears unaware of Lefebvre's work and the deep similarity between her own concepts and his earlier writings, evoking rather the Deleuzian concept of 'matter-*movement*' (54).[1]

This choice of reference points draws Bennett's work away from explicitly named structures of inequality such as race or class, and towards the more diffuse identity politics of poststructuralism. Identifying the limitations of new materialist theories for political thinking, Paul Rekret (2018) has argued that such theories, in focusing upon the interrelation between organic and non-organic forms, underestimate the capitalist reality in which such inter-relations are obscured and overwritten in the service of capitalist production. Rekret here turns to Marx and his argument in the *Grundrisse* that it is a function of capitalist wage production to separate the worker from the material world. New materialists, he argues, fail to identify the specific political structures through which such separation works – they enter into a dangerous philosophical abstraction and emphasis on individual subjectivity that severely limits their usefulness for collective political action. In contrast, in *Rhythmanalysis* Lefebvre declares, 'Instead of going from concrete to abstract, one starts with full consciousness of the abstract in order to arrive at the concrete' (2004 [1992]: 5). Declaring that his work consciously engages a 'critique from the left' (7), Lefebvre situates rhythms within a politics of capitalist exchange – rhythms, he declares, were not recognised by Marx and yet they are part of what is commodified into products by capital (6). And it is within this context that he seems able to address the lacuna that Rekret identifies. While meaning may be indeterminate and revocable in the post-postmodern period, rhythmanalysis offers a route towards considering this meaning alongside a concern for concrete structures of inequality in a methodology that is much more distinctly transglossic.

Resistant rhythms

As Peter Ely illuminates in his chapter for this volume, associations between Kunzru and Marxist thinking are themselves profitable – in both his short fiction and *My Revolutions* Kunzru addresses the potential of anti-capitalist thought. *Memory Palace* itself engages with this theme, read by Lucienne Loh as 'most critical of the presumed privileges of life in the developed world' (2019: 355). Embodying the transglossic notion of form as content, the text is equally committed to anti-capitalist process in its formal structures; when the artists include within their pieces text in the voice of Kunzru's protagonist, they break the convention of the sole author and posit an alternative communal voice that Kunzru has called 'the communal construction of civilization' (Wheeler, 2013). Yet the relation of rhythm to political structures need not be limited to those aligned with Marxist ideology. Indeed, recent scholarship on Lefebvre has examined how his Marxist-rooted theory might be transferred to a broader concern with power structures; thus we can consider how such rhythms are not only shaped by capitalist discourse, but also by the discourses of patriarchy, race and ableism that inform movement in everyday life (Reid-Musson, 2018). The association between Kunzru's attention to multimodal mobility and a politicised notion of rhythm draws attention to another aspect of the transglossic, namely a renewed authorial responsibility which places the author at the centre of socio-political movements. From the beginning of his career, with his rejection of the John Llewellyn Rhys Award for *The Impressionist* due to its sponsorship by the right-wing UK newspaper the *Mail on Sunday* and his work with English PEN, Kunzru has typified this outward-looking concern. The multimodal thus offers new avenues for the assertion of previously held conviction.

It is in this context that Kunzru's mobility can also be associated with an enduring concern with the experience of the other against dominant power structures. In a special issue of *The Sociological Review* devoted to urban rhythms, Smith and Hetherington (2013) argue that it is not enough to document rhythms, one must also conduct a methodology which identifies their consequences. Alongside this, the polyrhythmic can be associated with a range of philosophical positions offered by theorists including Jacques Derrida, Gilles Deleuze and Jean-Luc Nancy, which present the defiance of a singular sensory experience as a key route to opening up a space of expression for the other. Elsewhere (Upstone, 2014), I have written about this potential of this differentiation for what Edensor terms 'resistant rhythms'. As Tim Edensor (2010) notes, examining rhythms assists us to identify 'how power is instantiated in unreflexive, normative practices but also side-stepped, resisted and supplemented by other dimensions of everyday experience' (2). Such alternatives to the rhythms of consumerism, capital, and socially sanctioned schedules and activities can 'offer unconventional, sometimes utopian visions of different temporalities' (2010: 16). While they stabilise places and mark the fact that change is never absolute, rhythms also assert that place is conterminously never fixed, but rather is in a process of perpetual becoming; they maintain thus a belief in the production of place which challenges the association of mobility with non-place at the same time that they reject notions of object spatiality (see Edensor, 2012).

In this respect, the journey taken by Kunzru's readers is one in which otherness is sustained and sameness resisted at the level of formal interaction. As readers are taken through Kunzru's texts they move with and encounter within the text's spaces a polyrhythmia that can only be fully experienced in multimodality, as both text and image, and in *Twice Upon a Time* also sound. The texts' competing rhythms demand that the reader embraces the existence not of singular subjects but of hybrid, interwoven and dialogic presences. Multimodality in this regard has a particular resistive quality. In particular, it resonates with Emmanuel Levinas's construction of the encounter with the other as one which can only maintain the identity of that other if it moves beyond sight. This is revealed to great effect most famously by Jacques Derrida in his essay 'Violence and Metaphysics', in which he exposes the classical philosophical reliance upon seeing as a relation which looks to reduce difference to sameness and thus to obliterate the other's identity, and in the work of Jean-Luc Nancy, who emphasises the subjectivity of sight and its essential presence in community. The reference in *Twice Upon a Time* to auditory experience is of particular significance in asserting this ultra-visual dialogue. Interspersed with Kunzru's reflections on his own identification with New York in the text is the story of 1960s New York musician Moondog, who is blinded at age 16 and whose career unfolds from being a street musician to an avant-garde performer connected to some of the most well-known experimental composers. The pages in the part of the book dealing with Moondog's blindness are plain brown backgrounds, suddenly stripping the reader of the visual explosions of the previous pages. The blind, Kunzru writes, 'develop an appreciation for precision, repetition, knowability'.

This view is resonant with the representation of sound within the discipline of sonic ecology and its stress on noise as that which can productively denote space through its measurable patterns (see Atkinson, 2007). Kunzru references how Moondog uses 'snaketime' rhythms of sevens, fives and nines, the musician's own name for what he described as his unique sense of rhythmic style. Kunzru overlays his own recordings of the city with extracts of Moondog's music, replicating Moondog's own recordings, albums such as 'Street Scene' in which Moondog overlays his musical rhythms with recordings of New York street noise, interspersed with dialogue from film. While *Memory Palace* lacks a physical soundtrack, its own disjunctive qualities mirror this palimpsestic revelry and conjure a disruptive musical association – for Seth Wheeler (2013) Kunzru's text is 'a jazz refrain that the various artists riff off'.

These counter-canonical rhythms emphasise the potential of sound to construct an alternative subculture, but through Moondog's blindness they also literally assert the rhythmic space as a celebration of the other against an ableist dominant. Speaking of the 1990s, Kunzru notes his 'optimistic predictions of that era: the infinite possibilities of communicating online, the empowerment of disabled people, increased gender fluidity, end-runs around authoritarian censorship and the dissolution of the nation-state' (Kellogg, 2020). Of these themes, all but disability is a common focus in Kunzru criticism. Parallels here can be drawn between *Twice Upon a Time* and *Gods Without Men*, whose central character of Raj – a four-year-old boy with autism – is used by Kunzru to examine the 'shame and guilt that still hovers over disability' (Sanghera, 2011). Whereas that novel exposes the limitations of Kunzru's optimism, *Twice Upon a Time* utilises its form to defiantly advance it. Moondog's powerful ability to capture the city's rhythms is one that emerges from within rather than in spite of his blindness – he is not disabled, but rather powerfully enabled.

In the service of this embracing of difference, Kunzru capitalises upon the potential of rhythm to evoke spatio-temporal disruptions, a focus on rhythm as the articulation of a moment which, Lefebvre writes, cannot be captured in its multiplicity without 'the recollection of other moments and of all hours' (2004 [1992]: 36). The narrative of *Memory Palace* eludes conventional temporality: the internet, readers are told, is a thing from 'before the Withering'

(*MP*: 12), but the recourse to such mythical abstract framings is resonant with folklore – this is a post-apocalyptic future that feels like a feudal past. The very title of *Twice Upon a Time*, a quote from a line by Moondog, equally speaks to the concern of a single temporal moment in repetition. Multimodality is thus aligned with the multiscalar temporalities which rhythymanalysis is so suited to interpret (Edensor, 2010). What emerges in such a space is a version of Homi Bhabha's time-lag, the spatialised disjunction of temporality that pulls together varying subjectivities and opens the space for marginalised voices.

Critics rarely connect Lefebvre's work on rhythm to his tripartite construction of space as lived, conceived and perceived (exceptions are Cresswell, 2010 and the reading of this work by Revill, 2013). This is unfortunate given the close relationship between the two works and, in particular, how Lefebvre's wider work on space opens up a route to considering his relevance for contemporary debates regarding unequal access to public space. In his work on thirdspace geographies, heavily influenced by Lefebvre's writings, American geographer Edward Soja turns to Bhabha to examine how thirdspace geographies evoke the radical interruptive power of simultaneously real and imagined spaces to interrogate official power structures around space. In *Twice Upon a Time*, Kunzru's movement though his own thirdspace uncovers rhythms that speak to such subcultural presences. A series of pages reveal in fragments the varying sounds of the city, from Latin DJs to choir boys, to be brought together thus:

> All this in twenty minutes. Many simultaneous cities. NPR city, College Radio City, R'n'B City, above all the Latino City running in parallel to the Anglo one. Add to that the Internet streams and you have a sort of infinite parallelism – Armenian City, Punjabi City, Ethiopian City, Mandarin City, New Age City, Ambient City, Faery City, Evangelical City, Adult Contemporary City, Singles City, Sports City, Pet City … (2014a: n.p.)

Moondog has developed his own rhythms through a cross-cultural dialogue; resonant with Lefebvre's corporeal rhythms Moondog visits a Native American reservation as a child, where a chief teaches him 'the running beat, and alongside it the walking beat, which is also the universal heartbeat'. So it is that a radically differentiated subject evolves whose own rhythms are produced through and within the radically differentiated rhythms of their spatio-temporal locations. The interwoven rhythms of this moment draw attention to the radical newness of cultural production, which can be seen in the era of extinction rebellion, #MeToo and Black Lives Matter as a vital call to consider what difference cultural production makes. Such contexts are relevant because, as Atkinson (2007) explores in his work on sound ecology, sound rhythms in urban contexts can be a way to take over public space, to claim territory, or to interrogate official usage (2007: 1913). They contribute to what Kevin Hetherington (2013) defines as the city as archive, shaped in the process through which rhythms emerge from more abstract noise, a space which provides countercultural content that might interrogate the official archives of the library, map and museum. It is here, then, that *Memory Palace* and *Twice Upon a Time* find themselves once more in overlapping territory, both serving as alternative cultural repositories for memory and experience that offer the opportunity to facilitate new voices.

As these rhythms coalesce, Lefebvre's understanding 'that a rhythm is slow or lively only in relation to other rhythms (often our own: those of our walking, our breathing, our heart)' (2004 [1992]: 10) becomes a process of dialogue between competing measures, both human and material. How different then is this rhythm from the movement we might see in a figure such as the nineteenth-century *flâneur* – one who moves, certainly, but through a space represented largely as static, and with the focus almost entirely on a single subjectivity. Indeed, within the single subject rhythm is driven towards the resistance of singularity. There is, Lefebvre says, 'no rhythm without repetition in time and in space, without *reprises*, without returns [...] But there is no identical absolute repetition, indefinitely. Whence the relation between repetition and difference' (2004 [1992]: 6). Like Bhabha's mimicry in which the repetition of the dominant destabilises its foundations, rhythm undermines the possibility of a stable referent. On one page of *Twice Upon a Time*, the narrator recalls a scene of factory women, Spanish love songs on the radio, the machinery whirring and thudding and observes, 'there's something devotional about the tableau, the repetitive gestures, the white uniforms, the plaintive declarations of love'. This conjunction of rhythm and subjectivity marks a new, twenty-first century version of Lefebvre's polyrhythmia but points to the collective politics that rhythms create – the rhythm that, as Lefebvre tells us, may be captured by the group to enact change (2004 [1992]: 14) may belong to the group as well as the individual.

Such concern for the primacy of the individual in contemporary culture returns us to Marxist influences, but also to a furthering of the investigation into the nature of consciousness and selfhood that has preoccupied Kunzru in all of his novels. If *Twice Upon a Time* owes anything to literary antecedents, then it is to the work of J.G. Ballard, whom Kunzru has both interviewed and written on. In his introduction to Ballard's *The Atrocity Exhibition* (2014b) Kunzru quotes Ballard's description of his collage form as 'sample pages of a new kind of novel, entirely consisting of magazine-style headlines and layouts, with a deliberately meaningless text, the idea being that the imaginative content could be carried by the headlines and overall design, so making obsolete the need for a traditional text except for virtually decorative purposes' (2014b: paragraph 7). Kunzru describes Ballard's use of this form in the context of his reference to the writer Raymond Roussel and his autonomic writing machines, greatly influential to the Surrealist movement, which 'seem to open a road towards a poetry of the unconscious' (paragraph 9). Recognising an analogous impulse in Ballard's work, Kunzru goes on to say:

> Automatism is liberating, yes, but also sinister. *The Atrocity Exhibition* is a cousin of *A Clockwork Orange* and *The Manchurian Candidate*, books that display a deep anxiety about behaviorism, conditioning and free will. By the sixties, ideas about computing were beginning to percolate out into the wider culture, particularly through the newly fashionable discourse of cybernetics. Suddenly, it was apparent that information and control systems were embedded in the biology of the human organism, as well as into various forms of technology (notably missile guidance), a fact which made cybernetics key to the conduct of the Cold War. It was now open to conceptualize the media in an analogous way as a technology of control, a sort of guidance system which could be used to direct consumers towards desired goals. During the period he was working on *The Atrocity Exhibition* and *Crash*, Ballard (who had briefly worked at an ad agency) published a series of 'Advertisers Announcements' in *Ambit*. He conceived of these spreads in a conceptually rigorous way,

to the extent of paying the magazine's ad rate for the pages. 'Fiction,' reads the text of one, 'is a branch of neurology.' (paragraph 9)

Such analysis locates Kunzru's own formal strategies in *Twice Upon a Time* as concerned for the unconsciousness production of image as indicative of the associative practices within the human brain that parallel the information retrieval systems of computerised technology, affirming the deconstruction of Romantic selfhood evidenced in *The Impressionist* (2002), *My Revolutions* (2007) and *Red Pill* (2020).

The text in this sense is the flip-side of the humanisation of technology in *Transmission*, offering instead the technologised self that exists primarily in the random production of visual and text through neural pathways. In *Memory Palace* the very focus on memory and forgetting is a concern for consciousness and its corrupt, inexact science. Yet beyond this the novel suggests that the horror of the future is thus one in which objects are stripped of their connection to subjectivity. The narrator's future world has lost the ability to measure – accounting is the worst crime, and all terms of measurement are forbidden. Yet so too are ideas, and imagination. The world of the Wilding is one in which only material objects are valued. In this context the disjunctive rhythm of the dystopian text forges a path to the other and the disruption of authoritarianism. At the end of the narrative the narrator is about to die, imprisoned, and a member of the resistance visits him, allowing him to download one memory onto her consciousness. He chooses a memory of walking with his lover and their dog through green fields, the moment of anticipation just before they reach the top and see the view. While Loh declares the text 'unremittingly bleak' (2019: 355) this moment is decidedly one of hope, and that this promise is evoked by walking seems particularly pertinent; speaking of *Twice Upon a Time*, Kunzru has described his semi-conscious urban wanderings as indicative of the fact that 'you can't really write sort of top-down, panoptical version of any city. You can tell your city, and it might be completely different from the city that belongs to the person who is strap-hanging next to you on the subway. You have your geography. You have your markers. You have your sense of place. That's not necessarily completely shared, even though you are physically occupying the same space' (Tipper, 2014). Yet in the same article he asserts his belief that 'there is something noble about sharing the streets with other people' as a gesture against the capitalist gentrification of the city where privatisation of space inevitably shields the individual from contact with the other (Tipper, 2014). While the text examines the auditory territory of the iPod as one which negatively overrides the city's rhythms and creates 'a community of one', Kunzru's own walking exposes cross-cultural rhythms of the city's immigrant populations, its street artists, its underground musicians. As such, it questions the discourse surrounding 'Music listening while moving through public space […] as a way of creating a private auditory bubble for the individual' (Werner, 2015b: 197). This positive future is for those that Kunzru refers to as the 'multitaskers', those who can be both within the technological and the physical space. Within both these movements is the gesture towards a personalised and meaningful action in which rhythms are separate yet conjoined, the transglossic notion of simultaneity but also Alain Badiou's definition of love in *In Praise of Love* (2009), perhaps, as the 'two scene' (29), the 'paradox of identical difference' (25) in the occupation of the same space as an other without the absorption or loss of individual subjectivity.

Conclusion

While *Twice Upon a Time* celebrates the possibilities of the immersive multimodal e-book, the curators of *Memory Palace* speak of their text as examining the material alternative that exists within a context where text has become searchable and interactive, pushing the limits of the material form. The contrast between digital forms as spreading information and the book as communicative media for slower thoughts, for thinking, itself suggests the alternating rhythms of varying platforms. For Lefebvre, rhythm is a way to oppose linear calculation with the emphasis instead on the variable duration and length of notes in music as representative of irregular measures. These, however, are not to be confused with the immeasurable. Rhythm is multiplicitous, but it drives us not towards nonplace but to inhabitancy. Equally, texts such as *Memory Palace* and *Twice Upon a Time* embrace disjunctive rhythms within the context of meaning – their mobilities, both literal and metaphorical, are part of a distinct cultural moment. It is this holistic experience, this speaking across positions conterminously at formal and thematic levels, that makes these texts transglossic.

Reading *Memory Palace* alongside *Twice Upon a Time* invites a rhythmanalysis, not to prioritise one over the other but to observe how one's corporeal engagement through reading creates a human-material rhythm. As I read these books in my south-west London lockdown, the traffic noise, the hammering of a building site outside my window, drilling downstairs, my daughter's laughter on a phone call, my fingers tapping on the keyboard, the movement of my chest, my breath, these intersect with the textual rhythms of each piece and are transformed from the hedonistic rhythms of *Twice Upon a Time*, to the slowness of *Memory Palace*, one text symphonic with my breath, the other an arrhythmic interruption that brings the noises of the street into the room. In these polyrhythmic spaces we move with and hear an other outside ourselves.

Note

1 It is even more striking that those new materialists who focus readily on movement, most notably those working within the fields of sports and dance sociology, turn not to Lefebvre alongside their contemporary reference points, but more often to Deleuze, Foucault and Latour (see, for example, Markula, 2019; Gunaratnam, 2019).

References

Ahmed, Sara (2008). 'Multiculturalism and the Promise of Happiness', *New Formations*, 63, 121–138.

Ahmed, Sara, Claudia Castada and Anne Marie Fortier (eds) (2003). *Uprootings/Regroundings: Questions of Home and Migration* (London: Routledge).

Atkinson, Rowland (2007). 'Ecology of Sound: The Sonic Order of Urban Space', *Urban Studies*, 44:10, 1905–1917.

Badiou, Alain (2012). *In Praise of Love*, translated by Peter Bush (London: Serpent's Tail) .

Barad, Karen (2007). *Meeting the Universe Halfway: Quantum Physics and the Entanglement of Matter and Meaning* (Durham, NC: Duke University Press) .

Bennett, Jane (2010). *Vibrant Matter: A Political Ecology of Things* (Durham, NC: Duke University Press) .

Berlant, Lauren (2011). *Cruel Optimism* (Durham, NC: Duke University Press) .

Cresswell, Tim (2010). 'Towards a Politics of Mobility', *Environment and Planning D: Society and Space*, 28:1, 17–31.

Cresswell, Tim and Peter Merriman (eds) (2011). *Geographies of Mobilities: Practices, Spaces, Subjects* (Farnham: Ashgate).

Edensor, Tim (2010). 'Introduction: Thinking about Rhythm and Space', in Tim Edensor (ed.), *Geographies of Rhythm: Nature, Place, Mobilities and Bodies* (London: Routledge), 1–20.

—— (2012). 'Mobility, Rhythm and Commuting', in Tim Cresswell and Peter Merriman (eds), *Geographies of Mobilities: Practices, Spaces, Subjects* (Farnham: Ashgate), 189–203.

Elden, Stuart (2004). 'Introduction', in *Rhythmanalysis: Space, Time and Everyday* Life, by Henri Lefebvre, translated by Stuart Elden and Gerald Moore (London: Continuum), vii–xv.

Evaristo, Bernadine (2017). 'Interview with Hari Kunzru', *Brit Lit Berlin 2017*, https://writersmakeworlds.com/hari-kunzru/ (accessed 8 August 2022).

Gibbons, Alison (2008). 'Multimodal Literature "Moves" Us: Dynamic Movement and Embodiment in *VAS: An Opera in Flatland*', *Hermes: Journal of Language and Communication Studies*, 41, 107–123.

Gunaratnam, Yasmin (2019). 'Those that Resembles Flies from a Distance': Performing Research', *Mai: Feminism and Visual Culture*, May, https://maifeminism.com/those-that-resemble-flies-from-a-distance-performing-research/ (accessed 8 August 2022).

Hetherington, Kevin (2013). 'Rhythm and Noise: the City, Memory and the Archive', *The Sociological Review*, 61:S1, 17–33.

Kellogg, Carolyn (2020). 'An Alt-Right Mind-Bender for the QAnon Era: How Novelist Hari Kunzru Went Down the Rabbit Hole', *Los Angeles Times*, 26 August, www.latimes.com/entertainment-arts/books/story/2020-08-26/hari-kunzru-profile-for-his-novel-red-pill (accessed 8 August 2022).

Kunzru, Hari (2014a). *Twice Upon a Time: Listening to New York* (New York: Atavist Books).

—— (2014b). 'Introduction', *The Atrocity Exhibition*, by J.G. Ballard (London: Fourth Estate).

Lefebvre, Henri (1991 [1974]). *The Production of Space*, translated by Donald Nicolson-Smith (Oxford: Blackwell)

—— (2004 [1992]). *Rhythmanalysis: Space, Time and Everyday Life*, translated by Stuart Elden and Gerald Moore (London: Continuum).

Lefebvre, Henri and Catherine Régulier (2003). 'The Rhythmanalytical Project', translated by Imogen Forster, in *Rhythmanalysis: Space, Time and Everyday Life* (London: Continuum), 71–84.

Loh, Lucienne (2019). 'Hari Kunzru', in Daniel O'Gorman and Robert Eaglestone (eds), *The Routledge Companion to Twenty-First Century Literary Fiction* (London: Routledge), 346–359.

Markula, Pirkko (2019). 'What Is New About New Materialism for Sport Sociology? Reflections on Body, Movement, and Culture', *Sociology of Sport Journal*, 36, 1–11.

Plate, Liedeke (2015). 'How to Do Things with Literature in the Digital Age: Anne Carson's *Nox*, Multimodality, and the Ethics of Bookishness', *Contemporary Women's Writing*, 9:1, 93–111.

Reid-Musson, Emily (2018). 'Intersectional Rhythmanalysis: Power, Rhythm, and Everyday Life', *Progress in Human Geography*, 42:6, 881–897.

Rekret, Paul (2018). 'The Head, the Hand, and Matter: New Materialism and the Politics of Knowledge', *Theory, Culture & Society*, 35:7–8, 49–72.

Revill, George (2013). 'Points of Departure: Listening to Rhythm in the Sonoric Spaces of the Railway Station', *The Sociological Review*, 61:S1, 51–68.

Sanghera, Sathnam (2011). 'I Was Never in It for the Cash', *The Times*, 23 July, www.thetimes.co.uk/article/i-was-never-in-it-for-the-cash-5nvvgtdrvgp (accessed 8 August 2022).

Shaw, Kristian and Sara Upstone (2021). 'The Transglossic: Contemporary Fiction and the Limitations of the Modern', *English Studies*, 102:5, 573–600.

Sheller, Mimi, and John Urry (2006). 'The New Mobilities Paradigm', *Environment and Planning A*, 38:2, 207–226.

Smith, Robin James and Kevin Hetherington (2013). *Urban Rhythms: Mobilities, Space and Interaction in the Contemporary City* = *The Sociological Review*, 61:S1.

Tipper, Bill (2014). '*Twice Upon a Time*: Hari Kunzru', *Barnes and Noble Review*, 14 May, www.barnesandnoble.com/review/twice-upon-a-time-hari-kunzru (accessed 8 August 2022).

Ulin, David L. (2014). 'Hari Kunzru's Digital Tone Poem of New York', *Los Angeles Times*, 21 May, www.latimes.com/books/jacketcopy/la-et-jc-hari-kunzru-digital-tone-poem-new-york-20140521-story.html (accessed 8 August 2022).

Upstone, Sara (2014). '"Footprints are the only fixed point": Mobilities in Postcolonial Fiction', in Lesley Murray and Sara Upstone (eds), *Researching and Representing Mobilities: Transdisciplinary Encounters* (Basingstoke: Palgrave), 39–56.

Werner, Ann (2015a). 'Introduction: Studying Junctures of Motion and Emotion', *Culture Unbound. Journal of Current Cultural Research*, 7:2, 169–173.

——— (2015b). 'Moving Forward: A Feminist Analysis of Mobile Music Streaming', *Culture Unbound*, 7, 197–212.

Wheeler, Seth (2013). 'Memory Palace: Hari Kunzru Interviewed by Seth Wheeler', *3am Magazine*, 3 July, www.3ammagazine.com/3am/memory-palace/ (accessed 8 August 2022).

Yoder, Anne K. (2012). 'Plot, Rhyme, and Conspiracy: Hari Kunzru Colludes with His Readers', *The Millions*, 20 March, https://themillions.com/2012/03/plot-rhyme-and-conspiracy-hari-kunzru-colludes-with-his-readers.html (accessed 8 August 2022).

7

'The ghost is him': the echoes of racism, non-being and haunting in *White Tears*

David Hering

In *White Tears* two young hipsters, Seth and Carter, use the latter's inheritance to set themselves up as record producers. Carter becomes fixated on blues music, specifically its pre-war iteration, because the form is 'more intense and authentic than anything made by white people' (*WT*: 9). This culminates in their creation of a fake song, 'Graveyard Blues', for which Seth supplies a 'vocal' from a covert recording of an African American chess player in Washington Square; the pair attribute the track to the invented musician Charlie Shaw. Seth and Carter construct their digital recording to mimic the physicality of an old 78rpm record, with all the associated cracks and pops of shellac, but the electronic file itself has presence only on a hard drive. In that sense 'Graveyard Blues' is a classic Baudrillardian simulacrum, a copy that does not exist in its original form. But something else does exist: a malevolent presence conjured by the record, one that will return in search of justice. Charlie Shaw, we discover, was real, a budding Blues musician wrongfully arrested en route to a recording session back in the Jim Crow era. As was shamefully common at the time, Shaw was incarcerated on trumped-up vagrancy charges and made to undertake hard labour, dying unknown and unheard without ever having a chance to record his music. In *White Tears* this liminal object, with its alternating oscillation between presence and absence, speaks to a broader social concept of blackness as both object and non-existence, one which Kunzru weaponises by transforming this abject, non-existent, ghostly state into a violent narrative of revenge, revoicing and possession. In doing so, Kunzru enters into an extensive dialogue with the cultural history of music and racism, and the way in which particular African American musical forms become compromised by their reception and consumption.

Blues, non-being and objecthood

In W.E.B. Du Bois's famous formulation, the condition of blackness involves living at a remove from white society: 'I was different from the others [...] shut out from their world by a vast veil. I had thereafter no desire to tear down that veil, to creep through; I held all beyond it in common contempt, and lived above it in a region of blue sky and great wandering shadows' (2007: 3). Du Bois suggests a paradoxical topography, a zone of clear sky that is simultaneously a place of darkness. This location is not unique in African American notions of selfhood; perhaps its most famous incarnation is Ralph Ellison's eponymous *Invisible Man* (1952), who obtains a precarious state of continuously shifting visibility, moving ultimately to a room underground and out of sight that is, in an invocation of Du Bois's region, both void of natural light and blindingly lit by thousands of electric bulbs. In *White Tears,* Charlie Shaw has a similarly complex ontology. When the narrative begins he is an invention, a manufactured simulation of the kind of skeletal prewar country blues so beloved of Carter for its bleak authenticity, but as the novel progresses he attains new forms of personhood, and these forms are commensurate with the excavation of his past and the injustices he has suffered. To become incarnate, Shaw must move beyond the 'grey drizzle of static', the veil that imprisons him in the record and locks him out from the world, and creep through into the land of the living (*WT*: 270). This is a progression from Du Bois's studied abstinence from the world beyond the veil; rather than holding the world in contempt Shaw decides instead to hold it to *account*, to get those who have wronged him to 'pay me what you owe me' (*WT*: 53).

Shaw's spectral imprisonment within an object is indicative of a condition of non-being, one identified by a number of African American thinkers as being crucial to an understanding of the humanistic dynamic of racism. To be black, says Calvin L. Warren, is to 'lack being but have existence', to 'inhabit the world in concealment and non-movement' (2018: 13).

Warren's claim makes a nod to the earlier concept of the veil ('concealment') but suggests a further calcification of that position; rather than being able, as Du Bois does, to formulate a position from which to view the world beyond the veil, on Warren's view the condition of being black prevents autonomous movement. In a disturbingly haptic image, he illustrates the subject as being 'buried deep between layers of metaphysical violence' (2018: 29). The veil, here, becomes a crushing weight, a burial that paralyses the body and impedes autonomy. This movement from insubstantial agency to burial is dramatised in Kunzru's novel through Shaw's initial imprisonment within the song; it is perhaps no coincidence here that the business of shellac and vinyl recording involves the terminology of pressing and capturing, thus sealing the voice into a physical object, a ghost in a machine.

Before thinking about ghosts, however, it is essential to consider the object in which they are trapped. Frantz Fanon describes the condition of blackness, in similar terms to Warren, as a matter of being 'sealed into that crushing objecthood' (2008: 82), and this proves to be a useful way to think about how Kunzru dramatises musical objectification in *White Tears*. The pre-war blues of musicians like Charlie Patton and Skip James was not the prevailing and popular African American music of its day, but the form, and the records themselves, became fetishised by a group of primarily white collectors in the 1950s known informally as the Blues Mafia. In *White Tears* we are introduced to Chester Bly, an unscrupulous collector who intimidates elderly Southern African Americans into handing over their collections of old shellac 78s; in the dreamlike logic of the novel, he eventually steals a record that turns out to be 'Graveyard Blues', the phantom Charlie Shaw song later invented by Seth and Carter. Bly dies shortly afterwards in what is implied to be a supernatural murder. Bly is a fairly straight parody of the New York-based mid-century Blues collector Jim McKune; like McKune, Bly sets an arbitrary limit on the number of discs in his collection, treats the act of listening as a quasi-religious ritual, and dies in mysterious circumstances. Kunzru here parodies those collectors who, according to music researcher and producer Ian Nagoski, fixated on pre-war blues as 'this quasi-demonic, earthy, raw folk-music thing' (qtd. in Petrusich, 2014: 180). It is no coincidence that Bly's fixation on this object is correlated with his dismissal of the selfhood of living African Americans. When Shaw's sister, the lone owner of his record, is described by Bly's assistant Jumpjim, her selfhood is negated: 'her substance is absence' (*WT*: 168). The ontology implied by this substance/absence speaks to Warren's paradoxical assertion that black people are 'introduced into the metaphysical world as available equipment in human form' (2018: 6). Warren's description, hovering between the poles of metaphysics and equipment, indicates that subjugated condition of being both insubstantial and considered as raw materials, as an object-to-hand.

This condition of being equipment or raw materials speaks, inevitably, to the systematic objecthood suffered by African Americans during and after slavery. Shaw's arrest for vagrancy is a typical example of the injustices meted out to black Americans during the Jim Crow era, and the incarceration that follows is analogous to Warren's sedimented condition; Shaw is imprisoned, his voice silenced, buried deep within the walls of the penitentiary. However, the matter of burial is also important to Kunzru's novel because it speaks to the way that racism intersects with what Kathryn Yusoff terms 'the biopolitical category of nonbeing' (2018: 5). For Yusoff, slavery resulted in 'a geologic axiom of the inhuman in which nonbeing was made, reproduced and circulated as flesh', a phrase that invokes the movement from non-being to Warren's 'available equipment' (2018: 5). Yusoff is also interested in thinking more broadly about the history of geology itself as it pertains to race: 'Geology is a transactional zone in which ideas of origins, subjectivity, and matter are intertwined, with historical materialist roots that span a genealogy of dispossession, uprooting, and extreme violence' (2018: 26). This formulation has its basis, of course, in the working of the land by enslaved African Americans as well as those unlawfully imprisoned and, like Charlie Shaw, forced to perform hard labour on Southern soil. Shaw's song revolves heavily around the refrain 'Believe I buy me a graveyard of my own' (*WT*: 5). This line, inspired by Jim Jackson's 1927 song 'I'm Gonna Start Me a Graveyard of My Own', indicates a desire to own some land, even if it only belongs to the dead; in 'Graveyard Blues', however, this will allow Shaw to 'put my enemies all down in the ground', a reversal of the untimely and undignified death and burial he suffered at the prison (*WT*: 13). Fanon's 'crushing objecthood' is recontextualised, here, in terms of the sedimentation of the earth pressing down on Shaw's body. Through his description of Shaw's fate, Kunzru brings these different degrees of objecthood together. Treated effectively as a non-citizen, Shaw is forced into incarceration and made into a tool to work someone else's land. When he dies, his body abused and objectified, he is thrown into the same soil, pressed under and fossilised in a prefiguration of his non-consensual 'pressing' into the simulation of the virtual record by Seth and Carter. This process requires a continual oscillation between non-being and object, an ontology formed in negative terms. Yusoff's claim that 'blackness becomes what could be termed an *ontology without territory*' provides an appropriate representation of Shaw's liminality; revenant, he wants to buy a graveyard of his own to gain mastery over the territory that pressed him into concealment and non-being (2018: 81, emphasis in original).

This condition of existence between non-being and objecthood resembles something else: ghostliness. Shaw's haunting of Seth and Carter is predicated on a continuous shifting between the ethereal and the concrete, between the incorporeal voice and embodied possession, which climaxes in Shaw using Seth as his instrument to murder the members of Carter's family who own the prison group Walxr, an earlier iteration of which was responsible for his incarceration. However, before coming to the more specific matter of Shaw's revenge it is important to consider how the central motif of ghostliness in *White Tears* speaks to a similar ontology of blackness as that outlined by Du Bois, Fanon and Yusoff. In *Haunted Life* (2007), David Marriott considers the meaning of the racial slur 'spook' in the context of black ontology. The term itself does not have a clear origin but is thought to relate to the supposed invisibility of darker skin. The expression locates black skin as fearful in its relative obscurity – the racist myth of the black male predator is accentuated by the impossibility of gauging his proximity – but principally, the spook is insubstantial enough to be denied coherent selfhood. 'This is the reason for the alleged spookiness of blacks', says Marriott: 'to submit to it is to suffer dissolution' (2007: 2). While trying to undo the haunting Seth meets with two men, one of whom who he believes to be an embodiment of Shaw. This man is sitting in the back seat of a car, his arm the only visible part of his body, playing a 'chopped and screwed' version of 'Graveyard Blues' (*WT*: 172). In a moment of desperation, Seth tries to psychologically will this corporeal version of Shaw out of physical existence:

> Charlie Shaw is in the car and I need to speak to him. I need him to break his silence, to come out from behind the veil and say what it is he wants. If he doesn't explain, I'm scared that this will go on and

the next person it touches will be me. I am a good person [...] [Shaw's companion] is stepping towards me, holding out his arms wide, the palms of his hands open, herding us into our car. He makes me feel insubstantial. It is not logical to feel this way. I am alive, I think as I fumble with the car door. The ghost is him (*WT*: 174).

Seth inadvertently invokes Du Bois's veil by acknowledging that Shaw exists on its other side, and ultimately tries to push Shaw further back into that realm of obscurity. Seth's motivation is predicated on his belief that his and Shaw's corporeality are somehow inversely symbiotic; as Shaw's spirit grows in physical power, Seth will become insubstantial, diluted. As part of this effort to dispel Shaw, Seth makes implicit appeals to the kind of humanism that casts blackness into a zone of non-being: 'I am a good person [...] It is not logical to feel [insubstantial]' (*WT*: 174). In this sense his final remark attempts and fails to perform an illocutionary speech act; Seth hopes that by simply naming Shaw, and not himself, as the ghost, he can cast him back into nothingness, into an ontology without territory, into the simulation of the digital file that Carter describes as 'inhuman' (*WT*: 20). Seth's mistake here is to assume that the recording into which he tries to will Shaw is an inert object. When Seth and Carter construct 'Graveyard Blues' they do so in a parody of authenticity, whereby the recording will exhibit all of the aesthetic hallmarks of blues. By doing so, they confine the idea of the blues record to an artefact, an object with a sense of financial or collector's value. The record itself has other ideas. It resists its objecthood by becoming an open channel for the echoes of injustice and racism that constitute the blues as a form. In the words of Du Bois, it 'grope[s] toward some unseen power' (2007: 125).

Echoes and afterlives

These echoes found in the record might be usefully conceptualised as a version of what Saidiya Hartman calls 'the afterlife of slavery' (2008: 6). Hartman's concept relates to the kind of injustices experienced by African Americans – 'premature death, incarceration' – that are also suffered by Shaw. However, there is an additional way in which we might conceptualise Hartman's afterlives; as an echo of the voices of those same subjugated peoples in music: 'Guglielmo Marconi, the inventor of radio, believed that sound waves never completely die away, that they persist, fainter and fainter, masked by the day-to-day noise of the world. Marconi thought that if he could only invent a microphone powerful enough, he would be able to listen to the sound of ancient times' (*WT*: 43).

Seth's idea that sound waves persist across history acts as an unwitting analogy for the insistent afterlives of pain and inequality channelled through Blues music, one to which he is initially deaf. His mistake is to regard blues as an inert form, one ripe for pastiche, and a second-hand shortcut to authenticity. What Seth misses is the *persistence* of blues in the present, not just as a marker of injustice but as a process of preservation. In mistaking the blues as a passive form, Seth unwittingly lays himself open to its active, spectral quality. The supernatural conduit created by 'Graveyard Blues' exemplifies the persistence of sound waves as captured by Marconi's theoretical microphone, a persistence not merely the result of a passive echo, but of what Fred Moten and Stefano Harvey consider to be the 'transferability' of black performance, a process actively undertaken in order to 'constitute the "proof" that blackness is not or is lost or is loss' (2013: 49).

This active echo within the blues form originates, of course, long before Shaw's incarceration. 'Sound', remarks M. NourbeSe Philip in her collection *Zong!*, 'never stops in water' (2020: 203). Philip's book traces the memories of those enslaved people on the British slave ship *Zong* in the late eighteenth century and configures the massacre, in which at least 130 Africans were deliberately thrown overboard in order not to invalidate an insurance policy, as a series of vocal echoes. The awful persistence of sound in *Zong!* – the cries of the dying and the words of those who witnessed – is channelled through a restructuring of the report on the ship; Philip breaks open and reformulates the words of the captors and slaveholders in order to reveal the lives of the dead that lie behind their veil. This process is not entirely dissimilar to the way in which Shaw breaks out of the carapace of Seth and Carter's simulated recording; the repressed history of racial injustice cannot help but erupt through the tools of its instrumentalisation. For both Kunzru and Philip, the persistence of sound stands as an analogy for the endurance of the afterlives of slavery. The elements of Seth and Carter's recording of 'Graveyard

Blues' come from background noise or, to use a more musically appropriate term, from field recordings, an expression often used by white musicians who travelled to the South to record blues music in the 1930s and 1940s. The resurrection of Shaw from these apparently ambient elements indicates that the legacies of slavery are baked into the background hum of American culture. When Philip says that 'the ancients walk within us' (2020: 195) she is in part referring to this insistent and immanent noise. In her introduction to *Zong!*, Hartman makes the claim, one that we might synthesise with her concept of the afterlives of slavery, that these 'sonic compositions emerge from the hold of the ship' (2020: xi).[1]

Hartman's concept and Philip's collection frame the hold of the slave ship as a terrible musical instrument, one that acts as a sounding board reverberating across water and time, through and past abolition, Jim Crow, civil rights and the supposedly post-racial Obama presidency into the present of twenty-first-century racial injustice in which *White Tears* is set. Christina Sharpe theorises this movement as 'the wake':

> the track left on the water's surface by a ship; the disturbance caused by a body swimming, or one that is moved, in water; the air currents behind a body in flight; a region of disturbed flow; in the line of sight of (an observed object); and (something) in the line of recoil of (a gun); finally, wake means being awake and, also, consciousness. (2016: 21)

Sharpe's reverberating structure frames institutional and cultural racism as an endlessly expanding wave, one with its own 'coordinates and effects' (2016: 20). In theorising the wake, Sharpe returns to that Fanonian concept of non-being whereby 'consciousness of the body is solely a negating activity' (2008: 84). For Sharpe, it is important to theorise this 'state of being inhabited/occupied and also being or dwelling in' as a *processual* stage towards increased agency of the subject (2016: 20). This process can only be achieved by incorporating the wake into a contemporary ontology: 'we join the wake with work in order that we might make the wake and *wake work* our analytic, we might continue to imagine new ways to live in the wake of slavery, in slavery's afterlives, to survive (and more) the afterlife of property' (2016: 18, emphasis in original). This process of living *within* the afterlife of slavery operates in *White Tears* not only as a practice of living with generational and historical trauma, but also as what might be termed a process of possession of the kind practiced by Shaw's ghost, an actualisation of how Philip's ancients walk within. Of course, in Kunzru's novel this process of 'living within' is weaponised; Seth is forced by Shaw's ghost to experience the injustices suffered by African Americans, from unlawful arrest and interrogation to incarceration.

It would be a mistake to think of this process of wake and echo as taking place within a simple linear timeframe. Moten and Harney, thinking through the work of poet Nathaniel Mackey, draw upon the term 'mu', a word with a number of meanings but most commonly thought of as representing nothingness. Moten and Harney use the term to deliberately disrupt the sense of linearity involved in thinking about the afterlife of slavery: 'Where we were, where we are, is what we meant by "mu" [...] so it is we remain in the hold, in the break, as if entering again and again the broken world, to trace the visionary company and join it' (2013: 94). They align this formulation with the musical structure of Mackey's collection *Splay Anthem* (2002):

> [Mackey] speaks of mu in relation to a circling or spiraling or ringing, this roundness or rondo linking beginning and end, and to the wailing that accompanies entrance into and expulsion from sociality. But his speaking makes you wonder if music, which is not only music, is mobilised in the service of an eccentricity, a centrifugal force whose intimation Mackey also approaches, marking sociality's ecstatic existence beyond beginning and end, ends and means, out where one becomes interested in things, in a certain relationship between thingliness and nothingness and blackness that plays itself out in unmapped, unmappable, undercommon consent and consensuality. (Moten and Harney, 2013: 95)

This concept of circling and the rondo aligns the historically persistent trauma of black life in America with a musical structure, one that continues to circulate and return to the same theme time and time again; this also resembles the fugue structure invoked by Philip in *Zong!* (2020: 204). In *White Tears*, Kunzru uses a similar technique whereby the past is visible in the present and where life is also an 'aggregate of non-living processes', locating it within the object of the blues record (*WT*: 271). The old shellac 78 revolves, each sweep of the needle returning in a circular movement to a point beside its original position, slowly spreading outward with each revolution in the manner of Sharpe's wake. The linearity of the song, then, is always physically inscribed within a movement of partial return.

This concept of circularity should not, however, be thought of as a permanent trap. In fact, in *White Tears* this process bears more relation to an incantation, whereby the structure of the rondo (or to use a blues term, the refrain) is not merely repetitive but also, as with Kunzru's concept of the 'aggregate', exponentially productive. Of course, the process of listening to a record does involve the needle continually returning to a place adjacent to its origin point, but this is to forget the associated aggregation of the song itself, which unfolds simultaneously with the needle's partial return. Tyehimba Jess practices a similar technique in his poetry collection *Olio* (2016), which narrates the lives of African American musicians after emancipation but before audio recording technology. Towards the end of *Olio*, Jess instructs the reader to liberate the page itself from the fixed linearity of the book: 'cut thru the dotted perforation to free the comedians from the medium of two-dimensional tête-à-tête. Take the last lines and loop them into the first. The jokesters will gently coax their heads and feet together so you can listen to them sing three-dimensionally' (2016: 216). This gesture, whereby the musicians of *Olio* re-emerge from historical obscurity onto the page, and the page itself emerges physically from the book and into the world as a three-dimensional object, can also be seen in *White Tears*, when the playing of 'Graveyard Blues' immediately invokes a feeling in Jumpjim that 'Charlie Shaw's voice is looking for me' (*WT*: 166). The record conjures an active, productive presence rather than simply a repetitive, cyclical inscription.

This productivity is accentuated when Seth and Carter reinvoke Shaw's record by accumulating different components into a digital file. Digital audio editing, of course, allows the rearrangement of musical elements in a manner different to the way an analogue sound wave is inscribed on to a physical record. Seth describes the process of digital audio editing as productive of an entirely new space: 'There are ways you can use a studio. Things you can do that open up impossible spaces in the mind. You can put the listener in a room that doesn't exist, that couldn't exist. You can put them in an impossible room' (*WT*: 26).

Seth unwittingly acknowledges here the supernatural power that he and Carter are about to unleash via 'Graveyard Blues'; he even suggests that studio technology, specifically reverb, can make 'time reverse its flow', which could also act as a description of the temporal out-of-jointedness required for a haunting (*WT*: 26). This editing process, which ruptures the law of linear time, ultimately invokes Shaw's spirit, allowing him to leap into the present and carry out his revenge. This incorporates a weaponised version of the concept of the spook mentioned by Marriott; whereas Marriott initially suggests that the term invokes dissolution, Shaw's ghost instead manipulates spookiness to enact visibility and vengeance.

Verbing the noun

The eruption of Shaw's ghost recalls Avery Gordon's concept of haunting as a process of 'producing a something-to-be-done', located in that moment when 'the cracks and the rigging are exposed, when the people who are meant to be invisible show up without any sign of leaving' (2008: xvi). Here, the exposure of the rigging takes the form of that rupture of linearity occasioned by the editing of the digital file, which allows the spirit of Shaw, liberated from temporality, to enter the present. Gordon's sociological model of haunting is particularly useful when thinking about *White Tears* because she describes a process that inscribes social agency into the presence of the ghost itself. 'The ghost is [...] a social figure', she writes, 'and investigating it can lead to that dense site where history and subjectivity make social life. [...] Being haunted draws us affectively [...] into the structure of feeling of a reality we come to experience, not as cold knowledge, but as a transformative recognition' (2008: 8). Gordon's process can be taken to describe Shaw's ghost as an agent of revival and change; the haunting in *White Tears* necessarily involves Seth being drawn affectively into the reality of African American injustice. He experiences this reality – being arrested, interrogated and brutalised by the police – not as 'cold knowledge' but as an embodied process of 'transformative recognition'. This is not merely a matter of Shaw's revenge on Seth; it is also a making-real of the ghost's 'life world':

the ghost is a living force. It may reside elsewhere in an otherworldly domain but it is never intrinsically Other. It has a life world, in the strongest sense of the term, of its own. And it carries this life world with all its sweet things, its nastiness, and its yearnings into ours as it makes its haunting entry, making itself a phenomenological reality. There is no question that when a ghost haunts, that haunting is real. The ghost has an agency on the people it is haunting and we can call that agency desire, motivation, or standpoint. And so its desires must be broached and we have to talk to it. (Gordon, 2008: 179)

This talking need not necessarily be a conversation. In the afore-mentioned scene where Seth encounters Shaw hidden in the back of the car, his desperation is driven precisely because Shaw will not talk with him. Instead, to paraphrase Gordon, *he* has to talk to *it*. 'If some reality believes in you', Seth realises, 'then you must live it. You can't say no thank you. You can't say I don't want this. If horror believes in you, there's nothing to be done' (*WT*: 227). For Seth, this process inverts Gordon's 'something-to-be-done'; the ghost's purpose, that 'something', is to inscribe into its quarry that absolute *lack* of agency that Shaw experienced during his life.

This inversion, which flips Seth's something into nothing, sim-ultaneously converts Shaw's nothing into something. Gordon calls this agency 'the ghost's desire', and it is entangled here with the conversion of objecthood into subjecthood (2008: 179). This pro-cess aligns with a recent tradition of writers, theorists and critics rethinking black agency at the level of the noun. Two recent examples are particularly pertinent to *White Tears*. In a section of *Olio* titled 'Mirror of Slavery/Mirror Chicanery', Jess stages an overwriting of John Berryman's *Dream Songs* in the voice of the real-life musician Henry 'Box' Brown (2016: 71). *Dream Songs* is, of course, notorious for Berryman's employment of the minstrel figure Mr Bones, who regularly speaks to the protagonist Henry in dialect, Berryman performing a form of literary blackface:

Afters eight years, be less dan eight percent,
distinguish' friend, of coloured wif de whites
in de School, in de Souf. (2014: 67)

In *Olio*, Jess renames *Dream Songs* as 'Freedsongs', reconstructing the poems and overwriting them in the voice of the long deceased, never recorded Brown to narrate his escape from slavery, with Jess acting as medium (2016: 74). Crucially, this involves changing the linguistic function of the word 'blues' from noun to verb; Jess and Brown 'blues' the blackface of Berryman's poems, reinscribing the details of Brown's life over Berryman's minstrel songs. To blues, then, is to flip the nouning of African American objecthood into the verbing of active agency, to free the ghost hidden within the noun. This also occurs in Sharpe's use of 'wake': 'we join the wake with work in order that we might make the wake and *wake work* our analytic, we might continue to imagine new ways to live in the wake of slavery, in slavery's afterlives, to survive (and more) the afterlife of property. In short, I mean wake work to be a mode of inhabiting *and* rupturing this episteme with our known lived and un/imaginable lives' (2016: 18, emphasis in original).

Making the wake work also implicitly unlocks the meaning 'to wake', and perhaps also the past/present tension inherent in 'woke'. Again, the word's transition from noun to verb signals a shift from objecthood to agency. It is no coincidence that Sharpe goes on to use the language of both inhabitation and rupture to describe this moment, which requires the same resituating of both subject position and linearity common to Gordon, Jess and Kunzru. For the ghost to re-emerge the situation requires a dramatic change, a schism in time and personhood, that something-to-be-done that allows the spectral voice to speak on its own terms. In Kunzru's novel, the inhabitation afforded by the verbing of objects is Shaw's possession of Seth's body. When using 'reverb' in the studio, Seth says that time will 'reverse its flow'; a reverbing of the noun in *White Tears* allows Shaw the agency to terrify and direct Seth into an empathetic approximation of his own horrifying experiences (*WT*: 26). The principal verbing that occurs in *White Tears* is, I would suggest, that of the word 'spook'. If Marriott's description of the noun involves the black subject suffering dissolution, of being devoured by the world of white supremacy, then Shaw's ghost verbs 'spook' into the act of terror. As with Jess, bluesing here becomes an overwriting of whiteness, but Kunzru places a specific emphasis on fear as a governing principle of African American subjugation. In Shaw's life story, he is not only dissolved (he is 'thrown into silence and darkness', never to be recorded) but terrorised, subject to the full violence of the racist American carceral system under Jim Crow

(*WT*: 255). Captain Jack, the prison riding boss later namechecked in 'Graveyard Blues', carries out random acts of violence and murder to instil terror into the convicts. As his companions are killed apparently on a whim, Shaw is left to 'squeeze [his] eyes tight, hoping they don't come for me'; inevitably, they do (*WT*: 257). After his death, Shaw's re-emergence into the world is bound up with the infliction of that daily terror of violence, that spooking, on those who have inadvertently summoned him.

To understand the nature of Shaw's spooking, it is worth returning to a pivotal moment in *Black Skin, White Masks* (1952) where Fanon recounts a traumatising encounter with a young boy and his mother. The child, clearly inculcated to be terrified of Fanon, unleashes a stream of racial invective, culminating in the fear that Fanon is going to 'eat me up' (2008: 86). Marriott sees this racist terror not only as 'the child's fantasy of being devoured that attaches itself to a fear of blackness' but also, conversely, as an instance of the black subject's fear of 'being taken over by a racial imago – of being intruded upon, displaced, and fixated by an imaginary double [...] of having a phantom unconscious which appears to hate you' (2007: 211; 208). This scenario, which illustrates the two-way ontological terror on which racism thrives, is inverted by Kunzru in *White Tears*. Instead, it is *Seth* who is taken over by a hateful phantom unconscious, Seth who is made to suffer the constant terror of being displaced by an image of himself that he cannot control. When wrongly arrested by the police, one officer calls Seth a racial epithet, to which he responds, in vain, 'I did not hear that. I am not that' (*WT*: 206). Of course, it does not matter what Seth thinks or says, because the racial imago, like that experienced by Fanon in his encounter with the child, is inscribed on the self from an outside system. This is not the only element of Fanon's experience that Kunzru inverts. The white fear of being devoured finds its analogue in *White Tears* through Shaw's stage name, Wolfmouth, which indicates a predatorial appetite. However, when Shaw attacks Seth the process of devouring is reversed:

> Then he stuffed his hands into my mouth, pulling my jaws wide open, then wider still, until I was in excruciating pain. I tried to scream but I could not, and he stretched my jaws until they cracked, the top and bottom hanging a whole hands-width apart. [...] He pulled ever wider until he was able to fit, first one patent-leather pump, then

a knee, then a second shoe and a second knee into my mouth, and finally it was the work of a moment to climb inside entirely and disappear down my gullet like an eel down a chute. My jaws snapped back in place. Now I was the horse and he was the rider (*WT*: 249)

Seth's forced swallowing of Shaw, which results in the novel's bloody climax where the possessed Seth murders the owners of the Walxr prison group, enacts the displacement by a racial imago so feared by Fanon, but switches it to a white subject. The subsequent depiction of the murders themselves are overwritten by 'The Laughing Song', the mysterious B-side of 'Graveyard Blues' which consists entirely of the words 'ha ha ha ha' repeated for nearly four full pages and is 'the most terrifying sound' Shaw has ever heard (*WT*: 264–267). 'The Laughing Song' is the convergence and culmination of the themes of music and ghostliness in *White Tears*. For four pages, Shaw's music and voice take control of the white page, his repeating laughter a weaponised iteration of those echoes of the afterlives of slavery, bluesing and spooking in a moment of murderous, terrifying dominance, the refrain circling, rondo-like, around again and again, a ghostly record rupturing the objecthood of a 78 that may never have existed, bringing the subject out into the world for his revenge.

Conclusion

The closing chapter of *White Tears* takes place in prison, where Seth is incarcerated for the murders. In an ontologically unstable voice that moves between first and second person, he speaks of his newfound belief that 'there is no clear border between life and non-life' as he has four tears tattooed on his face by another prisoner, one for each person who has died as a result of his actions; the motor on the tattooist's needle is 'powered by a motor from an old CD player' (*WT*: 270; 271). This climactic image of a musical device inscribing black tears onto white skin suggests that the suffering courted by Seth has, finally, penetrated his flesh. Seth finds himself incarcerated like Shaw, abused by the white prisoners he will not join with in a show of racist solidarity, becoming the 'lowest of the low' (*WT*: 271). The grimly ironic *coup de grâce* with which the novel ends is Seth's final attainment of the authenticity he sought through the appropriation of 'the sound of the middle passage' (*WT*: 271). The implicit note in this coda is that Seth's initial perception of authenticity was a misreading, a failure to understand; these records instead embody a living, haunting echo of suffering and injustices that, while they deserve to be remembered, no one should wish to attain.

Note

1 We might also think here of the famous chapter from Toni Morrison's *Beloved* in which the young girl in the middle passage recounts her harrowing experiences in a dissonant series of echoes and recurrent images (1988: 248).

References

Berryman, John (2014). *77 Dream Songs* (New York: Farrar, Straus and Giroux).

Du Bois, W.E.B. (2007). *The Souls of Black Folk* (Oxford: Oxford University Press).

Fanon, Frantz (2008). *Black Skin, White Masks* (London: Pluto Press).

Gordon, Avery (2008). *Ghostly Matters: Haunting and the Sociological Imagination* (Minneapolis: University of Minnesota).

Hartman, Saidiya (2008). *Lose Your Mother: A Journey Along the Atlantic Slave Route* (New York: Farrar, Straus and Giroux).

Jess, Tyehimba (2016). *Olio* (Seattle & New York: Wave Books).

Mackey, Nathaniel (2002). *Splay Anthem* (New York: New Directions).

Marriott, David (2007). *Haunted Life: Visual Culture and Black Modernity* (New Brunswick, NJ: Rutgers University Press).

Morrison, Toni (1988). *Beloved* (London: Picador).

Moten, Fred and Harney, Stefano (2013). *The Undercommons: Fugitive Planning and Black Study* (New York: Minor Compositions).

Petrusich, Amanda (2014). *Do Not Sell at Any Price: The Wild, Obsessive Hunt for the World's Rarest 78rpm Records.* (New York: Scribner).

Philip, M. NourbeSe (2020). *Zong!* (London: Silver Press).

Sharpe, Christina (2016). *In The Wake: On Blackness and Being* (Durham, NC: Duke University Press).

Warren, Calvin L. (2018). *Ontological Terror: Blackness, Nihilism and Emancipation* (Durham, NC: Duke University Press).

Yusoff, Kathryn (2018). *A Billion Black Anthropocenes or None* (Minneapolis: University of Minnesota, 2018).

8

'Food for the wolves': the rise of the alt-right in *Red Pill*

Kristian Shaw

The political events of 2016 brought debates surrounding nationalism and cosmopolitanism (and their apparent contradictions) firmly to the fore as academics and cultural commentators attempted to account for Brexit and the unexpected electoral success of Donald Trump. Hari Kunzru's *Red Pill*, published in 2020, gestures to these alarming political developments across Western societies, articulating the ways in which the internet and memetic discourses played a significant role in the run-up to the 2016 US presidential election. Drawing on a personal interview with Hari Kunzru, this chapter will reveal how the semi-autobiographical elements of *Red Pill* reflect his fervent critique of the contemporary political moment; more specifically, the novel captures Kunzru's own experiences during his research on far-right message boards – which became the drivers of alt-right content – where sincerity and empathy fail to register in hyper-ironic online environments of mockery and trolling. Interrogating the political consequences of these cultural shifts, the chapter will also detail how *Red Pill* calls subtle attention to the sharp rise in xenophobic resistance to immigration following the Syrian refugee crisis; a development which proved to be a fertile breeding ground for the spread of far-right ethno-nationalism, as evidenced in Trump's electoral victory, the fateful event towards which the narrative inexorably tends. Such a reading reinforces a broader commentary on Kunzru's earlier body of work, advancing his authorial curiosity with the haunting signifiers of race, the politics of which scar the historical legacy, and contemporary horizon, of the United States.

The detached cosmopolitan

The novel's unnamed protagonist, an independent scholar, leaves his wife and child in Brooklyn to begin a three-month writing residency at the Deuter Center for Social and Cultural Research in Wannsee near Berlin.[1] The Center, located near the venue of the 1942 Wannsee Conference where the "Final Solution to the Jewish Question" was planned, is named after a post-war industrial chemist famous for developing titanium dioxide, a pigment known for its bright white colour and ability to reflect light into dark spaces. Whiteness, and the historical impulse to cosmetically whitewash tenebrous histories, haunt the narrative from the outset. Deuter, the narrator notes, possessed 'a utopian streak', dedicated to fostering 'the full potential of the individual human spirit' (*RP*: 10) and promoting a Stoic commitment to openness and transparency. Serving as a 'microcosm of the wider public sphere', its scholars are expected to contribute to 'the development of their own communal space [...] pooling their thoughts in the public labour of scholarship' (*RP*: 24). The institute thus functions as a Habermasian discursive space in which academics and intellectuals can discuss critical and cultural theories across interdisciplinary divides – a micro-community markedly at odds with the cultural division being played out on a national level. On arriving at the Center, however, the narrator slowly perceives the values of the Center to be a front for data retention and panoptic surveillance, monitoring the websites academics visit and the amount of time they spend in workstations, with any shortfall in communal association or measurable outputs resulting in a stipend deduction. Despite being dependent on his prestigious fellowship, the protagonist rejects the Communal Workplace, describing the thought of human engagement as 'horrifying' and exhibiting disdain for the 'need for full participation' (*RP*: 39; 79). Attempts by management to convince the narrator that he is working alongside his academic colleagues, contributing to 'part of a common project, a man taking resolute communicative action', fail, and he finds he cannot align his research with the Center's plans for the 'future development of a transparent public sphere' (*RP*: 54; 60).

The creative Communal Workplace has the opposite effect on his productivity, forcing him to retreat to his isolated room and private thoughts, being accused of a lack of mutuality by both his fellow academics and the institute (echoing the fate of Arjun in Kunzru's earlier novel *Transmission*). The combative, right-wing, Jordan Peterson-esque Edgar, who goes on to write a book on the dangers of social liberal thought, 'Wrongthink: The Authoritarian Left and the New Religion of Social Justice', suggests this supposed right to privacy 'was no more or less than the right to lie. To misrepresent yourself to the world. It incubated fraud and corruption' (*RP*: 98). Meditating on Edgar's harsh appraisal, the narrator comes to view his research project on the construction of the lyrical self, which initially sets out to provide a 'definitive case for the revolutionary potential of the arts', to have become little more than an argument with himself, standing for 'some wider problem that I was having' (*RP*: 11; 17). Harbouring anxieties about the forthcoming US presidential election, and isolated on a campus which draws a veil over disquieting histories – functioning as a 'precise objective correlative of my emotional state' – the narrator begins to question his liberal humanist values: 'if the world changed, would I be able to protect my family?' (*RP*: 8; 6). His partner Rei's confident faith in the US election polls, and reassurance that 'We're smart people. If it comes, we'll see it coming' (*RP*: 75), foreshadows the events of November 2016 and proves to be a key instance of liberal complacency, as the narrator's fears regarding the spread of authoritarian populism across the world are proven to be well founded. Indeed, in contrast to Rei, a human rights lawyer for a non-profit, who retains a faith in the 'essential reasonableness of the world', the narrator recognises the forthcoming presidential election to be only one small component of a more widespread political movement troubling his consciousness, acknowledging that 'the rising tide of gangsterism felt global' (*RP*: 75). This incessant liberal self-flagellation, questioning whether his independent scholarship and absorption 'in my little projects, my lofty thoughts and scribblings' (*RP*: 76) neglects real-world problems around him, gestures to an emergent belief in the inability of the academic sphere to actively confront political and cultural developments. As Kunzru puts it, at no point in the novel does the narrator 'think of himself in relation to others. It's always about this interior set of resources. He's a real liberal in that strict sense, one who can't imagine being in relation to others' (qtd. in Day, 2020).

Locked away in his claustrophobic room, the narrator becomes obsessed with a violent US cop show, *Blue Lives*; the title gestures to the countermovement which emerged in response to Black Lives Matter and aimed to draw attention to the damaging violence committed against police officers as opposed to the effects of police brutality. *Blue Lives* captures the public's demand for emotional narratives which manufacture and exacerbate divides between rival parties, reflected in the theatrical histrionics of the 2016 US presidential campaign. Kunzru's narrator realises *Blue Lives*' sadistic and aggressive cop, antihero Carson, espouses counter-Enlightenment philosophies predicated on a destructive nihilism and quotes liberally from the works of French philosopher Joseph de Maistre, who opined that any rational justification of government would result in violence and chaos. In alluding to right-wing fascism's intellectual history, Kunzru hints that the novel, like his performative television show *Blue Lives*, contains 'a subtext smuggled into the familiar procedural narrative' (*RP*: 70). Kunzru states, 'I wanted [the narrator] to have this contact with this very specific German Romantic tradition, because I see that playing out on the alt-right and I see the attractiveness of a certain vision of the noble outsider, the man apart from the world'; the narrator's initial challenge to his privacy is then supplanted by this 'more profound challenge that comes with his discovery that what he considers unquestionable is absolutely questioned all around him and is becoming a part of the social world, the political world' (qtd. in Shaw, Chapter 9 in this volume). Yet the question remains: how does Kunzru's seemingly superfluous interrogation of personal privacy and academic detachment connect to the historical echoes of totalitarianism or relate to the novel's broader commentary on contemporary US politics? The answer lies in the formal structure of the novel. Kunzru fractures his autodiegetic narrative by integrating a short chapter entitled *Zersetzing* (Undermining) – taken from a form of psychological warfare employed by the German Stasi – a development of his short story 'A Transparent Woman' published in *The New Yorker* in June 2020.

Inspired by time spent in East Berlin, *Zersetzing* details the narrator's brief acquaintanceship with Monika, a cleaner at the Deuter Center, as she documents the coercion and exploitation of her earlier years, forced to become an informer for the Stasi in 1980s East Berlin. Speaking on his decision to utilise Monika's account as the central 'wedge' of his novel, rupturing the autodiegetic flow, Kunzru concedes 'some readers will experience this "story within a story" as a distraction, or criticize it as a rupture in the formal unity of the book' by dragging the reader away from his protagonist's oppressive inner torment; however, 'even though it's only indirectly related to the travails of my narrator, it feels absolutely central to what I'm trying to do' (qtd. in Treisman, 2020). As Kunzru goes on to explain, the short story enables him 'to use the past as a way to illuminate the present', developing the sense that 'one's own life is the product of longer-time scales, larger systems', creating clear parallels with the current political moment and delivering a cautionary tale on the dangers of corroding public trust. *Zersetzing* may disrupt and disturb the narrative, but the short interference simultaneously illustrates the significance of historical inheritance to global developments and is crucial to understanding the wider organising logics underpinning the narrative. Though the development of historical parallels between post-war Germany and twenty-first-century American society may seem a tenuous narrative thread, Kunzru affirms that the lingering impulses of totalitarianism continue to infect the present: 'Americans have learned that, even without the Communist Party or the Stasi, freedom can still slip away', with 'far more pervasive forms of surveillance and control' (qtd. in Treisman, 2020) emerging under capitalist democracies. Written in the first person, Kunzru's fictionalised account also functions as an intimate link between the erosion of political freedom and the narrator's own questioning of selfhood – an enduring theme in Kunzru's body of work. Yet the narrator fails to understand the warning in Monika's life story and hurtles towards his own destruction, becoming consumed with the actions of *Blue Lives'* creator, Gary Bridgeman, who goes by the pseudonym Anton (alluding to the *anonymous* nature of online activity which will shape later developments in the narrative). Anton soon undermines the narrator in a related, if far less dangerous, manner than those under Stasi control.

The American sublime

In a bizarre chance encounter, the narrator meets Anton at a party in Berlin and confronts him with the charge of racism for mocking the multicultural diversity of Berlin, a city 'polluted by immigrants' (*RP*: 174). Anton's swift dismissal of the narrator as a naïve liberal protected within his academic bubble, claiming his ineffectual shame tactics no longer hold any power, establishes an adversarial dynamic that will define subsequent events of the narrative. Seemingly drawing on ideas advanced by Oswald Spengler and Friedrich Nietzsche, Anton takes pleasure in bathing in liberal tears and believes himself to be engaged in a civilisational struggle against the multicultural agenda of intellectual elites and the liberal system in his efforts to form a white ethnostate, a Herrenvolk democracy to counter demographic change. Kunzru therefore aligns his fictional antagonist with the alt-right, a far-right movement grounded in internet activism which wages a culture war against liberal orthodoxy, identity politics and globalism; the term has since become a catch-all for white supremacists, paleoconservatives and libertarians disillusioned with multiculturalism, political correctness and the political establishment. However, the alt-right proves to be a mercurial organisation that resists easy definition, enjoying its own vernacular and iconography. In George Hawley's study of the movement's origins, evolution and methods, he acknowledges that its precise genealogy is difficult to locate given its similarities with older, far-right white nationalist movements, but 'should be treated as an entirely new phenomenon' on the basis of its 'atomized, amorphous [...] and mostly anonymous' (2017: 50; 3) nature on blogs, forums and message boards. The movement rallied behind Donald Trump during his presidential campaign, while Trump, in kind, brought alt-right strategist Steve Bannon on board as a member of his political staff, creating a symbiotic relationship that strengthened and energised both parties in the process. Like Trump, the alt-right attracted attention and visibility through provocations and sensationalism, relying on similar rhetorical manoeuvres to convey they shared the concerns of conversative voters. As a result, the oppositional rhetoric of the alt-right tapped into a wider discontent with the state of the union – exploiting a moment of political instability – and proved seductive to disenfranchised voters across the nation. The alt-right is, of course, simply a resurrection and rebranding of age-old racisms and forms of authoritarianism, the historical echoes of which continue to reverberate in the present. Despite attempts by the alt-right to achieve an air of legitimacy by cloaking its ideology under more intellectualised formations, strategically distancing their nationalist rhetoric from racially coded discourse and articulating the merits of patriotic duty, Stephanie Hartzell argues 'white nationalism is white supremacy and efforts to downplay this interconnection are part and parcel of white supremacist rhetorical strategy' (2020: 143).

As Angela Nagle notes, the alt-right is preoccupied with 'European demographic and civilisational decline' and considers academic culture and 'cultural Marxism' (2017: 12) to be destructive stimuli in weakening Western societies. Attacking detached Habermasian spaces such as the Deuter Center, Anton asserts the 'so-called morality' of liberal ideology is just 'paralysis [...] they'd delegated their power of action to others, men who weren't frozen rabbits, who could do what needed to be done' (*RP*: 170), betraying early warning signs of his alt-right nationalist credentials.[2] Appropriately, the chance encounter, rather than being a tenuous narrative thread, highlights that alt-right harassment often 'occurs spontaneously rather than as the result of a preconceived plan'; scholars and journalists who attempt to make contact and understand the movement simply receive 'dishonest (or just baffling) answers' (Hawley, 2017: 88; 4). Anton's attack on cultural Marxism in particular is rather revealing (given the attendant anti-Semitic undertones in his rhetoric), as the alt-right position cultural Marxist beliefs as part of a conspiracy against Western societies and their values, believing media outlets and academia to be encouraging this liberal propaganda. For Kunzru, this oppositional dynamic characterises the current political divide, concerning the struggle between cosmopolitan human rights and a nihilistic disregard for the machinations of power. The 2016 US presidential campaign became 'a contest not so much of ideologies as realities, duelling world-pictures that rely on different sources of information' (Kunzru, 2020b). Anton's calm and measured responses to the narrator's incensed outbursts is a productive political tactic employed by the alt-right that Hawley terms 'highbrow white nationalism' (2017: 26); this discursive strategy eschews the racist vitriol and violent attacks associated with white supremacist groups in favour of academic discussion and an intellectual tone in order to insinuate ethonationalist dogma back into political debates, concealing white supremacy under the slightly more seemly guise of white nationalism.

Anton accuses the narrator of nurturing a vague and ineffectual cosmopolitan outlook: an abstract universalism based on thin commitments to global others. His moral posturing is not followed by active cosmopolitan engagement, equating to solidarity at a distance. Taking Anton's attack on his *gestural* cosmopolitanism to heart – 'you have a sentimental wish to help other people far away, nice abstract refugees who save you from having to commit to anybody or anything real' (*RP*: 176) – the narrator determines to prove the practical application of his ethico-political outlook. After all, not only did the narrator apply to the Deuter Center to avoid 'being burdened by the practical aspects of daily existence', but the timeframe of the novel coincides with the Syrian refugee crisis, strengthening Anton's assault on recent changes to European demographics: 'It was the year they all came, more than a million refugees crossing Europe, massing at fences, drowning in the Mediterranean, hunted by vigilantes in the Bulgarian woods' (*RP*: 11; 155). His attempt to form an authentic connection with a refugee and his daughter, grasping for 'a small act of charity in a fallen world' that will alleviate the suffering of the 'global poor' (*RP*: 190), fails, as he is reduced to offering money in the absence of any other tangible offering. In the process, he is mistakenly believed to be soliciting the refugee to sell his daughter and ejected from the secure facility.

For the narrator, the fate of the nameless refugee communicates his own potential alienation when confronted with the ethnonationalism of the alt-right, perceiving in 'the freemasonry of dark-skinned men who meet in white places' (*RP*: 156) the solidarities required to endure xenophobic hatred. Anton's desire to retreat into an ethno-nationalist stance articulates Eric Kaufmann's (2018) notion of 'whiteshift', the fear held by far-right factions that rising immigration levels and demographic changes threaten the primacy of white majorities – who are being replaced by a non-white population – and erode the cultural imaginaries of Western societies. It is worth noting (given the European setting of the novel) that 'whiteshift' also gained purchase across Europe, particularly in France, where far-right politician Éric Zemmour rejuvenated and propagated Renaud Camus's 'great replacement theory' in response to unwanted mass migration and demographic growth. As Paul Gilroy reminds us, a retreat to the securities of 'racial hierarchy' and nationhood equates to a 'defensive gesture' and operates as a 'stabilizing force' in the face of cultural change (2005: 6). White resentment, then, became the channel through which alt-right discursive narratives could flow. In advocating for an entrepreneurial capitalism and aggressive ethno-nationalism at odds with the narrator's liberal traditions, Anton promotes a form of 'neo-illiberalism' (Hendrikse, 2018) grounded in authoritarian and fascistic tendencies, seeking to destabilise the seemingly liberal institutional structures of the media and academia. Emotive economic threats such as job scarcity can thus be framed as the direct result of immigration and changing demographics; accordingly, the incitement of nativist impulses by the alt-right – such as the 'cruel tribalism' cultivated by Anton which dispenses with 'public politics altogether' in favour of 'the raw exercise of power' (*RP*: 226; 227) and decries liberal attitudes that undermine European civilisation – resonates within various subcultures, reaching broader publics, and unites disparate factions under the same amorphous umbrella. His anti-cosmopolitan agenda, then, becomes a form of discursive empowerment with both his television show and his political stance a means of ridiculing what he perceives to be the floundering cosmopolitics of Western societies.

Whilst walking in Berlin, the narrator recognises this potent capacity of immigration as an emotive and divisive political resource; following Angela Merkel's decision to provide aid to Syrian refugees crossing the Mediterranean, the city is littered with 'stickers with English slogans: Refugees Welcome No Borders [...] Wievel ist zuviel? "How many is too many?"' (*RP*: 154–155). Perceiving in Anton's 'Euroskeptic' sentiments a more general resistance to Merkel's belief in the need for pooled sovereignty and open borders, he realises the nationalist tendencies of the alt-right are part of a wider global trend against cosmopolitan hospitality: '*Europe en danger*. These things were clues, signs of the new dispensation' (*RP*: 214; 203, italics in original).[3] After all, the alt-right's vision of what can be termed the *American sublime* excludes fresh waves of migrants and refugees from the national vision in an effort to resist the cultural heterogeneities of the inferior present, maintain faith in a nativist myth of ethnic unity, and cling to the unchecked entrepreneurism of the American dream. A form of analogical thinking emerges in which historical ideologies are resuscitated in the present while contemporary developments are perceived in terms of their relation to the more idyllic past. As Neal Curtis writes, 'the belligerent nationalism of the radical right [...] has its own form of temporal politics that seeks to tie the future to a reanimated myth of past strength, unity and supremacy. Against these attempts to close off the future in favour of the present and the past' (2020: 165). Trump's divisive language during his election campaign, incessantly repeating his 'Make America Great Again' slogan, tapped into a nostalgia for a past untainted by the politics of progress, with a reductive homogenisation of the body politic positioned as a legitimate step in recovering the nation's sacred (if fallacious) politico-historical consciousness and rewriting white power back into the national narrative. Kunzru's attempt to tie the alt-right to more historical manifestations of fascism is, therefore, understandable, as the politics of the Alt-Right equates to 'a politics of the dead, the dying and the decadent – representing every conceivable regressive ideology from colonialism to eugenics, patriarchy to pollution' (Curtis, 2020: 178). David Neiwert touches upon a related idea in his projection of an 'Alt-America', which he defines as 'an alternative universe that has a powerful resemblance to our own, except that it's a completely different America, the nation its residents have concocted and reconfigured in their imaginations' (2017: 33). The eliminationist rhetoric and atavistic nativism of a projected Alt-America thus poses a direct threat to democratic institutions and the public sphere. As Kunzru (2020) rather appropriately notes, white nationalist message boards during the 2016 US presidential campaign 'felt like an alternate reality, one where a Donald Trump presidency was not only possible but inevitable'.

The narrator's failure to deliver a *mot juste* to refute Anton's claims haunts his daily work; although he remains unpersuaded by Anton's perception of political culture, failing to undergo any radical conversion process and remaining within his academic echo chamber, he begins to question his unquestioning defence of cosmopolitan ideals. As David Hollinger (2002) reminds us, while older universalist conceptions of cosmopolitanism adhere to a normative ideal – involving an overriding loyalty to humanity as a whole – newer, more pragmatic cosmopolitanism(s) are required to address and reconcile the synergy of local and global processes and the need for politically viable engagement rather than an empty solidarity with global others; in other words, making cosmopolitanism a practical – rather than simply theoretical or intellectual – endeavour, in order to 'bring cosmopolitanism down to earth, to indicate that cosmopolitanism can deliver some of the goods ostensibly provided by patriots, provincials, parochials, populists, tribalists, and above all nationalists' (Hollinger, 2002: 229). As the securities of the postwar period are slowly eroded in the twenty-first century, while the drivers of political nationalism take on new and insidious forms, Kunzru forces his fictional mouthpiece to re-evaluate the significance of why these steps were taken. Following his encounter with Anton, the narrator asks his wife, plainly and straightforwardly, 'Why do you believe in human rights?' (*RP*: 198), questioning the very foundations of his liberal worldview.

Due to the atavistic and nihilistic philosophies at the heart of *Blue Lives*, he begins to worry that the show is a performative gateway drug for the alt-right – a red pill designed to inculcate nationalist ideologies in the minds of the electorate – representing a personal threat to his family, political beliefs and way of life. Kunzru acknowledges the novel's title comes from Lana and Lilly Wachowski's seminal 1999 science fiction film, *The Matrix*, in which the hacker protagonist Thomas Anderson, operating under the alias Neo, is offered two pills. While the blue pill will allow him to continue living in blissful ignorance of the underlying systems governing reality, the red pill holds the potential to reveal the 'true' version of reality. Anton thus appears as an anarchic figure in the vein of Chuck Palahniuk's Tyler Durden, attempting to wake the narrator from his liberal dreaming. Nagle notes that the notion of being 'Red Pilled' took root on 4chan subforums, with the alt-right using the metaphor to describe a 'racial awakening' from 'the mind-prison of liberalism' (2017: 88). For the alt-right, most Americans 'live in a fantasy world, believing myths propagated by progressives. But a person who takes the red pill is suddenly aware of purported biological racial differences, problems associated with racial diversity, and various conspiracy theories about Jewish subversion'

(Hawley, 2017: 83). Indeed, the deployment of the red pill metaphor is situated in the narrator's epiphanic acknowledgement that many of his fellow citizens perceive a very different reality, one in which liberal cosmopolitan ideology is to blame for many current ills. His subsequent breakdown reflects this epiphany, as the slow haemorrhaging of private anxieties into the public sphere gestures to Kunzru's broader commentary on the creeping influence of far-right ideologies in contemporary politics.

Anton's success in seeping into the narrator's consciousness is also indicative of the astonishing success of the alt-right in disseminating their ideas and ideologies without the support of mainstream bodies. Moreover, the narrator's inability to disregard his provocations – and focus instead on his own research – anticipates the failure of US mainstream media to ignore the antagonistic behaviour of the alt-right and, instead, inadvertently perpetuate the circulation of racist discourses in efforts to discredit such notions. The denunciation of the alt-right by Hillary Clinton reinforced and legitimised this propagation of xenophobic material, invigorating the alt-right, and created a feedback loop that reshaped the 2016 election. Clinton positioned the alt-right as the enemy, legitimising them as the natural opposition to her liberal institutional ideology.[4] Under this reading, the alt-right was an online monster provided with a more stable offline platform by the misguided, if well-intentioned, actions of the democratic mainstream. In taunting the narrator at his workplace – spouting mystical ethno-nationalist beliefs concerning the 'shared destiny of northern Europeans' (*RP*: 181) that serve as the antithesis to the Deuter Center's enlightened liberal philosophy – Anton as an adversarial presence thus embodies the antagonism of the alt-right, his ideological struggle with the narrator representative of a wider political opposition between the regressive, xenophobic nationalism of alt-right agitators and the ineffectual gestural cosmopolitanism of centre-left progressives. Moreover, Anton's successful strategy draws attention to the ways by which voices of intellectuals and specialists slowly lost ground to populist thinkers or ordinary citizens during 2016 as voters embraced a movement away from measured, political responses in favour of passionate rhetoric and emotive storytelling. According to Kunzru, post-truth narratives are a political threat precisely because they 'bring forth all sorts of possibilities for totalitarianism. Fundamentally, there's a big move beyond democratic politics or against democratic politics coming from the right [...] who want to dispense with the public sphere altogether' (qtd. in Shaw, Chapter 9 in this volume). The alt-right certainly dismantle Al Gore's contention that the Internet 'is perhaps the greatest source of hope for reestablishing an open communications environment in which the conversation of democracy can flourish' (2007: 260). Greater global awareness does not result in a solidarity by connectivity; rather, the racial logics of white supremacy assume new forms in the digital domain.[5]

Shadows of the future

After the narrator is expelled from the Center for his increasingly unstable behaviour, he decides to follow Anton to his Paris film screening and expose the fascist nihilism at the core of *Blue Lives*. His irrational ranting at the screening leads to the narrator becoming a victim of online trolling and 'doxxing' – a vicious process of intimidation and shaming via the release of personal information online – in a systematic campaign of psychological cyberwarfare to discredit and devalue his academic standing and liberal worldview. It is from this point in the narrative that Kunzru documents how the online power of the alt-right bleeds into the public domain and shapes real-world discursive exchanges, with 'the occult power of their content leaking out into the offline world' (*RP*: 279). First, the narrator finds his own photo, taken at the Paris screening, utilised for a disparaging social justice warrior meme. In *Make America Meme Again* (2020), an investigation into the digital rhetorics of the alt-right, Heather Suzanne Woods and Leslie A. Hahner document how the movement weaponised memes as a strategic means of garnering support for Trump on online forums and eliciting outraged responses from liberal quarters. Memes, which they define as 'concepts and images that spread virally across culture, largely through social media platforms' (2020: 2), are proven to have a surprising suasory power in shaping public perceptions of key political issues and weakening processes of democratic deliberation. Co-opting the rhetorical and conceptual tactics of *détournement* from the Situationists, the alt-right deploy humour, hyper-irony and absurdism in their memetic discourses to conceal their racist

agenda and appeal to sympathetic mainstream audiences.[6] The proliferation and dissemination of memes is a form of trolling itself,
also known as 'lulz' (a corrupted form of 'lol' – laugh out loud –
meaning to derive pleasure from someone else's pain or distress). In
an article for *The New York Review of Books* in March 2020, 'For
the Lulz', Kunzru explains how memes are motivated by their 'lulz'
value – describing Anton as a 'human shitpost' who embodies the
worst aspects of alt-right digital excess and cyber trolling. Hawley
argues the alt-right 'injected itself into the national conversation
when it mastered the art of trolling', sowing discord online often
without any political purpose: 'a troll may be looking for nothing
but a moment of nihilistic amusement' (2017: 19; 20). Anton
seemingly subscribes to troll behaviour, advancing claims so incen-
diary and offensive that the narrator cannot help but become emo-
tionally invested in attempting to forge a dialogue. Kunzru thus
demonstrates how the online performativity of trolling overlaps
and operates in a dynamic interplay with real life, revealing the
distorted ideology hiding behind the computer screen.

The narrator's previous academic monograph is subsequently
torn apart online, dismissed as a 'mongrel book' negatively
influenced by the 'most degraded type of postmodernism' and cele-
brating a dangerous 'rootless cosmopolitanism' (*RP*: 218) in its critique of Eurocentrism. Scrolling through far-right message boards,
littered with Nazi references and racist caricatures, he concludes
Anton is masterminding an online troll farm dedicated to propagating far-right content. Hiding behind his 'lulz', Anton can deploy
irony and comedy as valid protective shields against charges of
racism, with his pseudonym serving as a secure disguise within the
liberal creative industries of Los Angeles, enabling him to troll in
plain sight of American culture. On a European civilisation reddit
the narrator finds a poster, whom he assumes to be Anton under
another pseudonym, claiming northern Europeans suffer from a
predisposition to cosmopolitan ideals such as openness, hospitality
and mutuality, allowing immigrants to take over Western societies.
The post ends by asserting Western democracy must be 'abandoned
for something more muscular' (*RP*: 216) in a Hobbesian vision
of the near future, a disturbing platformisation of neo-fascism.
Kunzru's authorial decision to utilise a suburb of Berlin for his creative interrogation of the incipient impact of the far right in US

politics is rather appropriate. According to Hawley, the alt-right draws on the influences and symbolism of the European New Right, sharing their disdain for immigration, political correctness, cosmopolitan ideals and multicultural societies. Indeed, for the American white supremacist and political activist Richard Spencer – who popularised the usage of alt-right as a descriptive term (and on whom Anton seems to be partly based) – the alt-right operates as 'the banner of European white identity politics' (qtd. in Hawley, 2017: 68).

Much like the haunting spectrality of *White Tears*, narrative events and locations within *Red Pill* hover between presence and absence, their clear visibility obscured by the limited and unreliable perspective of the narrator. He takes his Pynchonian paranoia concerning Anton to logical extremes, considering all events to be fateful indicators containing an ominous logic, part of a larger plot designed to further the alt-right cause. The novel contributes to this destabilisation of the self by generating a series of narrative indeterminacies and uncertainties, signals without signification. Those narrative gestures – seemingly carrying some concealed meaning or sinister legibility – which cannot be translated into his interpretative scheme are quickly screened out. There is no final illuminating pattern for the narrator to decipher and fight back against the 'rising tide of gangsterism'; rather, he is locked into a cycle of endless regression and despair. In the process, his research project on the construction of the lyrical self is sidelined as he himself is subject to uncertainty and dispersal in his search for an unlocatable threat. The narrator's inability to write or communicate is reflective of the failure of the centre and left to find the right words to articulate their growing concerns about the right-wing shifts in contemporary US politics. Further, his fruitless quest for meaning and signification is intimately related to the Democratic quest of interpreting emergent, alternative modes of communication fostered and propagated by the alt-right – which serve as an insurgent and subversive counterforce to centre-ground politicking – and negotiating their own limitations in scaffolding the concerns of voters.

It is difficult to ascertain what the narrator hopes to achieve in his pursuit of Anton, other than to discredit his beliefs or hope that Anton will somehow simply abjure his ethno-nationalist tendencies and embrace a liberal mindset. As Kunzru explains, 'Anton's blithe dismissal of the narrator's spluttering indignation' exposes 'a certain complacent high liberalism' which contributes to the proliferation of nativist rhetoric (qtd. in Shaw, Chapter 9 in this volume). In his downward spiral of obsession and declining mental health, the narrator stalks Anton to an island off the west coast of Scotland, mistakenly expecting to locate him in a ramshackle bothy used for one of his film screenings, but instead finds himself isolated and even further ensnared within Anton's supposed matrix. And yet, the unoccupied bothy also gestures to the nihilistic ethos at the heart of Anton's ethno-nationalist project: an ultimately empty ideological structure which relies on white mysticism and outdated nativist rhetoric to distract attention from the post-truth posturing. Though Kunzru affirms the race of the narrator is not a catalyst for Anton's trolling, the narrative articulates the ways in which harassment disproportionately affects people of colour; by attempting to hunt down Anton, the narrator believes himself to be confronting a destructive manifestation of *whiteness*, the historical echoes of which continue to shape the contemporary moment. As Whitney Phillips notes, the online digital behaviour of trolls certainly amplifies public debates, but they 'are born of and fueled by the mainstream world – its behavioural mores, its corporate institutions, its political structures and leaders' (2015: 169). The rambling incoherence and abject terror of the narrator closes 'An Apocalypse'; his misguided belief that all global crises are integrant offshoots of Anton's regressive ethno-political project details the extent to which the narrator increasingly conflates the micro and the macro in the 'universalization of [his] own panic' (*RP*: 226) concerning the forthcoming presidential election.

While *Red Pill* contains echoes of 1970s systems novels such as Don DeLillo's *Running Dog* (1978) and Thomas Pynchon's *Gravity's Rainbow* (1973), the novel is more than an exercise in collage. The final section of the novel, 'Home', presents a more stable reliable narrative voice, explaining the chain of events during the narrator's disappearance to his time spent in a Glaswegian psychiatric hospital to correct his manic episodes. The narrator begins to adjust to the familiar rhythms of domestic life, but his return simply marks the traumatic continuation of his cultural anxieties 'clothing themselves in flesh' (*RP*: 278) as the centre ground falls away beneath him. Though his therapist dismisses Anton as merely a small-time screenwriter incapable of wielding such cultural power, she fails to perceive how memetic discourses operate through dynamic and unpredictable informational flows that contravene the traditional linear dissemination of political content: 'the internet had changed things. There were underground currents, news modes of propagation. It wasn't even a question of ideas, not straightforwardly, but feelings, atmospheres, yearnings, threats' (*RP*: 267). From this perspective, the narrator's displaced cultural anxiety surrounding the US presidential campaign and wider geopolitical landscape, as well as his breakdown concerning the atavistic future emerging on the horizon and the belief that he is a 'porous barrier' between the decline of social liberalism and the rise of the online alt-right, bears some semblance of rationality: 'my madness, the madness for which I've been medicated and therapised and involuntarily detained, is about to become everyone's madness' (*RP*: 280).

Appropriately, *Red Pill* concludes on Election Night, 8 November 2016, when Donald Trump delivered one of the most shocking upsets in US political history. Kunzru explicitly avoids using Trump's name before election night – his haunting presence in the narrative exacerbated by his absence. Despite the narrator's insistence that for months he has 'been trying, as far as possible, to avoid thinking about this election' (*RP*: 273), his narrative has been a subconscious monologue on that very event. While Rei, who has been involved in organising fundraising events for the Clinton campaign, cultivates a passionate belief in the return to a stable status quo, for the narrator Trump's surprising electoral victory, marking a defining moment when the alt-right's battle to capture 'the hearts and clicks of voters', substantiates his inner fears (Woods and Hahner, 2020: 1). Rei's Brooklynite circle, perceiving Clinton's victory to be a predictable inevitability, are representative of the liberal complacency that characterised the 2016 presidential election, their failure to diagnose symptomatic ailments in the body politic allowing the pseudo-intellectual right to take hold of the national narrative by disseminating emotive disinformation across social media. As Kunzru admits, the narrative allowed him 'to poke a stick at a certain set of New York liberal verities' (Shaw, Chapter 9 in this volume). Clinton's emotionless and elitist campaign, running on the fatuous message of 'Stronger Together' in a moment of political instability and economic crisis, proved vulnerable when faced with Trump's predilection for a grand American narrative that promised a return to past glories and cultural homogeneity, serving as the marginalised alternative to the political establishment.

In their meticulous analysis of the 2016 US presidential election, Pippa Norris and Ronald Inglehart find that the economic grievances of American citizens were driven by conservative citizens with 'authoritarian orientations' (2019: 363) who create clear-cut 'Us' and 'Them' group dynamics when framing their national imaginary. The racist and nativist rhetoric employed by populist leaders, as well as leading cultural commentators such as Anton, allows them to appeal to 'diverse groups with heterogeneous grievances, to communicate messages to unsophisticated publics' (2019: 75). The unnuanced rhetoric of populism and alt-right nativism is suited to social media and extremist social movements in this respect. While populist ideas can exert a positive influence on the political landscape, helping to 'reduce corruption, strengthen responsive governance, expand the issue agenda [...] and reengage participation among groups alienated by mainstream party politics', Norris and Inglehart accentuate that authoritarian populism exploits fears relating to national security and immigration, fostering an inward-looking nativism and paving the way for 'rule by strongmen leaders, social intolerance, and illiberal governance' (2019: 461).

The positioning of Anton as a baleful personification of what Kunzru specifically terms 'whiteness' (*RP*: 260), and the embodied influence of the alt-right on the US Presidential campaign, comes to fruition when the narrator spots him at a Trump victory party surrounded by raucous Republicans in MAGA hats. Kunzru's description of his own reaction to the shocking result, 'a moment of stunned incomprehension at this unprecedented intrusion of the real into the world on the other side of the screen' (2020), reinforces the reading of the narrator as his fictional mouthpiece. As an authoritarian agitator, Anton seemingly subscribes to Trump's desire to 'Make America Great Again' as well as his paranoid conspiracy theories and diagnosis of immigration as the key issue affecting US global dominance and capitalist growth; his fascination with the idea of 'north' connecting with the wider public desire to reclaim a mythical golden past where American society was more ethnically homogeneous and reliant on its Northern European heritage.

If Kunzru's novel tends towards absurdism, it is perhaps indicative of the disjointed state of American political discourse as the nation struggles to reconcile its past politico-historical consciousness, present state of political turmoil and future cultural direction for the twenty-first century.

In a speech following Trump's election victory, Richard Spencer, the president of the white supremacist National Policy Institute, directly cited the practical application of 'meme magic' in dismantling the liberal consensus: 'though we may use these terms half-jokingly, they represent something truly important, the victory of will [...] We willed Donald Trump into office, we made this dream into reality [...] America was, until this last generation, a white country, designed for ourselves and our posterity. It is our creation and our inheritance, and it belongs to us' (Spencer, 2017). Spencer's cries of 'Hail Trump! Hail Our People! Hail Victory!', as audience members gave the Nazi salute in celebration, make it difficult to distance Trump from the nativism of his alt-right standard bearers. The narrator's direct reference to the unexpected power of this 'meme magic' (*RP*: 279) echoes Kunzru's own sentiments on election night, when he observes 'anons' on alt-right forums – the reference to the anonymous mobilisation of online identities a further elucidation of the origins of Anton's name – proclaiming that their 'occult system' had willed Trump's victory into being (Kunzru, 2020). That being said, it would be a mistake to suggest Trump shares the politics of the alt-right, or that the alt-right perceive in Trump the means to their ends. The alt-right merely backed his campaign in the hope his audacious (if popular) political identity would embolden the public to give voice to their concerns surrounding immigration, normalise xenophobic rhetoric and open America's Overton window to allow their nativist ideology to enter the room. The movement serves as a grotesque sideshow to Trump's broader appeal; the temptation for autocracy was already inherent in the system.

Indeed, Milner and Phillips (2016) argue Trump 'tapped into prejudices bigger and older than the internet: hateful racial stereotypes, oppressive gender norms, sweeping anti-elitism, and good old fashioned fear of the other. [...] Online or off, memes emerge when resonant ideas spread within and across social collectives. Factual, objective truth isn't a requisite if [the] underlying idea connects and compels sharing'. From this perspective, it is difficult to perceive the alt-right as a new alternative; rather, they serve as the latest manifestation of white supremacist racial rhetoric that has haunted American history. T.L. Anderson echoes Milner and Phillip's analysis, claiming 'Trump's political ascendance to the White House was not an aberrant phenomenon, nor is the GOP's embracement of the Alt-Right. Both occurrences result as the predictable evolution of using race as a strategy to cultivate and galvanise white resentment for over 50 years, building upon a legacy of exclusion that is centuries old' (2019: 93). The election of Joe Biden on 3 November 2020 may appear as the restoration of the status quo, but America's desire for political storytelling – a grand narrative that gestures to the cultural dominance of the nation's past – continues to haunt the body politic. On 6 January 2021, thousands of Trump supporters attacked the Capitol building in Washington, DC to protest his defeat in the presidential election – a situation exacerbated by Trump's claims that the election was stolen from him as part of a liberal conspiracy. Trump's refusal to condemn white nationalism, advising the neo-fascist Proud Boys to 'stand back and stand by', as if waiting for further instruction, almost seemed an endorsement of racial violence and gave succour to alt-right groups populated by figures such as Anton.

Conclusion

The closing scene of the novel reinforces Kunzru's commentary on the limitations of normative models of universalist cosmopolitanism that fail to confront or resolve the discordant and conflictual cosmopolitics of the contemporary global arena. Whereas, for Anton, 'hospitality is the greatest sin', the narrator resists any red pill awakening by recognising the need for a more pragmatic politics of cultural engagement to confront nativist ideology. Spotting a teenager sporting a hoodie that reads 'We Only Love Family', the protagonist interprets the sentiment to represent 'a retreat from some wider and more expansive kind of love [...] Alone, we are food for the wolves. That's how they want us. Isolated. Prey. So we must find each other. We must remember that we do not exist alone'

(*RP*: 283). His encounter with Anton, then, does serve a progressive function, forcing the narrator to radically reorientate his detached academic perspective around a more engaged, cosmopolitan relational imaginary of solidarity, openness, mutuality and collectivity. In expressing a deep concern over the sudden and violent shifts towards right-wing populism and amplification of nativist rhetoric in Western societies, Kunzru communicates literature's affective capacity to challenge the troubled regressive narratives of our political moment.

Notes

1 The narrative events almost mimic Kunzru's own fellowship at the American Academy in Berlin in 2016.

2 The cover design for *Red Pill* utilises Caspar David Friedrich's *Wanderer Above the Sea of Fog* (1817); Friedrich was a German Romanticist painter praised by the Nazis for attaching nationalist sentiments to landscape paintings.

3 Kaufmann finds far-right attacks on refugee shelters in Germany tripled between 2013 and 2014, before quadrupling in 2015 after the Syrian refugee crisis (2018: 481).

4 Although Anton does not espouse a misogynistic approach in the novel, the alt-right's support of Donald Trump was strengthened by their staunch resistance to Hillary Clinton in particular. The *Red Pill* forum on Reddit is inundated with anti-feminist posts and threads dedicated to ways of stalling the perceived oppression of white males in Western society.

5 As I have argued elsewhere in relation to *Transmission* (Shaw, 2017), Kunzru's early career in journalism, working for *Wired UK*, ensures he is well placed to comment on the myth of digital cosmopolitanism and the means by which the internet – rather than improving forms of commonality, dialogue and exchange – often contributes to societal disjuncture.

6 The narrator recognises a Pepe meme on the IT technician's T-shirt at the Deuter Center – a cartoon frog who gained traction on alt-right forums and became a white nationalist icon for his implied ironic dismissal of societal expectations. Trump would later acknowledge the Pepe meme online, invigorating his alt-right supporters, amplifying division and tying his campaign to claims of white supremacy.

References

Anderson, T.L. (2019). 'Herrenvolk Democracy: The Rise of the Alt-Right in Trump's America', in Christine M. Battista and Melissa R. Sande (eds), *Critical Theory and the Humanities in the Age of the Alt-Right* (Cham: Palgrave Macmillan), 81–99.

Curtis, Neal (2020). 'Countering Idiotism 2.0: "Relational Imaginaries" and Common Futures', *New Zealand Sociology*, 35:2, 165–188.

Day, Meagan (2020). 'Hari Kunzru's Novel *Red Pill* is a Literary Document of the Age of the Alt-Right', *The Wire*, 22 December, https://thewire.in/books/hari-kunzrus-novel-red-pill-is-a-literary-document-of-the-age-of-the-alt-right (accessed 8 August 2022).

Gilroy, Paul (2005). *Postcolonial Melancholia* (New York: Columbia University Press).

Gore, Al (2007). *The Assault on Reason* (New York: Penguin).

Hartzell, Stephanie (2020). 'Whiteness Feels Good Here: Interrogating White Nationalist Rhetoric on Stormfront', *Communication and Critical/Cultural Studies*, 17:2, 129–149.

Hawley, George (2017). *Making Sense of the Alt-Right* (New York: Columbia University Press) .

Hendrikse, Reijer (2018). 'Neo-illiberalism', *Geoforum*, 95, 169–173.

Hollinger, David A. (2002). 'Not Universalists, Not Pluralists: The New Cosmopolitans Find Their Own Way', in Steven Vertovec and Robin Cohen (eds), *Conceiving Cosmopolitanism: Theory, Context, and Practice* (Oxford: Oxford University Press), 227–239.

Kaufmann, Eric (2018). *Whiteshift: Populism, Immigration and the Future of White Majorities* (London: Allen Lane).

Kunzru, Hari (2020). 'For the Lulz', *The New York Review of Books*, 26 March, www.nybooks.com/articles/2020/03/26/trolls-4chan-gamergate-lulz/ (accessed 8 August 2022).

Milner, Ryan and Whitney Phillips (2016). 'Dark Magic: The Memes That Made Donald Trump's Victory', *US Election Analysis 2016: Media, Voters and the Campaign*, www.electionanalysis2016.us/us-election-analysis-2016/section-6-internet/dark-magic-the-memes-that-made-donald-trumps-victory/ (accessed 8 August 2022).

Nagle, Angela (2017). *Kill All Normies: Online Culture Wars from 4chan and Tumblr to Trump and the Alt-Right*. (London: Zero Books).

Neiwert, David (2017). *Alt-America: The Rise of the Radical Right in the Age of Trump* (New York: Verso Books).

Norris, Pippa and Ronald Inglehart (2019). *Cultural Backlash: Trump, Brexit and Authoritarian Populism* (Cambridge: Cambridge University Press).

Phillips, Whitney (2015). *This is Why We Can't Have Nice Things: Mapping the Relationship Between Online Trolling and Mainstream Culture* (Cambridge, MA: MIT Press).

Shaw, Kristian (2017). *Cosmopolitanism in Twenty-First Century Fiction* (Cham: Palgrave Macmillan).

Spencer, Richard (2017). 'NPI 2016, Full Speech', 21 November 2016, www.youtube.com/watch?v=Xq-LnO2DOGE (no longer available).

Treisman, Deborah (2020). 'Hari Kunzru on Privacy, Surveillance, and Paranoia', *The New Yorker*, 29 June, www.newyorker.com/books/this-week-in-fiction/hari-kunzru-07-06-20 (accessed 8 August 2022).

Woods, Heather Suzanne and Leslie A. Hahner (2020). *Make America Meme Again: The Rhetoric of the Alt-Right* (New York: Peter Lang).

9

'In the wake of all that': a conversation with Hari Kunzru

Kristian Shaw

The following conversation took place online on 28 January 2021 in the midst of the COVID-19 pandemic.

KS: Hi Hari. Lovely to see you again. I understand you're now a Professor at NYU. Are you enjoying your time there?

HK: Yeah, so I teach mainly graduate classes there. It's a Creative Writing department rather than an English Literature department. I'm encountering a lot of people here who don't read anything other than contemporary writing but I'm trying to introduce them to a bit of literary history and works in translation. That's quite interesting – trying to introduce people to other European traditions or Latin American fiction. It's been useful for me as a writer because it's forced me to own a lot of my own positions on subjects, and also to re-read, which I never used to do very much. It's a nice department. It's a very interesting group of people. There's Zadie Smith, Claudia Rankine, Jonathan Safran Foer, Jeffrey Eugenides, Katie Kitamura, Nathan Englander. It's a really a strong group of people to be working with.

KS: That's fantastic. With that in mind, I'd like to start by talking about place. You now live in New York with your wife and children. Over your last few novels, *Gods Without Men*, *White Tears*, *Red Pill*, there has been a real concentration on the American landscape and history. Is this where you feel your focus will remain?

HK: Well, it wasn't my intention. My intention was to be here for nine months. That was thirteen years ago. I suppose I always had a very strong interest in American fiction. The writers I was excited by when I was 20 were people like Thomas Pynchon and Don DeLillo. That kind of systems novel tradition that I wasn't seeing so much in British fiction at the time. I had a keen interest in this sort of maximalist, magic realist type writing that people like Salman Rushdie were doing.

My intention coming to the US was *not* to write about the US. I had a project that was an Indian historical novel, set at the Mughal court. I just discovered that I couldn't write it – there was various reasons for that. I really underestimated how strange and absorbing it would be to be in a different place. I figured I knew New York reasonably well. It was just another place where I would be thinking about whatever I was thinking about. Instead, the question of 'what was this place' became important to me and the Mughal novel collapsed. I was left in this potentially difficult situation. I had a fellowship at the New York Public Library so I had this wonderful office. I had these all these resources, the best stipend; I had everything I needed to write, except something to write. I was kind of freaking out. Some friends said, 'if you're not doing anything useful, why don't you fly out to LA and we'll drive to Joshua Tree'. I did that and had an intense experience in the desert. And then that became my rhythm for the next couple of years, actually. I decided to stay and I started getting more and more obsessed with the landscape of the Southwest and with the experience of being in these vast spaces. We don't really have an equivalent of those spaces in the UK. I mean there are sublime landscapes, mountainous landscapes, but this vast, open flatness was overwhelming to me.

Gods Without Men grew out of that. I had that very scary moment of trying to see if it would be accepted as an American novel, or whether I had fallen short in the voice, and it would be rather obvious. A sort of *outsider's* book. I was very happy that the book was received as an American novel. After that, I had decided to stay. I had fallen in love, I got married. In the first year or two I was in the US, I could really think of myself as being just outside it. I was an observer. It was like being a traveller anywhere. Then as I got more wrapped up in it, I felt more implicated. One of the big issues was, of course, the question of race and the history of race. I realised that there were things that were kind of unsayable for American writers. One of the uses of being an outsider was I could insert myself into the middle of a debate that I had no business being in, or certainly no ownership of. I could use the understanding I had of these things through my own background and place myself in this very ambiguous, uneasy place. I'm very interested in the idea of uneasiness. That's the course I'm teaching at the moment called the 'Uneasy Uncanny'. I'm very interested in how fiction can occupy a very ambiguous space and stage certain kinds of troubled situations without necessarily taking a polemic view on them. *Red Pill* does that, too, in a way. It tries to take these characters into this deeply troubling space and hold it open.

This is sort of how it's happened. I wrote *White Tears* and, again, that was well received here. Much better than it was in the UK. I discovered that the British publishing scene does not see stories about black America as commercial. At that point, there was beginning to be a break. I've been here long enough to feel slightly disconnected from some of the newest cultural scenes. I mean, when I left, Gordon Brown was still the prime minister, so I've been away for the Cameron period. I've always said I'll come back but I have not been spending that solid time or absorption in what it feels like to be in Britain. I've floated off into this position where, in some ways, I'm much more present in the New York literary conversation, which has its own dimensions. But I still feel very much an outsider to a lot of American political terms and conditions. I mean, things like guns, all the things that European people tend to find bizarre about the politics here. I still have my [British] head on.

I suppose it's true for a lot of people. It's certainly true for Zadie [Smith], who's now back in the UK. This idea of a national literature, which was always a term that was used to critically place people, is much less useful now. I have a number of other writer friends who hop around, spend periods of time in different places. I'm friends with the German writer Daniel Kehlmann. He's a big deal in Germany. And Valeria Luiselli. There are times that we've had lunches where it's me, Zadie, Valeria, Katie, Daniel and Nick [Laird], and we're all from very different kinds of positions. We're all temporarily in New York because of the academic industrial complex that pays us to be there. But we're all connected in different ways. Valeria is writing in English and Spanish. Daniel writes in German but lives in New York and has a lot of friends in the English-language scene. The idea of a cosmopolitan writer is very contested right now as well, especially in the wake of things like Brexit, and in the wake of an understanding of cosmopolitanism as colluding with neoliberalism in certain ways. But that's where we are.

KS: Absolutely. The first academic book that I wrote was called *Cosmopolitanism in Twenty-First Century Fiction* and interrogated the idea of that condition. And, obviously, the next five years pulled that apart. There's a great scene in *Red Pill* where the narrator is asked why he isn't writing literature about his own people. What is he doing there? It's positioned as just a passing comment but it's reflective of those arguments that would become quite important from 2016 onwards. That course on the uncanny sounds really interesting because, in a number of your novels now, we have these various identities being destabilised. Arjun in *Transmission* after he's disseminated the virus, Pran in *The Impressionist* when he's disoriented in the desert, the narrator in *Red Pill* after he's failed to track down Anton. Is this deconstruction of the self what you're interested in on your course as well?

HK: Yes, to some extent. I'm trying to do genre-adjacent material. I go as far as Shirley Jackson and the weird tale. So there is an openness to genre, but part of it is this idea of the familiar Freudian uncanny where there's this ambiguity between organic and inorganic, living and not living, as well as Mark Fisher's book *The Weird and the Eerie* [2016]. The idea of landscape and place being in some way infused with memories. *White Tears* was very much based on the idea of haunting and of being haunted as an inability to move forward into the future – always being dragged back into the past. So all these ideas about time and place and identity are all are all wrapped up in there. The work I'm teaching include relatively realist things like Elfriede Jelinek's *The Piano Teacher* [1983] and Javier Marías's *Tomorrow in the Battle Think on Me*

[1994], and also Anna Kavan's *Ice* [1967] and Samanta Schweblin's *Fever Dream* [2014]. [Schweblin] is wonderful. It's an ecological story about poisoning and a landscape which appears benign but is potentially hurting people. It's a little bit like the Tarkovsky film *Stalker* [1979]. You get this beautiful rural landscape but actually death is inscribed. Those kind of ideas fascinate me.

What you were saying about the dissolution or deconstruction of narrators has always been very important to me because I've always had a sense of myself as being very constructed. It's been clear to me that the elements of my own sense of myself would have been different had I had a different history or if my family had a different history. So the idea of an organic connection to place that's been around in the Brexit period is very alien to me. I didn't come across Judith Butler until much later. I didn't actually read Judith Butler until after the ideas were already in circulation. The idea of self as performance interests me. The idea of how much our personal identity is continuous and stable interests me. We need to feel that somebody is substantially the same throughout their lives and, if that's not true, if you can remake yourself beyond a certain point. What does that say about you? More recently, I've been reading a lot of neuropsychology, neurophilosophy about the self as an emergent product of the brain, as a kind of fiction, really. And of course, the novel as a form is very wrapped up with a particular idea of self. But these are all continual preoccupations of mine, often in a rather involuntary way, I think.

KS: Yes, that definitely came across, again, in *Red Pill*. The thing I picked up on was what you touched upon earlier. It was almost the tip of the hat to those systems novels of the 1970s associated with DeLillo or Pynchon. In *Gravity's Rainbow* [1973] you have Slothrop, who is lost in the zone and he scatters. There was definitely a little bit of that coming across in *Red Pill* and *Gods Without Men*, but they also move beyond what you expect from one of those postmodern texts, I suppose. I'm not sure how aware you are of what's written about your work in academia but some people will say you are a very postmodern writer, and other people will say you're moving beyond that moment and gesturing to a cosmopolitan optic or the cosmopolitan condition. To what extent would you categorise your work as postmodern? Do you ever consider yourself a postmodern writer?

HK: I do. When I started out I was headed for your job, really. I was trained as a critic and a philosopher. I did a Master's in continental philosophy and I still read a lot of that tradition. In a periodicity sort of way I'm too young to have been part of that moment in the 1960s and 1970s – that high postmodernist moment in fiction involving mostly American writers. Donald Barthelme was very important to me as a person who would examine the limits of fiction and create these constructions that made very apparent the impossibility of writing a character in an unselfconscious way. But I think, at the same time, that's what happens to any artistic form; its insights get absorbed into the fabric of the mainstream. So now you see writers, who wouldn't think of themselves as experimental or avant-gardist, using techniques that were associated with the avant-gardes of previous times. I mean, you see it every time a writer uses a flashback or frames their text as if it's a film shot. It's banal now, but it was a visibly avant-garde move in the 1960s.

As a fiction writer, I write in the wake of all that. The most postmodern book I've written is *The Impressionist*. It was a book that's about books. It's a book that's about that English tradition of going to India and finding yourself against the sensory access of the mystic East. In the Marabar caves scene there's a wonderful postmodern echoing moment there. Since then I've become less interested in doing that. In my head, I'm writing a much more *realist* surface. I talk a lot with David Mitchell and he's somebody who, like me, grew up reading a lot of genre science fiction and fantasy writing. We both have an unselfconsciousness about those things that wouldn't have been around before. That was me trying to make this case for myself as a realist writer, and then thinking, 'wait, does he do that'? But I don't think you need to do big formal Italo Calvino, Donald Barthelme type moves these days in order to have that understanding floating around in the background of your writing. It would be just repeating gestures. Like somebody painting a Jackson Pollock now. It wouldn't have the same meaning now. I've always been interested in the theoretical aspects of fiction as well.

KS: Yeah. I remember when we spoke a few years ago we discussed the emergence of several novels which drew on the deepening of global interconnection. You stated your desire was to reflect more of the 'messiness' of that connectivity because in reality things weren't quite so 'neat'. The pandemic clearly reinforces that sentiment and the risk factors associated with our global community of fate.

HK: Yeah, David [Mitchell] has a fondness for that. He's somebody for whom the interconnectedness becomes a source of aesthetic joy or a sublime moment. Even though the threads may be tiny there's a cosmic pattern and there's a form. My experience is that it's much more fragmented and much more jarring and disjointed. A very important novel for me was Roberto Bolano's *2666* [2004], simply because it has these long narratives that do not appear to connect to each other and you have to do this work as a reader. There's stuff going on in the silences, in the gaps, and that was very much my idea for *Gods Without Men*. I wanted to flip the reader to think, 'hang on, why are we now in 1850 with a Mormon silver miner?' There are things happening in between these narratives that come together but ultimately don't add up to a cosmic transcendence. It's adding up to an unknown that we have to negotiate always with things that are beyond our knowledge.

I had a good time reading this philosopher Timothy Morton. He's a real magpie philosopher. He posts things that aren't strictly academic philosophy but he's writing a lot about climate. Morton has this idea of hyperobjects – that we're enmeshed in these systems that are essentially beyond our ability to calculate or comprehend. Like, the effect of global warming is suprahuman and can't be apprehended totally from any individual position. So there's this sense that there's a world that's not on a human scale. Traditionally, we try to pull everything down to our own size. Our moral decisions, our understanding of the world all happens at our own scale. But our experience of the contemporary is actually quite a spooky experience of things coming out at us that we don't understand or know where they've come from. I've spent a lot of time in the last 24 hours thinking about GameStop [stock market saga] and the madness on the markets there. That's a wonderful example of a completely unlooked-for force that has emerged out of this complex system. I definitely think about complexity and emergence and all those sorts of ideas.

I was lucky enough recently to do an interview with a philosopher called Manuel DeLanda for the podcasts that I've been making. He's somebody who's a very rigorous anti-humanist systems theorist. He's got his wonderful way of relating these massive things right down to these tiny micro things. His way of thinking about things, which decentres the human, I find very interesting. To use these humanist terms and conditions of the novel – quite familiar domestic ways of characters interacting, people having their loves, their losses, their hopes and all this traditional activity of the novel – in the context of these much larger and mostly unknowable things. That brings you straight into ideas about haunting and the uncanny and a sense of not fully understanding things. I suppose that's why my work over the last few years has taken on this quite anxious, spooky tone.

KS: Yes, the globalisation of the uncanny. The globalisation of the strange. All these different kinds of uncanny elements, whether it's hauntology, which is integral to *White Tears*, but also that uneasiness of the self under globalisation. The most interesting thing about *Red Pill* is it could have ended up like a 900-page Pynchon novel because there were so many ideas in there. You move from German Romanticism to elements of phenomenology, all the way to the alt-right and Trump. Do you ever find yourself cutting a lot of material when you revise your drafts or retaining material for future use?

HK: Yes, there's this conversation to be had about what people will read now as well. At 21, what I wanted to do was to write *Gravity's Rainbow*. These massive, sprawling texts with interconnectivity and digressions. I think the advent of the internet made that much less attractive to me. Imagining that we exist outside of the material constraints for the moment, I do think that the old-fashioned 1970s systems novel prefigured an experience of connectivity that is part of our everyday now.

I have come to appreciate concision. I've come to appreciate things that don't exhaust everything. The exhaustiveness of the digressions in a David Foster Wallace novel, for example. He will flog that shit right down. I annoyed a lot of Foster Wallace people at one point. I reviewed *The Pale King* [2011], the unfinished final novel, and suggested that he would have made it worse by carrying on because one of his things was not knowing when to stop. Everything goes all the way down. The footnotes have footnotes and everything is driven into the ground, whereas, there's a lot to be said for pointing towards something and letting things fall away into silence. A short novel with a lot of arrows pointing outside it. This is more interesting to me formally right now than a big fat novel which attempts to nail everything or contain everything. *The Impressionist* is still the longest novel I've written but *Gods Without Men* was as far as I wanted to go with that expansiveness and scope. Right now I'm much more interested in the writing. Part of it is living with somebody [Katie Kitamura] who writes very concise minimal prose. You both infect each other that way. But I quite like the idea of carrying on making *more* work rather than trying to contain everything in one work.

KS: The thing I found quite interesting about *Red Pill* is that it features a nameless narrator who is almost a semi-autobiographical version of yourself. In your work for *The New York Review of Books* you've mentioned you spent a lot of time lurking around far-right message boards.

HK: Everyone's got to have a hobby.

KS: Yeah, that kind of browser history will attract attention. Was *Red Pill* reflective of your experiences as you encountered 4chan and far-right message boards where sincerity doesn't work in those hyper-ironic environments of trolling? Did the efforts of the narrator gesture to your desire to protect your family from the worst excesses of the current populist moment and a pervasive surveillance society?

HK: I could be coy but I gave this narrator a lot of my own biography. It was very difficult at a certain point. I realised I wanted to write about a writer because I needed him to be able to talk in a certain way about the things that he was experiencing. I wanted him to have this contact with this very specific German Romantic tradition, because I see that playing out on the alt-right and I see the attractiveness of a certain vision of the noble outsider, the man apart from the world. The American edition of the book has Caspar David Friedrich's *Traveller on the Sea of Fog* [1818] on the cover; as the appalled designer reminded me it is a complete cliche, but we wanted to have that in there and then mess with it. In a way, that was the requirement for the book. So I needed him to be a writer. I decided as a matter of principle that he shouldn't be white, because I like the idea of having non-white characters in stories that are not necessarily to do with their race. His non-whiteness turns up in *Red Pill* but it's not the main thrust of the thing. That can happen to a white writer, too, but I made him not white.

We've been through the period of autofiction. We've had a decade of autofiction and I've had a lot of contact with people who are really making that work. I've spent quite a lot of time with Karl Ove Knausgård and talked to him about writing. But I've never had his disgust. He says his project came out of a disgust with the fiction of the novel, whereas I've always found it easier to talk in a personal way by removing myself and creating characters. But I wanted to see if I could push myself into a ... I mean, maybe less Karl more Ben Lerner. Ben is a poet; he's got that lyrical first person in his novels. Teju Cole would be another. They have essayistic, direct digressions hung on a very lightly fictionalised first person and I wanted to see what that offered in terms of my own work. As it turned out, I ended up making a story again! It's very funny, the more you try not to write like yourself, the more like yourself you become.

I gave this guy some furniture of my own but it also allowed me to poke a stick at a certain set of New York liberal verities. One of the experiences of the Trump era for a lot of people has been that what they thought was mainstream and normal has vanished and their terms and conditions have been upended. I wanted to show somebody going through that so I made him a more comfy version of myself or a small 'c' conservative version of myself. His ideas about literature and lyric poetry are immediately challenged. Then there's the challenge that comes through surveillance and the whole idea of privacy as a space of experimentation for the self. I was reading things like Thomas Merton [American Trappist monk and writer]. I have a fondness for readings of Buddhist mystics and hermits like Han Shan. A part of me would quite like to live in a hut.

But there's a challenge to that idea of privacy there. Then there's the more profound challenge that comes with his discovery that what he considers unquestionable is absolutely questioned all around him and is becoming a part of the social world, the political world. Anton's blithe dismissal of the narrator's spluttering indignation, his 'you can't say that it's racist' thing, is the end run of what the Chans [4Chan users] did around a certain complacent high liberalism.

KS: I think it's also played out in that dynamic between different factions in the novel. When the narrator actually goes to the Deuter Center for his research fellowship, he encounters believers in that kind of Habermasian public space. The belief that the rational progress of humankind will be done by academic progress. It really is that harsh contrast between that belief, and then the alt-right, where everything is done with a hyper-ironic mockery and nothing actually means anything.

HK: Absolutely! Yeah, the big fight between liberals and the left, which I think to me needs to be talked about more, is between a fiction that the public space is a contestation of ideas and the best way forward will emerge out of this. That's why you mustn't shut down free speech because if your idea is better it will survive in the marketplace. The left says, 'look, you're disregarding the real relations of power. Thinking in this disembodied way is dangerous because it disregards the actual material conditions in which that debate is taking place'. And then, on the right, as you say, what they dispense with is the good-faith aspect of the Habermasian notion. For them, you can say it and not mean it. That muddying of the public, in fact, is almost like deliberately taking a dump in the public's mind.

Look at the aftermath of the insurrection on January 6 [2021]. Marjorie Taylor Greene is a gun-toting, QAnon-loving Congresswoman and brings forth impeachment articles against Joe Biden. So now there's *two* truths. They produce an alternative truth. Look at Kellyanne Conway's idea of alternative facts. I mean, there are people who relate this very specifically to a KGB, FSB mentality: admit nothing, deny everything, make counter-arguments. Always in this information warfare mode of seeing the world. Truth is not the desired outcome. Power is the desired outcome. We're now in a public space where even things that seem clearly true can be contested by unsupported alternative explanations if they are just repeated enough or if they are put forward forcefully enough. This whole constant suspension of the ability to make decisions or to decide on the agreed facts before we even *get* to the Habermasian conversation about what we do.

This brings forth all sorts of possibilities for totalitarianism. Fundamentally, there's a big move beyond democratic politics or against democratic politics coming from the right in general and coming from very powerful people who want to dispense with the public sphere altogether. The idea of politics as a public activity, so central to how we all assumed things were going to go forward in the post-Cold War period, that, essentially, it would be a technocratic question of how we would achieve these goals – it's all been swept away. We're in a period where the rare exercise of power wishes to dispense with any appeal to the people in any meaningful way at all. We're all being battered and knocked about by this and it's a very interesting time to be a writer. It's a useful time to be a *fiction* writer because I do think fiction can stage these things and can help to understand these processes that don't have anything to do with the traditional procedures of democratic politics.

KS: The debate reminds me of your article for *The New York Review of Books*, 'Rival Realities', where those two different belief systems are exacerbated by the internet as well.

HK: Yeah, that's right. So, editorially, that was very interesting, because they felt the draft I submitted wasn't sufficiently distinguishing the truth from the fiction, but my rhetorical impulse in starting that off was to show these two rival realities with the understanding about which one I thought has value and meaning. But they were nervous that I wasn't double underlining enough. There was an editorial process where I had to say things like this argument is a lie and so on. That was interesting to me. It took American journalists years to say Trump was a liar. In 2016, they would not use that language, and that was very, very damaging. But maybe I fell into it myself by giving too much credence to the other position.

KS: Trying to be too balanced. That's one of the benefits of the novel, I suppose; you've got this medium through which to really unpack all these ideas at length. But your work has increasingly become multimedia and experimental – the highly visual *Memory Palace* in coordination with the V&A, the multilayered digital experience of *Twice Upon A Time* – what attracts you to these new forms of representation? As you've said the novel is a slow medium. Do you think the novel is losing its cultural power or merely adapting to work alongside emergent digital modes? And, in turn, providing the author with a discursive space in which to discuss current events?

HK: I mean, we're having the death of the novel conversation. If you sit down and think, 'right, I'm going to write a death of the novel essay for *The Atlantic*', you tend to be taking this position that we're coming after a great tradition where everything has already been said. That we are in this melancholic, T.S. Eliot, 'these fragments I have shored against my ruins' mode. But, for lots and lots of people, their stories have not been told yet. There's a separate conversation to be had about the limitations of the novel as a form by the material conditions of its production. If I want to do something that fucks around with fonts and pictures, where the cover is part of the story, there are barriers to all that formal experimentation. There are barriers in terms of the division of labour. There's also an economic set of questions: will it sell or how will the book club in Des Moines understand this thing?

That modernist formal experimentation has headed off into the art world where there is a support for that. There's a system behind that where they don't have a problem with accessibility. Art-world-adjacent people often sneer at commercial fiction because it is commercial and is having to be legible and function in that other space. So there's a set of limitations that I think make the novel less amazingly flexible than it could be like. I would love to be able to make things that do incorporate imagery. *Twice Upon A Time* was exciting to me because I could make these intellectual constructs using anything that came to hand. I could have the same set of procedures as I do as a novelist, making patterns and putting things adjacent to each other. But I could do it with all this different stuff. That's an idea that will come into its own somewhere down the line. The company that did that immediately went bust and *Twice Upon A Time* is not accessible, in any form at all now. People can't see it.

Podcasting has been interesting because it's a multimedia thing. You can use archive, you can use interview as a dialogic thing, you have other voices in there. So that's exciting to me too as a form. But in all these situations you have copyright law as a definite horizon. You can't quote beyond a certain time, you certainly can't use music, you can barely use two or three seconds of music as fair use. So there's a lot of things that keep the novel in its current form. But I think even with those limitations, and with the real bottleneck that you have as an artist of trying to make something that will, in some way, be still pleasurable for people who are not interested in or engaged in these complicated philosophical or political questions, they still want a story. I like stories and I like to tell stories.

[The novel] is still an incredibly flexible form. I think that's what makes it useful, partly because it's not a high modernist thing. I think every attempt to corral the novel into high modernism fails because it's the proverbial baggy monster. You can never have a novel that's as pure as a [Kazimir] Malevich white canvas. Because novel words refer to things; words get mixed up in the low and grubby business of life. As a writer, I've always been inclined to write non-fiction and journalism. The things that I start off writing as an essay find their way also into fiction and I used to worry that I should have clear blue water between the art and the commerce. Actually, the older I get, the more I feel that I'm very continuous in my practices: being a non-fiction writer, a journalist, and a person on the internet saying shit on Twitter. I think that's turning out to be a strength of the form in that you can put together these very complicated, heterogenous structures and put them out there under one cover. They can refer to all sorts of things.

I think the death of the novel position in general tends to be from an older white gentleman who feels a certain way about tradition. But people still buy a lot of novels. There may not be this idea of the novelist as grand priest or arbiter that you could point to, like Norman Mailer, in some previous version of the culture, but it's still part of the conversation and people still want to make them. We get so many people turning up at NYU wanting to be novelists. It's an insane thing to want to do! But they still want to do it.

KS: Absolutely. As you say, the podcast is a great medium for playing with boundaries and engaging with quite complex debates rather than writing a dense critical article on an issue. I've been enjoying your podcast series 'Into the Zone' during lockdown which you've described as your side hustle. The podcasts explore this idea that borders are never as clear as we think. This focus on border thought is a recurring theme in your work: the borders between online and offline life, between nation states, self and other, public and private. Is that driven by what you perceive as historical or emergent fractures in contemporary society?

HK: That's it, yeah, there's another interesting editorial process that goes on with the podcasts for the company. They have a certain horizon that you can't surpass. Will they let you do something that might be two and a half hours, if it goes to that length, or can I say the word 'heterogenous' in the podcast? I learned that there are ways of communicating in real time in someone's ear that work and they are not the same as written text. It's very interesting to me, like trying to explain Adorno in a podcast, or what is twelve-tone music? To try and do that in a way that's accurate but doesn't immediately become completely illegible to the person who is jogging or doing the washing up. That's an interesting challenge. There's a gatekeeping function of academic jargon and of art that isn't always necessarily functional. There are times when you do need to say the difficult word and unpack it because that's the only word that actually exists for that thing. But there are other times when you're just vaguely trying to sound like you're French. That's a bad set of habits. It's interesting to try and bring these complicated ideas into a public space where the rule of communication is that you can't use the jargon words. You must say it as simply as possible. That's a good discipline to try and have as a writer, it's an interesting problem to try and solve.

KS: Are some of these ideas going to feed into your next novel, *Blue Ruin*? *White Tears* dealt with blues music. *Red Pill* focused on the writing process and lyric poetry. I've read that *Blue Ruin* will concern contemporary art? A literary [Krzysztof Kieślowski] *Three Colours* trilogy?

HK: Yeah, that's absolutely part of it. I don't want to say too much about it just yet – I'll jinx it if I do. But the idea is *White Tears* is about music, *Red Pill* is about writing and *Blue Ruin* is about visual art. In a broad sense, it will take on questions of value and meaning and what it is to be an artist versus what it is to make objects. The market is a huge part of that. I mean, obviously, any conversation about contemporary art can get swamped by the related question of the art market. Those ideas interest me a lot. What I tend to do with all my work is to try to make everything resonate with everything else. If I have a set of interests that I'm writing an essay about, it will often also find its way into fiction, and vice versa. I just started this column at *Harper's Magazine* where I'm contracted to do six 2,500-word essays. The first one was about QAnon and conspiracy and I had a three-month lead time. I thought 'this is going to be a bit outdated by the time it comes out', but QAnon came back in a big way. I've just filed something about policing and criminal justice in the UK versus the US and the idea of abolition and defunding, and so on. I'm just trying to cook something up about productivity and lockdown and being a working person in a place where there's no workplace anymore.

After I finish this trilogy – it's a very loose trilogy, but it is a thematically linked trilogy – I might try and write something very different after that. But, for now, it's interesting to me because the present is so *present*. Certainly here in New York, this last year has been overwhelming with the pandemic and with Trump and with the new civil rights movement. It's been all been happening simultaneously right outside my door and also at an enormous distance because of lockdown and the isolation of that. The pandemic has clearly found its way into what I'm writing now. I think I've found a form and a story that will do that without it being about coronavirus in any straightforward way.

KS: It's almost inevitable that some of these events are going to bleed into fiction. Did you finish 2020 feeling slightly more positive with the downfall of Trump? Obviously, he is just one part of a global shift. The year did witness changes to structures of power as a result of Black Lives Matter protests and the need for some form of accountability. There were also some positive effects on the environment due to lockdown measures.

HK: Just speaking purely personally I was very freaked out. Between 2015 and 2017 I did not know how far this was all going to go. When you get into thinking like this you have to decide what's reasonable and what's excessive. In the same way that the guy who's buying a lot of canned food and guns is doing that. I could buy a gun. Here I am in the US, what would I fucking do with a gun? Even if I got into a situation where I needed the gun, I would probably not function very well. I've been playing out possibilities and wondering how far the collapse of American democracy was going to go. Was I going to suddenly wake up and find that I was essentially in Berlin and it was 1933? Shit. We had plans to move and try to have an escape plan if things got beyond a certain point. It's insane. That's a very extreme way to have to think in the background of continuing your everyday life.

So yes, I am feeling more positive now. It's a relief to me that the Trump presidency came to an end. It's a relief to me there seems to be some possibility that the pandemic will ebb during 2021 and I might find myself somewhere other than my few square blocks of Brooklyn. I feel we've got all the bigger questions still to deal with and, as you say, climate is the biggest of all those questions, but there are also still very major political shifts. Geopolitically, I do wonder what happens if American power ebbs in a multipolar world with China as a serious player. We seem to be in a position where

China is committing textbook genocide and no one can really talk about it. My children's world could be very dark indeed. But how I'm feeling in 2021 versus how I was feeling in early 2017, I'm better. I'm sleeping better.

KS: That's good. A notable feature of your novels thus far is their predictive power, their anticipatory potential in highlighting issues or concerns that, as we know, have gone on to become major developments. *Transmission*, for example, anticipates the racial discourses that were to emerge in Western populist movements a decade later. Your satirical depiction of the EU, reimagined as a Pan European Border Authority, reveals a Europe still stained by white hegemony and cultural prejudice, calling into question existing immigration policies and the preservation of racial hierarchies.

HK: I'd almost forgotten how into that I was at the time. I've always wondered why more fiction writers don't indulge their speculative tendencies in that way. I've always liked speculative fiction, genre fiction, because it will do that. But I think there's a point where pure speculation overweighs any possibility of running a plot through it. A lot of times you end up with a very creaky detective plot running through your imagined near-future world. It's interesting to think about dystopian fictions right now and how much less enticing they seem to me as a reader than they did a decade ago. I wrote *Memory Palace* as a dystopian piece of fiction. There is a sort of pleasure, which I think a lot of critics have discussed, about the form of dystopias. There is something interesting about imagining yourself after the end of everything. Those early nineteenth-century ones were cool, like [Mary Shelley's] *The Last Man* [1826], but it's not fun to think about that stuff right now. It feels almost indulgent to run made-for-Netflix dystopias set in a *Mad Max* landscape; whereas actually what we need to be doing is to be working out how we go on and how we can hold things together.

KS: It's interesting when dystopic things happen just how *ordinary* they are. Take January [2021] with the storming of the Capitol Building. It's never zombies. It's always the very banal elements of human life.

HK: Yeah, it's guys with landscaping businesses in the suburbs.

KS: That's true of British politics as well in a different way. These old-school, Eton-educated MPs in Westminster who try to embody the idea of the English sublime. Given we are now coming to terms with the fallout of Brexit after the transition period, what are your thoughts on Britain's future on the world stage?

HK: Over here, we've all been like fully focused on this [presidential] election and then the Georgia run-off. We have a two-year period now until the midterms when there's going to be a consolidation of the centre. Biden is appointing sensible people to various positions. There's going to be a weeding out of the Trump crazies but they're still on high alert in Washington for domestic terrorist attacks. The Republican Party is showing signs of regaining its confidence after three whole weeks of feeling a bit sheepish about leading an insurrection against American democracy. They're back on their bullshit. We have this two-year period where things will remain tense and then we'll see if the Republican base is still loyal to Trump. If the Republicans do well in those 2022 midterms then I don't think that's the narrative. I don't think this narrative of consolidation will have any longer-term meaning.

But I do think, in Britain, it does seem like you haven't had that massive moment of relief and hope that we've had here. [Boris] Johnson seems to be flailing and he seems very tired and personally weak. All his various failings as a leader and a human were very much exposed by the pandemic. Suddenly, it's the same only worse. Brexit seems to be ... I can't find any commentary which points towards any upside at all. As you say, the best you can do is this absurd Jacob Rees Mogg, British-fish-quota thing. A sort of jolly stiff-upper-lip joke. The absolute failure of that class of people to stand up for anything and the failure to govern in any meaningful way is terrible. I don't understand why the newly sanitised Keir Starmer Labour Party doesn't seem to be more popular. You'd have a pint of ale with Starmer and talk about the rugby. And isn't that what people want in Britain?

I do worry that the economic fallout of Brexit is going to be so extreme, in particular, the service industry-related stuff, all the financial services, which have been propping up the London economy for a long time. I saw that London's lost 800,000 people in the last twelve months. That's surely significant. If the game plan is to make the UK into a European Singapore – a little buccaneering trading nation that is going to attract lots of foreign capital and have laissez-faire rules for hiding it – I don't think that prosperity will trickle down in any meaningful way to the regions that expected Brexit to rebalance things. Cornwall, the North-east, all these parts of the UK that voted very heavily for Brexit, I think they'll be sorely disappointed and that will lead people to the stabbed-in-the-back argument, the old argument that gave rise to fascist formations. Britain's always been *fash*curious. I worry that if a sufficiently charismatic leader of the extreme right were to come around a lot of people would be absolutely down for that. So yeah, it would be nice if something straightforwardly positive would happen for the UK, because everybody needs a break.

KS: I think that's true across the board globally at the moment. A need for a break from the last five years. Much has been written and spoken about in recent years on the publishing scene and the identity of the author. Several authors have voiced a concern that they are often still hindered by a burden of representation. You mentioned earlier that the British publishing scene weren't as interested in stories of black America. How do you feel about the state of equality in British and American publishing right now?

HK: I can only really speak anecdotally but my sense of it is that a real critical mass has been achieved of young people of colour who are involved in making books. In writing them but also in publishing them and in all the other roles in publishing. As a result of that the conversation has really shifted. If you think about who was fashionable even relatively recently, like a decade ago, it's not the same names. People are much more excited about reading a whole new bunch of young, black American writers that are coming through right now. I don't know exactly how the Black Lives Matter thing has translated from the US to the UK but the cultural contexts are not the same. My sense of British publishing is that it's behind the curve. It's not as far along in this process of diversification as US publishing is.

There was, if I say this without names, an editor a few years ago at a British publishing house who wanted to bid on two books by black American writers. They were knocked back on both of them and told there was no interest in either of them and that they weren't commercial propositions for the British market. Those books were Colson Whitehead's *The Underground Railroad* [2016] and Paul Beatty's *The Sellout* [2015]. The fact that those stories could just be blocked by the sales team suggests that there is something very different going on. I mean, fine, people don't always want to read American stories – and those are very American stories – and there are black British stories that need to be told; if you look at something like *Small Axe* [2020], the Steve McQueen film series, that emerged out of black British culture and they've been rapturously received and opened up some spaces.

Here in New York you feel that there's now a way for writers of colour not to have to address a white audience as their primary audience. You don't have to translate your stuff for the proverbial white lady in the Midwest. You can speak in another way, you can speak to your readers, and that can translate out from there to whoever else wants to read it. Whereas, when I started publishing in the UK, there was a sense that whatever I did or said had to be understandable by this imagined white woman. The audience for fiction is predominantly female. I think that's an interesting truth about form. It has its own class position and has a certain level of income. That's a fact about the audience for literary fiction.

But the audience is becoming more diverse and there are plural audiences here in the US. It may be partly because it's a larger place with a larger market so that you can get to a critical mass – you can find a way of selling some books to people. But these stories being made, these stories being consumed, there is a critical apparatus to sustain an artistic movement without having to refer back to the previous set of gatekeepers. I don't know if that's present yet in the UK. I would hope that it's getting there. I mean, people like Nikesh Shukla and figures like Riz Ahmed are representing a newer kind of British culture. So it is there but I'm not sure that the publishing industry has quite opened up in the way I say. We've gone slightly beyond the period where postcoloniality was the only frame in which you could be accepted as a voice in the conversation. That was an interesting transition. The thirty-year transition from one thing to another. But I find it easier to function here, frankly, than I did in the UK.

KS: Thanks so much for your time, Hari.

HK: It's moving to me that there would be interest in making a volume of essays about my stuff. Nice talking to you.

Index

Printed in the USA
CPSIA information can be obtained
at www.ICGtesting.com
JSHW011818091223
53472JS00008B/2